MICROPROCESSOR SYSTEMS ENGINEERING

John Ferguson

ADDISON-WESLEY PUBLISHING COMPANY

Wokingham, England · Reading, Massachusetts · Menlo Park, California
Don Mills, Ontario · Amsterdam · Sydney · Singapore · Tokyo
Mexico City · Bogota · Santiago · San Juan

© 1985 Addison-Wesley Publishers Limited
© 1985 Addison-Wesley Publishing Company, Inc.

The programs presented in this book have been included for their instructional
value. They have been tested with care but are not guaranteed for any particular
purpose. The publisher does not offer any warranties or representations, nor does
it accept any liabilities with respect to the programs.

Cover design by Richard D. Dunn.

Originated direct from the author's w-p disks by
NWL Editorial Services, Langport, Somerset.

Printed in Finland by OTAVA. Member of Finnprint.

OTABIND
PAT. PEND.

British Library Cataloguing in Publication Data
Ferguson, John
    Microprocessor systems engineering. — (Small computer series)
    1. Microprocessors
    I. Title   II. Series
    621.3819'5835   TK7895.M5

    ISBN 0-201-14657-6

Library of Congress Cataloging in Publication Data
Ferguson, John
    Microprocessor systems engineering

    Includes index.
    1. Microprocessors   I. Title
QA76.5.F373   1985   001.64   85-4033
ISBN 0-201-14657-6

ABCDEF 898765

To Ann

ACKNOWLEDGMENTS

The publishers wish to acknowledge the following for permission to reproduce material: Comart Ltd. for Program 8.1 (p. 247); Digital Equipment Corporation for Figures 7.5 (p. 226), 7.7 (p. 228), 7.8 (p. 229), 7.9 (p. 230), 7.10 (p. 231); Hewlett Packard for Figures 6.26 (p. 180), 6.27 (p. 181), 6.34 (p. 187), 8.10 (p. 263); Intel Corporation for Figures 2.25 (p. 48), 2.27 (p. 50), 2.29 (p. 51), 2.31 (p. 58), 2.32 (p. 59), 5.25 (p. 158), 5.27 (p. 159), and for the use of mnemonics in Programs 2.9 (p. 55), 2.10 (p. 55), 2.11 (p. 55); Motorola Ltd. for Figures 2.36 (p. 68), 2.37 (p. 69), 2.38 (p. 70), 2.39 (p. 71), 2.40 (p. 72), 2.41 (p. 72), 2.42 (p. 75); Rockwell International for details of the AIM 65; Solartron for Figure 6.65 (p. 190), Thomson-CSF Components and Materials for Figures 6.48 (p. 201), 6.49 (p. 203), 6.50 (p. 204); and Van Nostrand Reinhold for Figure 2.18 (p. 35).

Contents

Preface

It would be difficult to ignore the explosive growth taking place in microprocessor applications. Typically these range from the now commonplace personal computer to complex control systems for instrumentation and machinery. Along with this expansion, the sophistication of the hardware and software tools needed to develop and maintain these applications has also grown.

The aims of this book are two-fold. Firstly, to familiarise the reader with the basics of both 8-bit and 16-bit microprocessor systems, examining their internal architecture and potential for interfacing to a number of peripheral devices. Secondly, to outline the different stages in the development of microprocessor applications, detailing many of the tools and techniques that are now commonplace in microprocessor development systems.

The book assumes no formal knowledge of computer science, but will probably benefit most those who have some experience of microcomputers, perhaps programming in BASIC or elementary assembly language. However, even complete beginners should find their way with the help of some of the texts listed in the 'Further reading' section at the end of each chapter.

Much of the material is based on a number of short courses run in conjunction with colleagues at MEDC. In particular, I would like to acknowledge substantial contributions from Tony Shaw and Louie Macari (now with James Howden and Company, Glasgow).

Thanks are also due to Bruce Orr of Hewlett Packard Ltd. for advice and help given on numerous occasions and to Hazel Wilson and Sheena Crawford for the many hours spent preparing the manuscript.

John Ferguson

Strathclyde University

Chapter 1

Introduction to microprocessor based products

The objectives of this chapter are:

- to provide an introduction to microcomputers, their components and vocabulary;
- to introduce the basic structure of a microcomputer and describe its operation;
- to highlight the diversity of microprocessor based products.

A microprocessor is a complex Integrated Circuit (IC) containing all the computational and control logic needed to run a small computer. The first microprocessor (the 4004) was produced by Intel in 1971 for a Japanese company manufacturing calculators. However, Intel soon realised its potential and proceeded to market it in the MCS-4 microcomputer. By the mid-seventies a number of more powerful 8-bit microprocessors, such as Intel's 8080 and its successor the 8085, the Zilog Z80 and Motorola's 6800 and 6809, fuelled the beginning of the 'micro revolution'.

The flexibility and power of the microprocessor has led to it generating a range of new products as well as greatly enhancing the features present in a number of everyday appliances: the microprocessor controlled oven offering a variety of cooking cycles ideally matched to each dish, and the microprocessor controlled scales that provide not only the total weight of any item of food, but also a breakdown of its fat, carbohydrate and protein content. Washing machines, cash registers, burglar alarms, cameras – the list is endless. All of these products have benefited from the inclusion of a microprocessor, providing increased performance at a low cost.

Microprocessors/microcomputers have brought increased productivity to both commerce and industry. Office automation, with the introduction of low cost personal computers, has simplified a number of routine tasks as well as altering our ideas on the management of information. The market place now contains a multitude of commercial software packages:

- word processors (e.g. WordStar, MultiMate), spelling and grammar checkers, all simplifying the monotonous task of document preparation and editing

1

- spreadsheets performing 'what if' type operations where managers can observe the consequences of altering input parameters, such as cost or availability, on their profits or performance (e.g. Supercalc, Lotus 1-2-3)
- general management of information with tools such as dBASEII

Along with these general purpose tools are the application specific packages on topics ranging from accountancy and inventory control, to the more esoteric, with a program evaluating the VAT rebate due to publicans on beer slops.

The impact within manufacturing industries has been less dramatic, hampered mainly by a lack of suitably qualified engineers who possess the experience required to integrate microprocessors/microcomputers into industrial systems. However, much work has been done in a number of application areas.

1. *Computer Aided Design (CAD)* has taken advantage of the growing sophistication of video graphics available on many microcomputers. Although originally the domain of the larger minicomputer, a number of CAD packages have been produced for micros providing the designer with a low cost set of tools that allow him to:

- generate drawings using some input device (e.g. graphics tablet, joystick, light pen, mouse)
- manipulate whole or part images with rotation, translation and zoom commands
- assemble large drawings from libraries of previous drawings and shapes
- analyse and evaluate a range of design parameters

2. *Computer Numerical Control (CNC)* of machine tools such as lathes or milling machines has been operational since the early sixties. The technique makes use of paper or magnetic tape to hold both instructions guiding the machining sequence, along with the dimensions of the final component.

The introduction of microprocessor based controllers has provided a number of benefits, including increased flexibility combined with cost savings. Many systems can be programmed using simple on-board keypads or have programming sequences downloaded from a central computing facility within the factory.

3. *Process Control*, where an operation is continuously monitored and corrective action taken if required, is ideally suited to a microprocessor system. Several strategies can be implemented, ranging from simple on-off control to the more complex proportional and three term control. Typical applications include the size monitoring of small components from a lathe. After machining, each piece is measured and the cutting tool adjusted to compensate for workpieces out of tolerance due to factors such as tool wear.

4. *Robotics* is probably the most widely known application of micro-

processors in engineering. The first generation robots were essentially simple pick-up and place devices. However, later generations make use of optical, pressure or ultrasonic sensors that allow them to adapt their behaviour according to the values of the sensed signals.

The current range of microprocessor applications is enormous. From instrumentation in scientific laboratories to the control of telephone exchanges, from the classroom to the amusement arcade, all are undergoing a revolution as a result of a tiny piece of silicon.

1.1   GENERAL ASPECTS OF MICROPROCESSOR BASED SYSTEMS

The organisation and operation of a microcomputer is similar in many respects to that of a large mainframe computer. However, the component count is greatly reduced by the use of large scale (LSI), or with more recent devices, very large scale (VLSI) integrated circuits. Unfortunately the price to pay for reduced size is reduced speed, with the result that microcomputers are generally much slower than larger discrete component systems.

Figure 1.1 shows a typical range of specialist integrated circuits (ICs) found in a microcomputer. The microprocessor plays the central role, acting much like the control centre of any system receiving information, interpreting it and then deciding what action to perform. However, the microprocessor is not free to do as it likes but must follow a set of instructions called a program. The memory chips store the program, together with any other information that may be required.

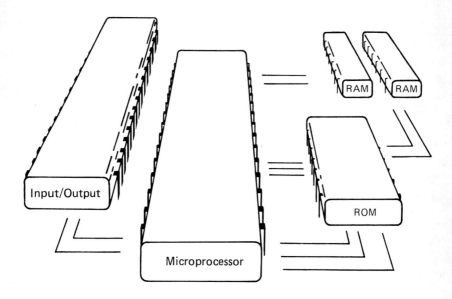

Figure 1.1   Some of the major components found in a microcomputer

In a microcomputer, memory is usually made up of two types: Random Access Memory (RAM) and Read Only Memory (ROM). The former (more appropriately termed read/write random access memory) can be used by the microprocessor to store information as well as to read information previously stored. The major disadvantage of semiconductor RAM is that it is volatile, with the result that all stored information is lost whenever the power supply is switched off. Some RAM devices use so little energy when not being accessed that they can be powered from batteries in the event that the supply fails or is switched off.

ROM, as the name implies, can only be read. Data is entered by a special programming device prior to installation within the computer. The non-volatile nature of ROM makes it ideal for many applications where the microprocessor has to execute a program immediately after power is applied, e.g. the system program in a washing machine controller, or the operating system controlling the keyboard and display on a personal computer.

A number of different types of ROM are currently in use. Mask programmed ROMs represent the most economic form for large volume applications, but have the disadvantage that programming has to be carried out by the chip manufacturer, and once performed cannot be changed. For small scale applications or for use during program development, Erasable Programmable ROMs or EPROMs are ideal. Low cost EPROM programmers allow local programming, and EPROM erasers provide a simple means of erasing the contents of a chip (using intensive ultraviolet light through a quartz window on the chip housing) in preparation for reprogramming.

A relatively recent innovation is the Electrically Alterable ROM or EAROM, that can be both programmed and erased within the micro-computer. Typical applications of these devices include storage of character codes and fonts in software configurable video display units and printers, as well as storing machining instructions in CNC machine tools.

A microcomputer must be capable of communicating with the outside world. Special purpose interface chips allow the microprocessor to accept data from devices such as keyboards, tape recorders and transducers, and to transmit data to displays, printers, etc.

System buses

Connecting the components together are three separate buses – the data bus, the address bus and the control bus. The address bus is a unidirectional or one-way bus made up of typically 16 lines. Onto this bus the microprocessor places logic levels (logic 0 is $\sim$ 0V and logic 1 $\sim$ 5V), generating one of 2^{16} or 65536 possible voltage patterns or addresses. Each pattern acts like a key, opening the door to a unique location within the computer, Figure 1.2. Once the door is open, the processor can then either read or write information to the selected location using the data bus. This is a bidirectional bus, containing eight lines (in an 8-bit microprocessor) connecting the processor's data pins to the other system components. These data pins can act as either inputs or outputs, depending on whether the microprocessor is receiving information (a

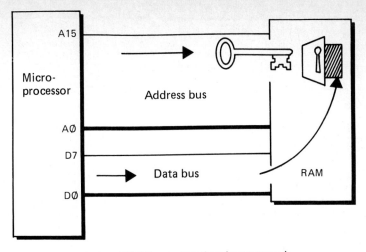

during a WRITE operation the microprocessor's
data pins act as outputs sending data to
the memory location selected by the address bus

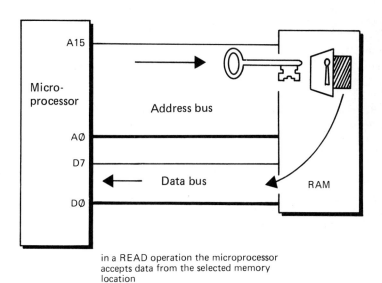

in a READ operation the microprocessor
accepts data from the selected memory
location

Figure 1.2 The microprocessor uses the system buses to
communicate with the other components

read or load operation) or transmitting information (a write or store
operation). Again, in a similar manner to the address bus, data is
transmitted in the form of voltage patterns, with a total of 2^8 or 256
patterns that represent the numbers 0 through to 255.

Finally, the control bus contains a number of signals that synchronise the data transfers between the microprocessor and supporting devices. Some of these control signals are generated by the processor and inform system components what action they have to perform, while others flag the microprocessor if some input/output device is in need of attention. The number and nature of control signals varies from one microprocessor to another. Chapter 2 provides details of those used by four popular processors.

Bits, bytes and hex
Each location within a computer's memory is capable of holding a voltage pattern in eight storage cells. Each cell represents a logical quantity called a *bit* and the group of eight cells forms a *byte*, Figure 1.3.

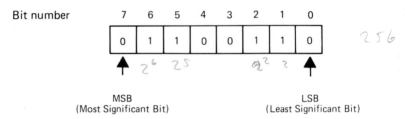

Bit number   7   6   5   4   3   2   1   0

| 0 | 1 | 1 | 0 | 0 | 1 | 1 | 0 |

MSB
(Most Significant Bit)

LSB
(Least Significant Bit)

Figure 1.3   Each memory location contains 8 bits

If a byte is thought of as a binary number, then each memory location is capable of storing numbers ranging from binary 00000000, i.e. zero, to 11111111, or 255 decimal. People find it awkward to deal with large binary numbers. A more convenient method of representing them is to use the *hexadecimal* number system, where numbers are evaluated to the base 16 instead of to the base 10, Figure 1.4.

Decimal	Binary	Hex
0	0000	0
1	0001	1
2	0010	2
3	0011	3
4	0100	4
5	0101	5
6	0110	6
7	0111	7
8	1000	8
9	1001	9
10	1010	A
11	1011	B
12	1100	C
13	1101	D
14	1110	E
15	1111	F

Figure 1.4   Hex is a convenient method of representing binary numbers

Hex is not the ideal solution. Beginners find it difficult at first, but it does provide a compact method of representing binary numbers by grouping them four bits at a time. A group of four bits has 2^4 or 16 possible values ranging from 0000 to 1111. If the numbers 0 to 9 represent the first 10 patterns, then extra symbols are required for the remaining 6. An arbitrary but now widely accepted choice is to use the letters of the alphabet A–F to represent the binary patterns 1010 to 1111. Using this notation, any 8-bit binary number or the contents of a memory location, can be represented as a 2-digit hexadecimal number, Figure 1.5.

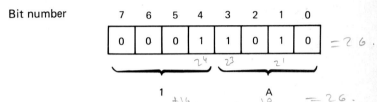

Figure 1.5   A 2-digit hexadecimal number can be used to represent
the contents of a memory location

A 4-digit number provides a convenient method of representing a 16-bit address with the address lines split into four groups of four and the pattern on each group represented by a single hex digit, Figure 1.6.

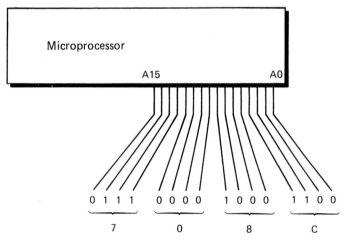

Figure 1.6   A 4-digit hexadecimal number represents the contents of
the address bus

Memory map
With hexadecimal notation, the address range of an 8-bit microcomputer extends from 0000 hex through to FFFF hex. The *memory map* shown in Figure 1.7 illustrates a common method of displaying the 65536 locations. Marks on the edge of the map divide it into 16 blocks of 4096 or 4 K locations (1 K represents 2^{10} or 1024 locations). A collective term used to describe 256 locations is 'page'; each 4 K block of memory contains 16 pages.

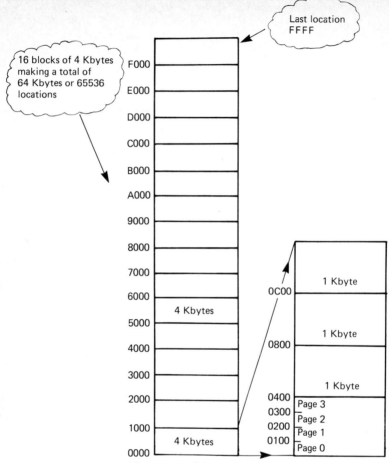

Figure 1.7 Memory map

Figure 1.8 contrasts the address space of an 8-bit microprocessor with the 1 Mbyte available to Intel's 16-bit processors, the 8088/8086. Both processors utilise a 20-bit address bus, allowing them to communicate directly with 2^{20} or 1048576 locations. In hexadecimal notation, each location is identified by a 5-digit hex number within the range 00000 hex to FFFFF hex.

Address decoding
In any microcomputer, a number of memory and input/output devices share the common system buses. To ensure that only one chip responds to any read or write operation, each device has a Chip-Select ($\overline{CS}$) control input. Only when this input is activated does the memory or I/O device respond to requests from the processor.

A circuit called an *address decoder* makes use of the chip-select inputs to position each component in the system's memory map. The following example should illustrate the technique.

Figure 1.8 Comparison of the memory maps of a typical 8-bit processor and Intel's 16-bit 8088/8086

Example A .2332 ROM has 12 address inputs (labelled A0 to A11) to access its 2^{12} or 4096 locations, Figure 1.9. Each location contains eight bits. The chip-select input disables output from ROM if held at logic 1.

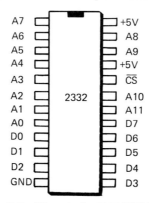

Figure 1.9 Pinout of a 2332 ROM chip

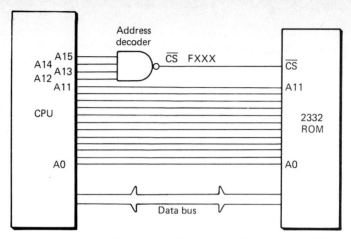

Figure 1.10 Simple address decode circuit to place ROM in block F

When the 2332 is installed in a system, the four most significant address lines, A15, A14, A13 and A12, from the microprocessor are not connected directly to the chip. It is these 'extra' address lines that are used by the address decoder to place the chip in the memory map.

Figure 1.10 shows one possible arrangement employing a 4-input NAND gate to position the ROM in block F of the memory map, i.e. in locations F000H to FFFFH. When address lines A15 to A12 are all driven high by the microprocessor, the output of the NAND gate is low, enabling the chip. (With a 4-input NAND gate all four inputs must be high before the output is driven low – if even one input is at logic 0, the output will remain high.)

Larger systems containing several memory or I/O devices make use of special purpose address decoder chips such as the 74LS138 'one out of

Inputs					Outputs							
Enable		Select										
G1	G2	C	B	A	Y7	Y6	Y5	Y4	Y3	Y2	Y1	Y0
A15		A14	A13	A12	CSF	CSE	CSD	CSC	CSB	CSA	CS9	CS8
X	H	X	X	X	H	H	H	H	H	H	H	H
L	X	X	X	X	H	H	H	H	H	H	H	H
H	L	L	L	L	H	H	H	H	H	H	H	L
H	L	L	L	H	H	H	H	H	H	H	L	H
H	L	L	H	L	H	H	H	H	H	L	H	H
H	L	L	H	H	H	H	H	H	L	H	H	H
H	L	H	L	L	H	H	H	L	H	H	H	H
H	L	H	L	H	H	H	L	H	H	H	H	H
H	L	H	H	L	H	L	H	H	H	H	H	H
H	L	H	H	H	L	H	H	H	H	H	H	H

H = High Level; L = Low Level; X = Irrelevant; G2 =G2A + G2B = always L (GND)

Figure 1.11 Truth table for 74LS138 one-of-eight decoder

eight' decoder. For each pattern of logic levels on the inputs only one of the chip's outputs is activated (driven to logic 0), Figure 1.11.

1.2 CATEGORIES OF MICROCOMPUTERS

The previous section introduced the three basic ingredients that form a microcomputer, namely the microprocessor, the memory and the peripheral interface. However, even with the same ingredients the diversity of applications has produced a wide range of micro products. Some systems are designed to act as low cost controllers, adding intelligence to appliances and games, others, like personal computers and small business systems, provide greater flexibility with interfaces for 'add-on' memory, disk drives, printers, etc. The available systems can be divided into the following categories:

- single chip microcomputers
- single board microcomputers
- multiple board bus systems

Single chip microcomputers

Single chip microcomputers reduce the component count, and hence the product cost, by combining the processor, ROM, RAM and some form of input/output, all in one package. Although the amount of on-chip memory is limited (up to 4 Kbytes of ROM and as little as 64 bytes of RAM), it is normally sufficient for most control applications.

Intel's 8051 has established itself as one of the more powerful single chip 8-bit microcomputers. Developed from the industry standard 8048, it boasts:

- 4 K × 8-bit ROM/EPROM
- 128 K × 8-bit RAM
- four 8-bit ports
- two 16-bit timer/event counters
- full duplex serial channel
- capability of use with up to 128 Kbytes of external memory
- powerful instruction set including multiply and divide

The 8051 is only one in the MCS-51 family of chips that include the 8031 and the 8751. Developed primarily for large volume applications, the 8051 contains on-chip mask programmable ROM that has to be programmed by the manufacturer. The 8031 has no on-chip ROM, and like most microprocessors, must make use of external memory. Finally, the 8751 comes complete with a quartz window and 4 Kbytes of EPROM in place of the mask programmable ROM.

The three members of the family are all pin compatible, with the 8751 ideally suited for development work, low volume applications and installations that require field updates to the system firmware (i.e. the program located in ROM).

Among the other popular single chip micros are the Zilog Z8 and National Semiconductor's INS 8073 (see Chapter 5, section 5.3), both of which have versions that include a BASIC interpreter in the on-chip ROM.

11

Figure 1.12 The ACT Apricot is an example of a modern high-density 16-bit single board computer

Single board systems

Early single board microcomputers centred around manufacturers' evaluation kits, simple controllers (e.g. MEDC board in Appendix B) and relatively low powered home computer systems. Evaluation kits provided (and still provide) an inexpensive method of gaining familiarity with a new microprocessor and its family of peripheral devices (e.g. SDK85, SDK86, KIM, National Semiconductor's SC/MP).

The latest breed of single board systems achieve higher component densities than ever before, with a number of manufacturers producing personal computers containing multiple 16-bit microprocessors, 256 Kbytes of RAM along with disk, serial and video interfaces, all on one printed circuit board, Figure 1.12. This improvement has been due to a number of advances in hardware technology, including:

- increased density in memory chips, with 64 K $\times$ 1-bit dynamic RAMs now commonplace
- the use of special purpose LSI peripheral controllers
- Uncommitted Logic Arrays (ULAs) condensing discrete logic circuitry into a single IC package
- multi-layer printed circuit boards

Growth in the number of single board systems is due to several factors. Firstly, single board micros are less expensive to produce than multiple board systems. Secondly they take up less room, providing a smaller, neater desk-top unit. Thirdly they are inherently more reliable, especially if subject to frequent movement, than systems utilising interconnection plugs and sockets.

Against these features, single board systems often provide a fixed set of functions, many of which are not required. However, for many applications the inherently low cost of such boards overrides any concern for functions left redundant.

To allow for additional functions, for example extra memory or a special purpose interface, many boards provide an expansion bus, either in the form of an edge connector or a set of on-board sockets (e.g. the BBC micro uses the former, whereas the IBM PC and the ACT Apricot employ the latter).

Multiple board bus systems
In multiple board systems a card frame holds a set of boards connected by a backplane or 'motherboard', Figure 1.13. In its simplest form a backplane is a printed circuit board with parallel tracks connecting a number of 'in-line' connectors.

Figure 1.13   Typical multiple board systems based on the S100 bus

A typical microcomputer might contain the following cards, Figure 1.14:

- a processor card holding the microprocessor and its associated control circuitry
- a memory card containing RAM and perhaps a small 'boot ROM' holding a short program that allows the microprocessor to initialise a floppy disk interface and then download a larger operating system program from the floppy disk into the RAM
- a floppy disk controller card containing the interface to one or more disk drives
- a serial and parallel interface card allowing the system to communicate with Visual Display Units (VDUs) and printers

Although initially expensive, multi-board systems are undoubtedly more flexible, allowing the user to select cards and build a system tailored

13

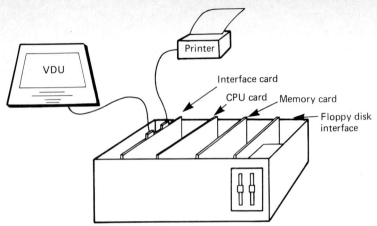

Figure 1.14 Cards found in a typical multiple board system

to his needs. Further, the availability of a range of processor cards makes it a simple task to update or change the microprocessor while still protecting the original investment in memory and peripheral boards.

Several bus structures are currently in use. Some are primarily manufacturer-specific (e.g. Intel's Multibus and Motorola's Exorcisor bus and Versabus), while others, such as S100, VME and STE, have wider support.

The first S100 system (the Altair produced by MITS in 1975) used a backplane containing 100 lines, together with 100 pin edge connectors. At this stage the bus was known as the Altair bus and it was some time later that it acquired the generic name 'Standard 100' bus or S100 for short (Appendix C). The bus proved extremely popular and before long a number of companies were producing S100 systems and add-on boards.

In 1981 the Institute of Electrical and Electronic Engineers published the IEEE 696/S100 standard that provided a firm definition of not only the signals on the bus but also their timing relationships to one another. This step helped overcome the small incompatibility problems experienced by many, and gave manufacturers a standard to work to. As a result, interest in the bus has grown, leading to several hundred companies currently producing S100 products.

Along with the wide range of peripheral interfaces and memory boards, the S100 bus now supports a number of 8-bit and 16-bit microprocessors, including 8080, 8085, Z80, 6502, 6800, 6809, 8088/86, 80186, Z8000, 68000.

Problems

    1.1 The following hexadecimal numbers represent voltage patterns on a microcomputer's address bus:

        a) 1234H
        b) A428H
        c) F2ACH
        d) FFFFH

Convert each to binary and indicate those in which address line A7 is at logic 1.

1.2 The hexadecimal number system evaluates numbers to the base 16. Conversion from binary to hex can be carried out by dividing a binary number into 'bundles' of 4 bits, each represented by a single hexadecimal digit. The octal number system evaluates numbers to the base 8 and requires only a three bit binary number to represent a single octal digit, e.g. binary 011111 would be 37 in octal or 1F in hex. Convert each of the hexadecimal numbers given in Problem 1.1 to octal.

1.3 What changes would you make to the address decode circuit, shown in Figure 1.10, to position the 2332 ROM in the address range:
  a) E000H–EFFFH
  b) A000H–AFFFH

1.4 Design an address decode circuit that makes use of the 74LS138 'one-of-eight' decoder to produce address select signals for the following eight memory areas:

  8000H–8FFFH/9000H–9FFFH/ . . . /E000H–EFFFH/F000H–FFFFH

(The truth table for the 74LS138 is shown in Figure 1.11)

1.5 A simple microcomputer requires only 4 Kbytes of ROM starting at 0000H and 1 Kbyte of RAM at FC00H. If each memory device is contained in a single package, describe an address decode circuit that would provide a chip select signal for each. (Assume there are no other devices in the memory map.)

FURTHER READING

General reading on the impact of microelectronics and 'the way ahead':

Evans, C., 1979. *The Mighty Micro*. London: Gollancz.

Feigenbaum, E.A. and McCorduck, P., 1984. *The Fifth Generation*. Reading, MA: Addison-Wesley/London: Michael Joseph.

A number of textbooks provide an introduction to microprocessor systems. Two sound books giving a step by step account are:

Downton, A.C., 1984. *Computers and Microprocessors*. Wokingham: Van Nostrand Reinhold.

Tocci, R.J. and Laskowski, L.P., 1979. *Microprocessors and Microcomputers: Hardware and Software*. Englewood Cliffs, NJ: Prentice-Hall.

For those wishing a textbook providing details of the application of microprocessors to industrial processes:

Kochhar, A.K. and Burns, N.D., 1983. *Microprocessors and their Manufacturing Applications*. London: Edward Arnold.

For further details of the S100 and other microcomputer bus standards:

Libes, S. and Garetz, M., 1981. *Interfacing to S100/IEEE 696 Microcomputers*. Berkeley, CA: Osborne/McGraw-Hill.

Poe, E.C. and Goodwin, J.C., 1981. *The S100 and other Micro Buses*. Howard Sams.

Chapter 2

Fundamentals of four popular microprocessors

The objectives of this chapter are:

- to illustrate the structure and operation of the microprocessor;
- to highlight the microprocessor's fetch and execute cycles;
- to describe those control signals common to a number of micro-processors;
- to provide a reference source for four popular microprocessors;
- to highlight, with the aid of several examples, some of the pro-gramming features peculiar to each processor.

Although the design and function of microcomputer systems can vary, all have one element in common, namely the microprocessor. The processor lies at the heart of the system forming the central processing unit of the microcomputer. This chapter begins by examining those features common to most microprocessors before providing an introduction to four popular processors:

MOS Technology 6502
Zilog Z80
Intel 8086
Motorola MC68000

The 6502 and the Z80 are 8-bit devices still widely used, especially in home computers and many commercial systems. However, both are starting to show their age as more and more 16-bit systems appear on the market. The 8086, Intel's first 16-bit microprocessor, brought with it new ideas, resulting in several manufacturers, notably IBM and ACT, adopting it (or its twin, the 8088), in a new generation of business machines. Finally, Motorola's 68000 represents a 'fourth generation' processor, making use of very large scale integration (VLSI) to provide one of the most powerful microprocessors produced to date.

2.1 THE MICROPROCESSOR

The tasks performed by the microprocessor can be summarised as follows:

- fetching instructions from memory
- decoding and obeying instructions
- performing logical and arithmetic operations on data
- transferring data to and from memory and I/O devices

Although the internal design of a microprocessor is extremely complex, most can be looked on as being made up of the three building blocks shown in Figure 2.1, namely:

Registers
Timing and Control Logic
Arithmetic/Logic Unit

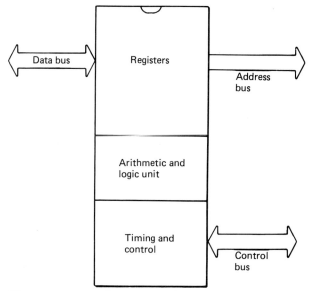

Figure 2.1   Main functional blocks in a microprocessor

Registers

Registers are a set of memory locations inside the microprocessor chip. Unlike locations within the system, which are referred to by number, each is given a name. The number and nature of registers varies from one chip to another, and to a limited extent reflects their performance. However, the registers examined here are common to most microprocessors, providing the means by which they read data and instructions, set up memory addresses and keep track of the current status.

Instruction register   When the processor fetches an operation code from memory it places it in the instruction register where it is decoded to determine what action has to be performed. This register is used automatically by the microprocessor and cannot be accessed by the programmer.

Memory address register On 8-bit microprocessors this is a 16-bit register that is used to hold the address of the instruction or data that is currently being accessed. A second 16-bit register (or program counter, to be described later) is used to point to the operation or instruction codes within a program.

Accumulator This is the main working register of the microprocessor and is involved with most data transfers. As the name suggests it stores data before an arithmetic or logical processing step and usually contains the answer after. Some processors have more than one accumulator, e.g. the 8086 has four.

Index registers Index registers are often used as pointers to elements in lists and tables, or as counters keeping track of the number of times a program loop has been executed.

Stack pointer register The stack is a region of RAM set aside for use by the processor (or the programmer) as a temporary 'notepad'. Whenever the processor is diverted from its main task (e.g. with a subroutine call or an interrupt) information relating to the return address in the main program is stored on the stack. The stack pointer register usually contains the address of the next available location within the stack, but sometimes points to the last item on the stack.

With some microprocessors the position of the stack is fixed in memory, e.g. the 6502 must have its stack in page 1, whereas with others the programmer is free to position the stack at any address.

Program counter A program is made up of a mixture of operation codes, data and addresses. Each new microprocessor instruction commences with an operation code and it is the job of the program counter to point to the position of the next code in memory. After an instruction has been fetched from memory the program counter is incremented until it points to the memory address containing the next operation code. Since the PC holds addresses it is a 16-bit register which is usually referred to in two parts

PCH Program Counter High (holds 8 high order bits of the PC)

PCL Program Counter Low (holds 8 low order bits of the PC)

Status or flag register The processor status register is a collection of status bits, or flags, that are set (logic 1) or cleared (logic 0) depending on the outcome of the previous instruction. Conditional jump or branch instructions use flags to make decisions and redirect program flow, e.g. branch if zero flag set; branch if carry flag clear.

Timing and control logic
The principal task of the microprocessor is to fetch and decode instructions from memory (the *instruction cycle*) and then to generate the control signals needed to carry out these instructions (the *execution*

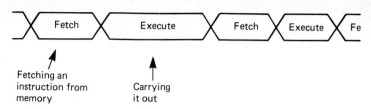

Fetch | Execute | Fetch | Execute | Fe

Fetching an
instruction from
memory

Carrying
it out

Figure 2.2   The processor alternates between instruction and execute
cycles

cycle). During program execution the processor is continually alternating
between these two activities, Figure 2.2.

A number of control signals enable the microprocessor to synchronise these functions with the other components in the microcomputer
system. Like the processor's registers the nature and number of these
signals varies from one manufacturer to another. However, those given
below are found in most systems.

Clock

The clock provides the heartbeat for the microprocessor driving it
from one instruction to the next. Normally a crystal or RC
(Resistor/Capacitor) network is used to provide the basic timing

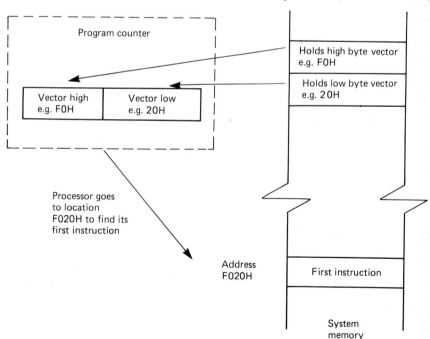

Figure 2.3   Some processors use vectors to load the program counter
at reset

19

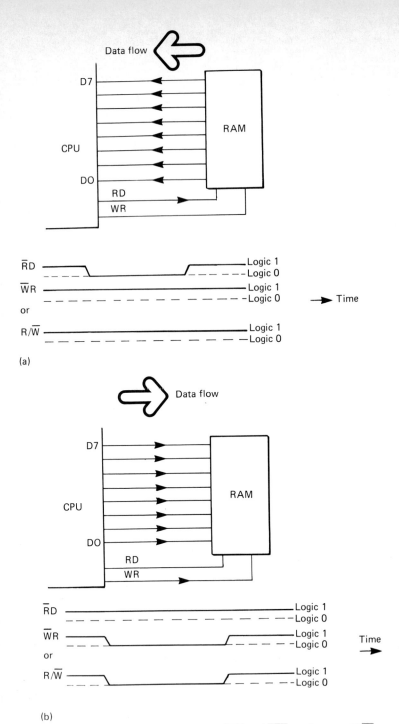

Figure 2.4 The processor uses either $\overline{\text{RD}}$ and $\overline{\text{WR}}$ strobes or a R/$\overline{\text{W}}$ line to inform other components of the direction of flow on the data bus: (a) memory READ; (b) memory WRITE

20

signal which is then fed to the microprocessor. Some processors then shape this raw signal providing high quality timing signals that are used by the microprocessor and surrounding components. Other microprocessors require external components along with the basic oscillator to generate these timing signals (e.g. the 8088/8086 uses an 8284 CLOCK generator/driver chip).

Reset

This input is used to reset most of the internal registers to zero before setting up the program counter to point to the first program instruction. With some microprocessors, for example the 6502, the PC does not point immediately to the first instruction but is loaded instead from two memory locations (vectors) that contain the low and high byte of the address of the first instruction, Figure 2.3.

$\overline{RD}$, $\overline{WR}$

The processor uses these signals to tell other components the direction of flow of information across the data bus. During a READ operation the $\overline{RD}$ strobe is activated informing peripheral devices that they have to pass data to the microprocessor. When the $\overline{WR}$ strobe is true the processor performs a WRITE operation with data passing from the processor to RAM or input/output device.

Some processors use only a single $R/\overline{W}$ (read/not write) line which is high for READ operations and low during WRITE operations, Figure 2.4.

$\overline{MREQ/IORQ}$

Both the Z80 and the 8086 include the program instructions IN and OUT which are designed especially for input/output programming.

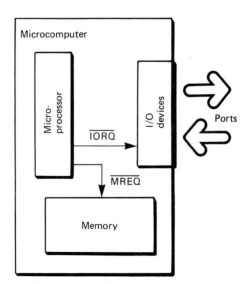

Figure 2.5 $\overline{MREQ}$ and $\overline{IORQ}$ lines are used by some processors to group devices into a memory map and a port map

21

When the processor uses any of these instructions it activates its Input/Output Request ($\overline{\text{IORQ}}$) line to enable devices on its I/O or port map. Any instruction dealing with memory mapped devices activates the Memory Request ($\overline{\text{MREQ}}$) line, Figure 2.5.

READY (WAIT)

This microprocessor input is used by slow memory or I/O devices effectively to slow down the processor giving them time to complete their task. On receiving a READY signal the processor enters a WAIT state where it 'marks time' until the READY signal is removed.

Slow devices that wish to use this facility are used along with a circuit called a *wait state generator*. When the processor addresses the slow device it also enables the wait state generator which then produces a READY signal of sufficient duration for the slow device, Figure 2.6.

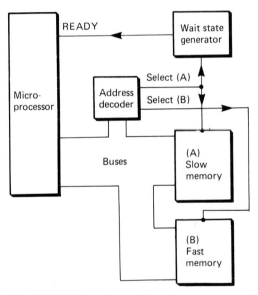

Figure 2.6 The READY input is used by slow memory or I/O devices (in conjunction with a WAIT state generator) to 'slow down' the processor

HOLD/HLDA

Normally it is the microprocessor that controls the system buses establishing addresses on the address bus and exchanging data over the data bus. However, some peripheral devices are capable of taking over the system buses and performing operations directly with memory in a process called Direct Memory Access (DMA). The HOLD input on the processor is used to request use of the system buses. When the microprocessor detects this signal it completes its current instruction before disconnecting itself by 'floating its tri-state' lines. It then acknowledges transfer of control using the Hold Acknowledge (HLDA) output, Figure 2.7.

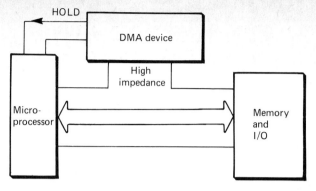

DMA device requests buses using HOLD

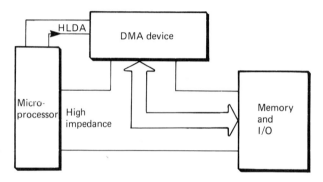

Processor hands over buses and acknowledges

Figure 2.7 The processor uses its HOLD/HLDA lines to handshake
with a device performing DMA

Interrupts ($\overline{\text{INT}}$ or $\overline{\text{IRQ}}$/NMI)

Interrupt inputs on a microprocessor allow external devices (e.g.
clock chips, keyboards, transducers etc.) to demand attention,
diverting the processor from normal program flow into another
program called an Interrupt Service Routine. On some processors
Interrupt Request ($\overline{\text{INT}}$ or $\overline{\text{IRQ}}$) inputs are level sensitive initiating an
interrupt whenever they are at logic 0. Many Non-Maskable
Interrupts (NMI) inputs are edge sensitive only triggering action
when they pass from logic 1 to logic 0. A second major difference
exists in that $\overline{\text{INT}}$ or $\overline{\text{IRQ}}$ interrupts can be masked (ignored) by the
processor if an interrupt disable bit is set in the processor status
register. Non-maskable interrupts, as their name suggests, cannot.

Arithmetic/Logic Unit (ALU)

The microprocessor's ALU allows it to perform a range of arithmetic and
logical operations e.g. addition, subtraction, ORing, ANDing etc. (and with

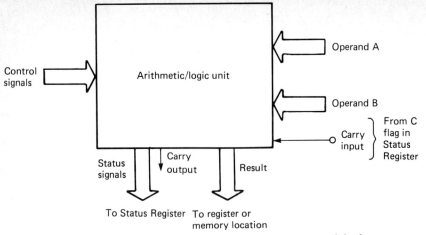

Figure 2.8 Processor's arithmetic/logic unit – simplified

some more modern chips multiplication and division). The process carried out depends on program instruction i.e. the operation code read from memory. Figure 2.8 illustrates the signals used by the ALU. Register or memory contents are entered together with current details of the processor's status. The result of the operation is then returned in a register and the flags are updated to reflect the result (e.g. the zero flag would be set if the result was zero).

2.2 THE 6502

The 6502 is the most popular of the 6500 family of 8-bit microprocessors manufactured by MOS Technology. Several versions of the chip are now available ranging from the common 6502 running at 1 MHz to the 6502C at 4 MHz. The chip has made its major impact in the home computer market with manufacturers Apple, Acorn, Atari and Commodore making use of its simple yet powerful architecture.

Like most of its contemporaries the 6502 requires only a single five volt power supply together with an external clock generator circuit. The chip itself uses this signal to produce two 'non-overlapping' signals, phase 1 and phase 2, that are used to control timing throughout the microcomputer system.

The 6502 was modelled closely on Motorola's 6800 and can operate happily with the latter's family of peripheral devices (e.g. 6820 peripheral interface, 6845 video controller). Its popularity has arisen due to its increased performance with two index registers and a more powerful set of addressing modes.

Programming model

The 6502 contains only six principal registers – an 8-bit accumulator (A), two index registers (X and Y), a 16-bit program counter (PC), an 8-bit stack pointer (SP) and an 8-bit processor status register (P), Figure 2.9. The programmer is restricted to page 1 (0100H to 01FFH) for the system stack.

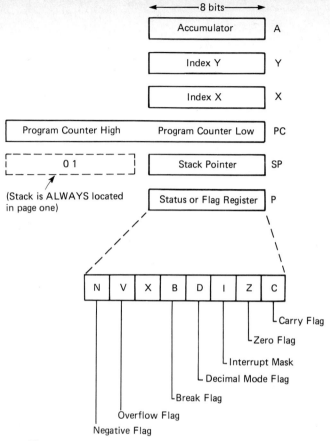

Figure 2.9   6502 programming model (including flag register)

Since the most significant byte of all stack addresses is 01H the processor only requires an 8-bit stack pointer register to hold the least significant byte.

Figure 2.10 gives an alphabetic listing of all the instruction mnemonics. Although there are only 55 instructions in the list, the 6502 uses 145 different *op-codes*. The difference arises from the fact that most instructions can be used with a range of *addressing modes*. In simple terms addressing modes are the different ways the microprocessor can perform its task. For example, the LDA instruction could be used to:

- load the accumulator with a number given in the program – *immediate addressing*
- load the accumulator with the contents of a memory location whose address is given in the program – *absolute* or *direct addressing*
- load the accumulator from an element in a list of numbers using either the X or Y register to point to the chosen number – *indexed addressing*

ADC Add Memory to Accumulator with Carry
AND 'AND' Memory with Accumulator
ASL Shift Left One Bit (Memory or Accumulator)

BCC Branch on Carry Clear
BCS Branch on Carry Set
BEQ Branch on Result Zero
BIT Test Bits in Memory with Accumulator
BMI Branch on Result Minus
BNE Branch on Result not Zero
BPL Branch on Result Plus
BRK Force Break
BVC Branch on Overflow Clear
BVS Branch on Overflow Set

CLC Clear Carry Flag
CLD Clear Decimal Mode
CLI Clear Interrupt Disable Bit
CLV Clear Overflow Flag
CMP Compare Memory and Accumulator
CPX Compare Memory and Index X
CPY Compare Memory and Index Y

DEC Decrement Memory by One
DEX Decrement Index X by One
DEY Decrement Index Y by One

EOR 'Exclusive-Or' Memory with Accumulator

INC Increment Memory by One
INX Increment Index X by One
INY Increment Index Y by One

JMP Jump to New Location

JSR Jump to New Location Saving Return Address

LDA Load Accumulator with Memory
LDX Load Index X with Memory
LDY Load Index Y with Memory
LSR Shift Right One Bit (Memory or Accumulator)

NOP No Operation

ORA 'OR' Memory with Accumulator

PHA Push Accumulator on Stack
PHP Push Processor Status on Stack
PLA Pull Accumulator from Stack
PLP Pull Processor Status from Stack

ROL Rotate One Bit Left (Memory or Accumulator)
ROR Rotate One Bit Right (Memory or Accumulator)
RTI Return from Interrupt
RTS Return from Subroutine

SBC Subtract Memory from Accumulator with Borrow
SEC Set Carry Flag
SED Set Decimal Mode
SEI Set Interrupt Disable Status
STA Store Accumulator in Memory
STX Store Index X in memory
STY Store Index Y in memory

TAX Transfer Accumulator to Index X
TAY Transfer Accumulator to Index Y
TSX Transfer Stack Pointer to Index X
TXA Transfer Index X to Accumulator
TXS Transfer Index X to Stack Pointer
TYA Transfer Index Y to Accumulator

Figure 2.10 Alphabetic listing of 6502 instruction set

Addressing Modes
Absolute or direct
Zero page
Immediate
Indexed absolute
Indexed zero page
Implied
Indirect
Indirect indexed
Indexed indirect
Relative
Accumulator

Figure 2.11   Summary of 6502 addressing modes

All the operations above have the same effect – namely the accumulator is loaded with a number. The way the processor sets about the task is different in each case and it is the job of the programmer to choose the best technique for the job in hand.

Figure 2.11 summarises the addressing modes for the 6502. Not all the modes are available with each instruction and the programmer should consult a detailed instruction list.

Programming examples

In common with most 8-bit microprocessors the 6502 was not designed to perform arithmetic, supporting only two arithmetic instructions:

ADC   Add with Carry

SBC   Subtract with Complement of Carry

The 8-bit size of the accumulator restricts the number range that can be used with each of these instructions to 0–255. If larger numbers, fractions or negative numbers are required the programmer has to write routines that perform the required task using these basic instructions.

```
               11   ;ROUTINE TO PERFORM 16 BIT ADDITION OF  3580H + 2749H
               12   ;THE ANSWER IS PLACED IN MEMORY LOCATIONS 0300H,0301H
               13
               14         ORG      0200H
               15
0200 A980      16         LDA      #80H       ;LOW BYTE OF FIRST NUMBER
0202 18        17         CLC                 ;ENSURE CARRY CLEAR
0203 6949      18         ADC      #49H       ;ADD TO LOW BYTE OF THE SECOND NUMBER
               19                             ;ANSWER NOW IN ACCUMULATOR
0205 8D0300    20         STA      0300H      ;STORE LOW BYTE OF ANSWER IN 0300H
0208 A935      21         LDA      #35H       ;GET HIGH BYTE OF FIRST NUMBER
020A 6927      22         ADC      #27H       ;ADD TO HIGH BYTE OF SECOND NUMBER
               23                             ;TOGETHER WITH ANY CARRY
020C 8D0301    24         STA      0301H      ;HIGH BYTE OF ANSWER IN 0301H
               25
               26   ;ROUTINE COMPLETE.................ANSWER IN 0300H,0301H
               27
               28
```

Program 2.1   6502 performing 16-bit addition

Program 2.1 gives an example of a routine that could be used to obtain the sum of two 16-bit numbers. The routine begins by adding the two least significant bytes and storing the least significant 8-bits of the answer in memory location 0300H. Any carry that is generated is added in with the addition of the two most significant bytes. The high byte of the answer is then placed in location 0301H.

```
                    32  ;SUBROUTINE TO DISPLAY A TEXT MESSAGE
                    33  ;ROUTINE MAKES USE OF SUBROUTINE "OUTPUT"(NOT GIVEN) TO
                    34  ;PLACE ASCII CHARACTERS IN THE 'A' REGISTER ON THE SCREEN
                    35
        (FF88)      36  OUTPUT   EQU     0FF88H    ;START ADDRESS OF DISPLAY ROUTINE
                    37
                    38           ORG     0200H
                    39
0200 A200           40           LDX     #00       ;USE 'X' AS COUNTER,SO SET TO
                    41                              ;ZERO AT START
0202 BD020E         42  NEXT     LDA     MESS,X    ;GET CHARACTER FROM MESSAGE
0205 20FF88         43           JSR     OUTPUT    ;ONTO SCREEN
0208 E8             44           INX               ;INCREMENT X
0209 C92A           45           CMP     #"*"      ;DOES 'A' REGISTER CONTAIN THE
                    46                              ;END OF MESSAGE MARKER
020B D0F5           47           BNE     NEXT      ;IF NOT BACK FOR NEXT CHARACTER
020D 60             48           RTS               ;SUBROUTINE COMPLETE
                    49
020E 5448495320     50  MESS     ASC     "THIS IS THE MESSAGE *"
                    51
                    52
```

Program 2.2   Using indexed addressing to display a text message

Program 2.2 illustrates a useful subroutine found in many large programs. The routine uses indexed addressing to display a simple text message on a microcomputer's screen. A string of ASCII characters making up the message is placed in memory starting at location MESS i.e. 020EH. An asterisk, ASCII code 2AH, is used as an end of string marker.

```
                    56  ;SUBROUTINE TO CONVERT BYTE IN ACCUMULATOR TO
                    57  ;TWO ASCII CHARACTERS AND DISPLAY
                    58
                    59  ;OUTPUT   EQU     0FF88H    ;START ADDRESS OF DISPLAY ROUTINE
                    60
                    61           ORG     0200H
                    62
0200 AA             63  CONVERT  TAX               ;SAVE BYTE IN 'X' REGISTER
0201 29F0           64           AND     #0F0H     ;GET TOP HEX DIGIT
0203 4A             65           LSR     A         ;MOVE IT INTO LEAST SIG. POSITION
0204 4A             66           LSR     A         ;(eg 80H -> 08H)
0205 4A             67           LSR     A
0206 4A             68           LSR     A         ;SHIFT COMPLETE
0207 200217         69           JSR     ASCII     ;CONVERT NIBBLE TO ASCII
020A 20FF88         70           JSR     OUTPUT    ;ONTO DISPLAY
020D 8A             71           TXA               ;ORIGINAL DATA BACK INTO 'A'
020E 290F           72           AND     #0FH      ;GET BOTTOM HEX DIGIT
0210 200217         73           JSR     ASCII     ;CONVERT NIBBLE TO ASCII
0213 20FF88         74           JSR     OUTPUT    ;ONTO DISPLAY
0216 60             75           RTS               ;SUBROUTINE COMPLETE
                    76
                    77  ;SUBROUTINE TO CONVERT L.S. 4BITS (NIBBLE) TO ASCII
                    78
0217 C90A           79  ASCII    CMP     #0AH      ;NUMBER (1->9) OR LETTER (A->F) ?
0219 9003           80           BCC     OK        ;BRANCH IF NUMBER
021B 18             81           CLC
021C 6907           82           ADC     #7        ;ADD 7 FOR A->F
021E 6930           83  OK       ADC     #30H      ;ADD 30H FOR ALL
0220 60             84           RTS               ;ACCUMULATOR NOW CONTAINS ASCII
```

Program 2.3   A hex to ASCII conversion routine

The routine begins by setting X equal to zero and then loading the accumulator with the first character in the message. Subroutine OUTPUT then displays the character and X is incremented to point to the next character. Finally the compare instruction checks the current contents of the accumulator for the end of string marker *.

Any program that is used to display the contents of memory locations in hex will include a subroutine to convert an 8-bit binary value to two ASCII characters. Program 2.3 performs this task. The routine converts the most significant 4 bits (nibble) to ASCII before the least significant nibble. The routine makes use of another subroutine ASCII to check the nibble lies between 0 and 9 or A to F and provide the offset required, namely 30H or 37H.

```
                89 ;ROUTINE TO STORE TEXT IN AN INPUT BUFFER
                90 ;SUBROUTINE "INPUT"(NOT GIVEN) IS USED TO GET
                91 ;CHARACTERS FROM THE KEYBOARD.
                92 ;INPUT BUFFER STARTS AT 2000H AND HOLDS UP TO 4KBYTES
                93
      (FFA0)    94 INPUT    EQU     0FFA0H      ;ROUTINE TO GET ASCII CODE FOR
                95                              ;CHARACTER FROM KEYBOARD INTO 'A'
                96
      (0080)    97 POINT    EQU     80H         ;0080H AND 0081H USED AS POINTERS
                98
                99          ORG     0200H
                100
0200 A200       101 START   LDX     #0          ;SET X TO ZERO (NOT USED)
0202 A900       102         LDA     #00         ;SET UP POINTERS TO START OF BUFFER
0204 8580       103         STA     POINT       ;LOW BYTE FIRST
0206 A920       104         LDA     #20H        ;NOW HIGH BYTE
0208 8581       105         STA     POINT+1
                106
020A 20FFA0     107 AGAIN   JSR     INPUT       ;GET CHARACTER
020D 8180       108         STA     [POINT,X]   ;STORE IN BUFFER
020F C92A       109         CMP     #"*"        ;WAS IT END MARKER ie"*"
0211 F00A       110         BEQ     FINI        ;IF SO FINISHED
0213 E680       111         INC     POINT       ;INCREMENT POINT
0215 D0F3       112         BNE     AGAIN       ;IF NOT ZERO STRAIGHT BACK
                113                             ;FOR NEXT CHARACTER
0217 E681       114         INC     POINT+1     ;IF POINT GOES TO ZERO THEN
                115                             ;INCREMENT HIGH BYTE ie POINT+1
0219 C930       116         CMP     #30H        ;BUFFER FULL ?
021B D0ED       117         BNE     AGAIN       ;IF NOT BACK FOR ANOTHER
021D            118 FINI                        ;ROUTINE FINISHED
```

Program 2.4   Using indirect addressing to load a text
buffer

Finally, Program 2.4 illustrates how the 6502's powerful indirect addressing mode can be used in a routine to store text in a buffer. Memory locations 0080H and 0081H are used as pointers or vectors to the next available location within the buffer. The routine begins by initialising the vectors to point to the first location i.e. 2000H. The subroutine INPUT obtains a character from the keyboard which is then placed in the buffer using the indexed indirect instruction

```
STA [POINT,X]
```

Again this routine uses the * as an end of text marker.

6502 Microprocessor description
The 6502, like many other processors, is housed in a 40 pin dual in-line package, Figure 2.12. The 16-bit address bus is capable of driving at least

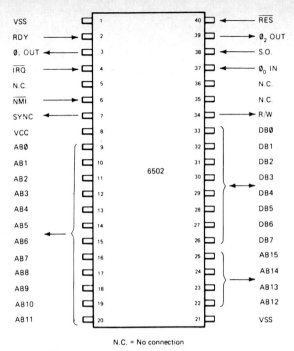

Figure 2.12 The 6502 microprocessor

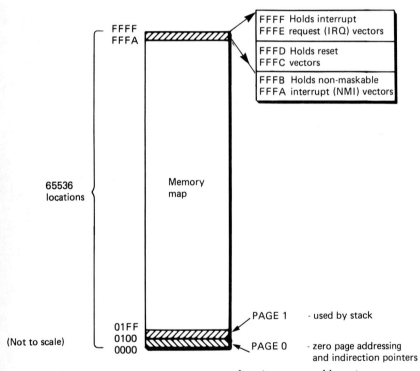

Figure 2.13 6502 memory map showing reserved locations

one standard TTL load and provides the processor with an addressable memory range of 65536 locations, Figure 2.13. Each of the 8 data bus pins is connected to an input and an output buffer. The latter is tri-state and like the address bus capable of driving one standard TTL load.

In a similar way to the 6800 the 6502 uses a 2 phase clock to control system timing. During phase 1 the processor sets up a valid memory address and selects either a READ or WRITE operation using the R/W̅ line. Data is then exchanged during the phase 2 clock pulse, Figure 2.14. In both READ and WRITE operations data must be stable at least 100 ns before the falling edge of phase 2 (for a 1 MHz clock). When performing a READ operation the processor latches data into its internal registers on the falling edge of the phase 2 clock.

Other processor signals   The 6502 signal lines are almost identical to those given earlier in the general introduction. Any differences or further details are shown below:

R̅E̅S̅ (pin 40)

The RESET signal is used to initialise the processor from a power down condition or to regain control. Normally this line is held at

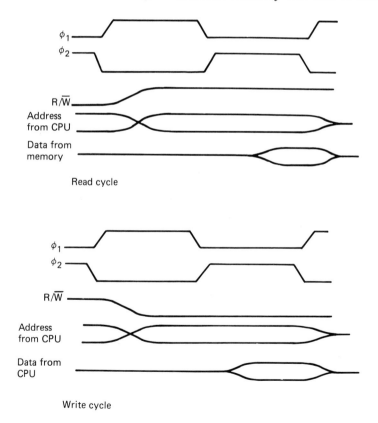

Figure 2.14   6502 READ and WRITE cycles

logic 1 using a pull up resistor. When the processor is reset the line is brought down to logic 0. On returning to logic 1 it begins the start-up procedure shown in Figure 2.15. Firstly the processor waits 6 clock cycles, to allow any external devices to recover from the reset, before going to locations FFFCH and FFFDH to find the low and high bytes respectively of the address of the first instruction, Figure 2.3.

SYNC (pin 7)

The processor uses its SYNC output to 'mark' those machine cycles when it is fetching an op-code from memory. The line is normally low going high at the start of phase 1 during an op-code fetch. Often this line is used together with the READY input signal to SINGLE STEP the processor.

SO (pin 38)

The Set Overflow line is effectively a single-bit input port that sets or clears the overflow flag, in the processor status register. The input is edge sensitive setting the flag on a falling edge (high to low) and clearing it on a rising edge (low to high). The SO input is useful when some external device requires rapid service, e.g. a program can detect a transition within 4 clock cycles (i.e. within 4 microseconds if using a 1 MHz clock).

NMI (pin 6)

After receiving a falling edge on the Non-Maskable Interrupt the 6502 first completes its current instruction before pushing its program counter and status register on the stack. After this the processor follows a similar sequence to that carried out on reset, going to locations FFFAH and FFFBH to find the low and high bytes of the starting address of an Interrupt Service Routine. Program control then transfers to this routine which should be terminated with a Return from Interrupt (RTI) instruction. The RTI instruction restores the PC and the status register and returns the processor back to its original program.

During the interrupt routine the I flag (interrupt disable) is set preventing any further interrupts by the $\overline{\text{IRQ}}$ input.

$\overline{\text{IRQ}}$ (pin 4)

This Interrupt Request input will initiate a sequence very similar to that following a non-maskable interrupt. However, there are some important differences:

1. The $\overline{\text{IRQ}}$ input will only cause an interrupt if the interrupt disable bit in the processor status register is clear (0). This gives the programmer control over $\overline{\text{IRQ}}$ interrupts, using the instructions:

    SEI   Set Interrupt Disable
    CLI   Clear Interrupt Disable

Figure 2.15   6502 activity at RESET

2.   The $\overline{\text{IRQ}}$ pin is level sensitive.

Like the NMI, $\overline{\text{IRQ}}$ uses vectors to find its interrupt service routine. Locations FFFEH and FFFFH, Figure 2.13, contain the low and high bytes of the new program counter. Again `RTI` is used as a final instruction to return control to the original program. The interrupt disable flag is automatically set at the start of an interrupt routine. (If the application requires that the processor is still sensitive to $\overline{\text{IRQ}}$ interrupts during an interrupt routine, it is up to the programmer to clear the interrupt disable flag using the `CLI` instruction.)

2.3   INTRODUCTION TO THE ZILOG Z80

The Z80 was designed as an enhanced version of Intel's popular 8080, providing an extensive instruction set, including the entire 8080's as a subset, together with indexed addressing and block move and search instructions. Additional hardware features comprise:

- non-maskable interrupt capability
- vectored priority interrupt structure
- on board refresh counter for dynamic RAM

Undoubtedly part of the success of the Z80 is due to its ability to execute 8080 code enabling it to make use of a vast software base. In particular Digital Research's operating system CP/M (Control Program for Microcomputers), which is 8080 based, has become a standard used for numerous program languages and applications packages in both industry and commerce.

Programming model
Unlike the 6502 described in the previous section, the Z80 is a register orientated processor with eighteen 8-bit and four 16-bit registers, Figure 2.16. An unusual feature of the Z80 is its alternative register set, A',B'...L'. Only one set of registers can be active at any time; however, some special instructions allow the programmer to switch quickly from one set to another.

General purpose registers   The A register is the processor's main working register and takes part in all logical and arithmetic operations. The other six general purpose registers are grouped in pairs, namely, B and C, D and E, H and L. Many instructions use the contents of a register pair to point to

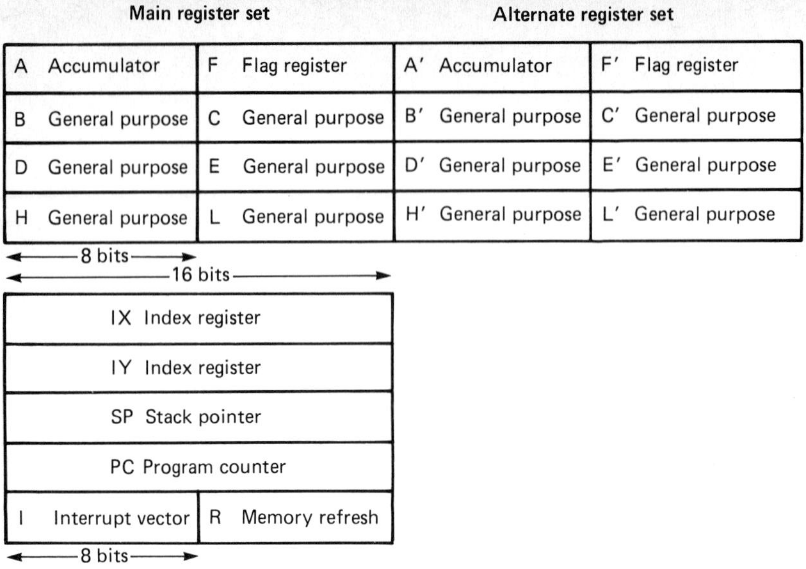

A	Accumulator	F	Flag register	A'	Accumulator	F'	Flag register
B	General purpose	C	General purpose	B'	General purpose	C'	General purpose
D	General purpose	E	General purpose	D'	General purpose	E'	General purpose
H	General purpose	L	General purpose	H'	General purpose	L'	General purpose

◄——8 bits——►
◄————————16 bits————————►

| IX Index register |
| IY Index register |
| SP Stack pointer |
| PC Program counter |

| I | Interrupt vector | R | Memory refresh |

◄——8 bits——►

Figure 2.16   Z80 programming model

the address of data in memory, an extremely useful technique called *register indirect addressing*.

The index registers IX and IY are used primarily as pointers with lists or tables. Since each is 16-bits wide they give the programmer the ability to locate or position data anywhere within the system's memory map.

Special purpose registers   The Z80 uses a full 16-bit stack pointer that points to the last location containing data on the stack. With the Z80 the programmer has the flexibility of locating the stack at any position within the system RAM.

After the microprocessor has decoded an instruction code it automatically increments the Program Counter (PC) by either one, two, three or four, depending on the length of the current instruction, to point to the start of the next instruction.

To support a vectored interrupt facility the Z80 employs an interrupt vector register I. The I registers hold part of an address used by the processor to locate an interrupt service routine (described later).

The refresh register is not normally used by the programmer. Effectively it is a counter that increments every time the processor fetches an op-code from memory. Its contents are placed on the lower 7 bits of the address bus at the end of an op-code fetch cycle and used in many systems to refresh dynamic RAM (see Z80 processor description).

Finally the processor status or flag register, Figure 2.17, contains a collection of bits that reflect the outcome of previous instructions.

Instructions and Addressing Modes   The Z80 is definitely a programmer's microprocessor with no less than 158 instructions including block

34

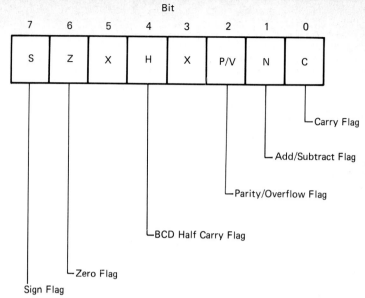

Figure 2.17 Z80 flag register

Mnemonic	Symbolic operation	Comments
8-bit Loads		
LD r,s	r ← s	s ≡ r,n,(HL),(IX+e),(IY+e)
LD d,r	d ← r	d ≡ (HL),r,(IX+e),(IY+e)
LD d,n	d ← n	d ≡ (HL),(IX+e),(IY+e)
LD A,s	A ← s	s ≡ (BC),(DE),(nn),I,R
LD d,A	d ← A	d ≡ (BC),(DE),(nn),I,R
16-bit Loads		
LD dd,nn	dd ← nn	dd ≡ BC,DE,HL,SP,IX,IY
LD dd,(nn)	dd ← (nn)	dd ≡ BC,DE,HL,SP,IX,IY
LD (nn),ss	(nn) ← ss	ss ≡ BC,DE,HL,SP,IX,IY
LD SP,ss	SP ← ss	ss = HL,IX,IY
PUSH ss	$(SP-1) \leftarrow ss_H : (SP-2) \leftarrow ss_L$	ss = BC,DE,HL,AF,IX,IY
POP dd	$dd_L \leftarrow (SP) : dd_H \leftarrow (SP+1)$	dd = BC,DE,HL,AF,IX,IY
Exchanges		
EX DE,HL	DE ↔ HL	
EX AF,AF′	AF ↔ AF′	
EXX	$\begin{pmatrix} BC \\ DE \\ HL \end{pmatrix} \leftrightarrow \begin{pmatrix} BC' \\ DE' \\ HL' \end{pmatrix}$	
EX(SP),ss	$(SP) \leftrightarrow ss_L, (SP+1) \leftrightarrow ss_H$	ss ≡ HL,IX,IY

Figure 2.18 Z80 instruction set

Mnemonic	Symbolic operation	Comments
Memory Block Moves		
LDI	(DE) ← (HL),DE ← DE+1	
	HL ← HL+1,BC ← BC−1	
LDIR	(DE) ← (HL),DE ← DE+1	
	HL ← HL+1,BC ← BC−1	
	Repeat until BC = 0	
LDD	(DE) ← (HL),DE ← DE−1	
	HL ← HL−1,BC ← BC−1	
LDDR	(DE) ← (HL),DE ←DE−1	
	HL ← HL−1,BC ← BC−1	
	Repeat until BC = 0	
Memory Block Searches		
CPI	A−(HL),HL ← HL+1	
	BC ← BC−1	
CPIR	A−(HL),HL ← HL+1	A−(HL) sets
	BC ← BC−1, Repeat	the flags only.
	until BC = 0 or A = (HL)	A is not affected
CPD	A−(HL),HL ← HL−1	
	BC ← BC−1	
CPDR	A−(HL),HL ← HL−1	
	BC ← BC−1, Repeat	
	until BC = 0 or A = (HL)	
8-bit ALU		
ADD s	A ← A + s	
ADC s	A ← A + s + CY	CY is the
		carry flag
SUB s	A ← A − s	
SBC s	A ← A − s − CY	s≡r,n,(HL)
AND s	A ← A∧s	(IX+e),(IY+e)
OR s	A ← A ∨	
XOR s	A ← A ⊕	
8-bit ALU		
CP s	A − s	s = r,n,(HL)
		(IX+e),(IY+e)
INC d	d ← d + 1	
		d = r,(HL)
		(IX+e),(IY+e)
DEC d	d ← d − 1	

Figure 2.18 Continued

Mnemonic	Symbolic operation	Comments
16-bit Arithmetic		
ADD HL,ss	HL ← HL + ss	
ADC HL,ss	HL ← HL + ss + CY	ss≡BC,DE,
SBC HL,ss	HL ← HL − ss − CY	HL,SP
ADD IX,ss	IX ← IX + ss	ss≡BC,DE, IX,SP
ADD IY,ss	IY ← IY + ss	ss≡BC,DE, IY,SP
INC dd	dd ← dd + 1	dd≡BC,DE, HL,SP,IX,IY
DEC dd	dd ← dd − 1	dd≡BC,DE, HL,SP,IX,IY
GP ACC. & Flag		
DAA	Converts A contents into packed BCD following add or subtract.	Operands must be in packed BCD format
CPL	A ← $\overline{A}$	
NEG	A ← 00 − A	
CCF	CY ← $\overline{CY}$	
SCF	CY ← 1	
Miscellaneous		
NOP	No operation	
HALT	Halt CPU	
DI	Disable Interrupts	
EI	Enable Interrupts	
IM 0	Set interrupt mode 0	8080A mode
IM 1	Set interrupt mode 1	Call to 0038$_H$
IM 2	Set interrupt mode 2	Indirect Call

Rotates and Shifts

RLC s CY ← 7 ← s

RL s CY ← 7 ← 0

RRC s 7 → 0 → CY

RR s 7 → 0 → CY

SLA s CY ← 7 ← 0 ← 0

SRA s 7 → 0 → CY

SRL s 0 → 7 → 0 → CY

s≡r,(HL), (IX+e),(IY+e)

RLD 7 4|3 0   7 4|3 7 (HL) A

RRD 7 4|3 0   7 4|3 0 (HL) A

Figure 2.18 Continued

Mnemonic	Symbolic operation	Comments
Bit S, R, & T		
BIT b,s	$Z \leftarrow \overline{s_b}$	Z is zero flag
SET b,s	$s_b \leftarrow 1$	$a \equiv r,(HL)$
RES b,s	$s_b \leftarrow 0$	$(IX+e),(IY+e)$
Input and Output		
IN A,(n)	$A \leftarrow (n)$	
IN r,(C)	$r \leftarrow (C)$	Set flags
INI	$(HL) \leftarrow (C), HL \leftarrow HL + 1,$ $B \leftarrow B - 1$	
INIR	$(HL) \leftarrow (C), HL \leftarrow HL + 1,$ $B \leftarrow B - 1$ Repeat until B=0	
IND	$(HL) \leftarrow (C), HL \leftarrow HL - 1,$ $B \leftarrow B - 1$	
INDR	$(HL) \leftarrow (C), HL \leftarrow HL - 1,$ $B \leftarrow B - 1$ Repeat until B=0	
OUT(n),A	$(n) \leftarrow A$	
OUT(C),r	$(C) \leftarrow r$	
OUTI	$(C) \leftarrow (HL), HL \leftarrow HL + 1,$ $B \leftarrow B - 1$	
OTIR	$(C) \leftarrow (HL), HL \leftarrow HL + 1,$ $B \leftarrow B - 1$ Repeat until B=0	
OUTD	$(C) \leftarrow (HL), HL \leftarrow HL - 1,$ $B \leftarrow B - 1$	
OTDR	$(C) \leftarrow (HL), HL \leftarrow HL - 1,$ $B \leftarrow B - 1$ Repeat until B=0	

Jumps		
JP nn	$PC \leftarrow nn$	
JP cc,nn	If condition cc is true $PC \leftarrow nn$, else continue	$cc \begin{cases} NZ & PO \\ Z & PE \\ NC & P \\ C & M \end{cases}$
JR e	$PC \leftarrow PC + e$	
JR kk,e	If condition kk is true $PC \leftarrow PC + e,$ else continue	$kk \begin{cases} NZ & NC \\ Z & C \end{cases}$
JP (ss)	$PC \leftarrow ss$	ss=HL,IX,IY
DJNZ e	$B \leftarrow B - 1$, if B=0 continue, else $PC \leftarrow PC + e$	

Calls		
CALL nn	$(SP-1) \leftarrow PC_H$ $(SP-2)| \leftarrow PC_L, PC \leftarrow nn$	
CALL cc,nn	If condition cc is false continue, else same as CALL nn	$cc \begin{cases} NZ & PO \\ Z & PE \\ NC & P \\ C & M \end{cases}$

Restarts	
RST L	$(SP-1) \leftarrow PC_H$ $(SP-2) \leftarrow PC_L, PC_H \leftarrow 0$ $PC_L \leftarrow L$

Figure 2.18 Continued

Mnemonic	Symbolic operation	Comments
Returns		
RET	$PC_L \leftarrow (SP)$, $PC_H \leftarrow (SP + 1)$	
RET cc	If condition cc is false continue, else same as RET	
RETI	Return from interrupt same as RET	
RETN	Return from non-maskable interrupt	

$$cc \begin{cases} NZ & PO \\ Z & PE \\ NC & P \\ C & M \end{cases}$$

Figure 2.18   Continued

1.   *Immediate mode*:   The location following the op-code contains the data operand.

2.   *Extended immediate mode*:   The locations following the op-code contain a 16-bit data operand.

3.   *Modified page zero addressing*:   This mode is used to initiate a subroutine jump to any of eight locations in page zero. Commonly called subroutines can be placed at these locations and be accessed by a single-byte instruction called a restart.

4.   *Relative addressing*:   This uses a 1-byte displacement address in the range $+127$ to -128 from the current address plus 2, thereby supporting relocatable code.

5.   *Extended or absolute addressing*:   The full 16-bit memory address is specified by the two operand bytes.

6.   *Indexed addressing*:   A displacement is added to one of the two index registers to form the final address. This is useful for look-up tables.

7.   *Register addressing*:   The op-code contains data specifying a particular register.

8.   *Implied addressing*:   The addressed register, such as the accumulator, is implied within the instruction.

9.   *Indirect addressing*:   A 16-bit register pair, such as HL, contains the operand address.

10.   *Bit addressing*:   Three bits of the op-code specify a particular bit of a memory location to be manipulated.

Figure 2.19   Z80 addressing modes

moves and tests for individual bits in memory or registers, Figure 2.18. The designers of the Z80 took advantage of 12 unused op-codes in the 8080, using some of them directly for new instructions and others as 'doors' to additional op-code tables each capable of supporting up to 256 new codes. Figure 2.19 summarises the addressing modes available on the Z80.

Programming examples
The first Z80 example, Program 2.5, illustrates the register indirect addressing mode loading the accumulator with the contents of a memory location pointed to by the HL pair. This useful technique gives the programmer the flexibility of pointing to data anywhere within the system memory map. After complementing the accumulator the HL pointers are incremented and the complement stored in location 8101H.

```
               3  ;SIMPLE ROUTINE TO COMPLEMENT THE CONTENTS OF  ..
               4  ;LOCATION 8100H PLACING THE RESULT IN 8101H.
               5
               6         ORG      8000H
               7
8000 218100    8         LD       HL,8100H    ;SET HL PAIR TO 8100H
8003 7E        9         LD       A,[HL]      ;GET DATA FROM 8100H
8004 2F       10         CPL                  ;COMPLEMENT 0->1,1->0
8005 23       11         INC      HL          ;SET POINTERS TO 8101H
8006 77       12         LD       [HL],A      ;STORE COMPLEMENT IN 8101H
```

Program 2.5   Z80 routine illustrating register indirect addressing

Program 2.6 shows a short routine to add the numbers 1 through 8. The processor's B register is used to hold the current number and the A register to hold the current total. Like most counting loops the program begins by setting the total equal to zero; exclusive ORing the accumulator with itself is a quick method of clearing the A register. The program then continues to add the series of numbers in the order 8, 7, 6 etc. using the ADD A,B instruction.

```
LOCATION OBJECT CODE LINE      SOURCE LINE

               1  "Z80"
               2
               3  ;ROUTINE TO FIND THE TOTAL OF THE NUMBERS 1 TO 8
               4  ;USE A TO HOLD THE TOTAL AND B THE CURRENT NUMBER
               5
               6          ORG     8000H
               7
8000 AF        8          XOR     A          ;SET A EQUAL TO 0
8001 0608      9          LD      B,08H      ;USE B AS COUNTER
8003 80       10  NEXT    ADD     A,B        ;ADD NEXT NUMBER TO TOTAL IN A
8004 05       11          DEC     B          ;OBTAIN NEXT NUMBER
8005 C28003   12          JP      NZ,NEXT    ;BACK FOR MORE IF B<>0
```

Program 2.6   Program loop to sum the numbers 1 to 8

The next routine compacts two ASCII characters (assumed to lie in the range 0 to 9, A to F) to a single 8-bit byte, Program 2.7. This type of packing routine is usually found in communication programs or simple monitor routines where a series of ASCII characters representing data are packed together to form 8-bit binary before being loaded into memory.

40

```
                      3 ;ROUTINE TO PACK TWO ASCII CHARACTERS (0 TO 9,A TO F) TO..
                      4 ;HEX NUMBER IN C REGISTER. ROUTINE USES THE SUBROUTINE ..
                      5 ;"INPUT" (NOT GIVEN) TO OBTAIN  ASCII CHARACTER IN THE A
                      6 ;REGISTER
                      7
                      8
                      9
        (0300)       10 INPUT     EQU       0300H       ;START ADDRESS OF INPUT ROUTINE
                     11
                     12
                     13           ORG       8000H
                     14
8000 0E00            15 PACK      LD        C,0         ;CLEAR C REGISTER..USE TO BUILD BYT
8002 CD0300          16           CALL      INPUT       ;GET FIRST ASCII CHARACTER
8005 CD800B          17           CALL      CONVERT     ;CONVERT TO HEX
8008 CD0300          18           CALL      INPUT       ;GET SECOND ASCII CHARACTER
800B CB21            19 CONVERT   SLA       C           ;USE THIS TO MOVE FIRST ..
800D CB21            20           SLA       C           ;..CHARACTER INTO M.S. 4 BITS
800F CB21            21           SLA       C
8011 CB21            22           SLA       C
8013 D630            23           SUB       30H         ;STRIP OF 30H FROM ASCII IN A
8015 FE0A            24           CP        0AH         ;IS REMAINDER > 9 ie. A TO F ?
8017 FA801C          25           JP        M,FINI
801A D607            26           SUB       07H         ;MUST BE A TO F ..SO CONVERT
801C 81              27 FINI      ADD       A,C         ;MERGE TOP AND BOTTOM NIBBLE
801D C9              28           RET                   ;FINISHED.. HEX VALUE IN C
```

Program 2.7   ASCII to hex packing routine

The routine uses the C register to build up the 8-bit byte from the two ASCII characters. Subroutine CONVERT makes the conversion from ASCII to a 4-bit nibble by stripping off either 30H or 37H from the ASCII code (the former for numbers, the latter for letters).

Finally Program 2.8 illustrates one of the Z80's powerful block move instructions. LDI, LDIR, LDD and LDDR can all be used to transfer a block of data from one place in memory to another. Register pair BC should be preset to the number of bytes to be transferred, register pair HL to the starting address of the source block, and register pair DE to the start address of the destination block.

The example makes use of the LDIR instruction (load and increment repeatedly) to move 0400H bytes from 2000H to 4000H as follows:

1.   The first byte is moved from address 2000H to 4000H using the HL and DE register pairs as pointers.

2.   The HL and DE registers are incremented by one to point to the next byte in each block.

3.   The byte count is decreased by one.

4.   If the byte count (BC) is not equal to zero then the instruction continues.

```
                      3 ;USING THE LDIR INSTRUCTION TO MOVE A BLOCK OF CODE
                      4 ;FROM 2000H TO 4000H
                      5
                      6           ORG       8000H
                      7
8000 212000           8           LD        HL,2000H    ;SET UP SOURCE POINTER
8003 114000           9           LD        DE,4000H    ;SET UP DESTINATION POINTER
8006 010400          10           LD        BC,0400H    ;SET BC FOR NUMBER OF BYTES
8009 EDB0            11           LDIR                  ;DO IT
```

Program 2.8   Using the LDIR instruction to perform a
block move

Z80 processor description

Figure 2.20 shows both the logic functions and the pin configuration of the Z80. Several versions are available offering a range of clock speeds (2.5 MHz, 4 MHz and 6 MHz) together with a low powered model suitable for hand-held or battery back-up applications. All versions require only a single +5 V supply and a single clock input Φ. Both of these features are improvements over the 8080.

The 16-bit address bus and the 8-bit data bus along with some of the control bus pins are tri-state (i.e. they can all be switched into a high impedance state) allowing external circuitry to take over the system buses in a process called Direct Memory Access (DMA).

Pin descriptions

A0 – A15

Address bus used to select both memory and I/O devices.

D0 – D7

Bi-directional data bus used for data exchanges between the processor and memory or I/O devices.

$\overline{\text{BUSREQ}}$ (pin 25)

An external device would use this line to gain control of the system buses. During the time it has control it will probably perform direct memory access, e.g. some floppy disk controllers can perform DMA transferring data directly to or from the system memory. When the processor detects that $\overline{\text{BUSREQ}}$ is active it forces its system bus pins into a high impedance state so that the external device can use the buses to communicate directly with memory.

$\overline{\text{BUSACK}}$ (pin 23)

The processor uses this output to signal devices requesting the system buses that the lines are now in a high impedance state. The external device can then take control.

$\overline{\text{M1}}$ (pin27)

This processor output indicates that the current machine cycle is an op-code fetch, Figure 2.21. $\overline{\text{M1}}$ (machine cycle 1) is also used along with $\overline{\text{IORQ}}$ to provide an interrupt acknowledge signal to I/O devices.

$\overline{\text{MREQ}}$ (pin 19) $\overline{\text{IORQ}}$ (pin 20)

In 6502 and 6800 systems any I/O devices are placed in the memory map and treated by the processor as if they were memory. The Z80 follows the approach developed by Intel providing two maps: a 64 Kbyte memory map used only for memory devices and a separate port map for I/O devices, Figure 2.22a. With this strategy the programmer uses IN and OUT instructions to access I/O devices in the port map and the range of memory instructions e.g. LD A,(0200H) to access memory devices.

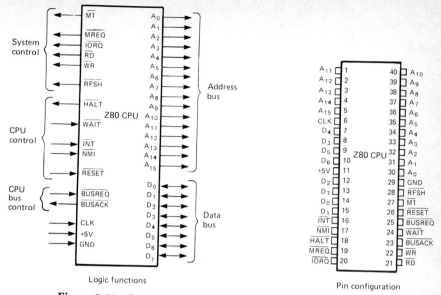

Logic functions

Pin configuration

Figure 2.20 Logic functions and pin configuration of Z80

When the Z80 performs `IN` and `OUT` instructions it places a valid I/O address on the lower half of the address bus and activates the IORQ line. On performing memory instructions Memory Request (MREQ) is activated, Figure 2.22b.

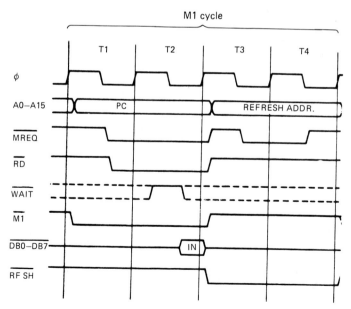

Figure 2.21 Z80 op-code fetch cycle (M1 cycle)

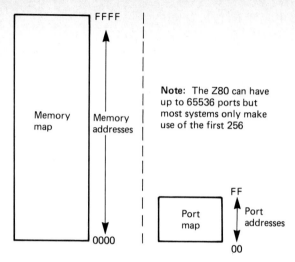

Figure 2.22a Memory and port maps

Note: The Z80 can have up to 65536 ports but most systems only make use of the first 256

$\overline{\text{RD}}$ (pin 21) $\overline{\text{WR}}$ (pin 22)

The read and write control lines are used by the processor to inform memory and I/O chips of the direction of data flow on the data bus, Figure 2.23.

$\overline{\text{RFSH}}$ (pin 28)

This microprocessor output defines a time during which the lower seven bits of the address bus contain the contents of the refresh register. If the system contains dynamic memory this address can be used along with other circuitry to perform a refresh operation.

$\overline{\text{WAIT}}$ (pin 24)

This microprocessor input is used by slow memory devices to lengthen the read or write cycle by injecting extra T or wait states.

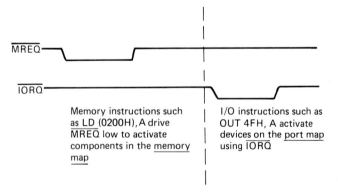

Memory instructions such as LD (0200H), A drive $\overline{\text{MREQ}}$ low to activate components in the memory map

I/O instructions such as OUT 4FH, A activate devices on the port map using $\overline{\text{IORQ}}$

Figure 2.22b $\overline{\text{MREQ}}$ and $\overline{\text{IORQ}}$ signals

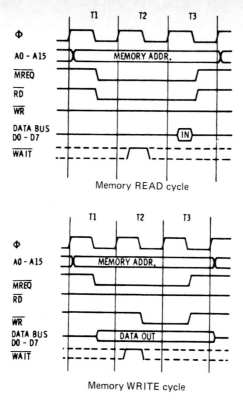

Figure 2.23   Z80 memory read and write cycles

$\overline{\text{HALT}}$ (pin 18)

When the microprocessor encounters a HALT instruction it will automatically execute the no operation instruction (NOP) to maintain the refresh operation for dynamic memories. The processor will remain in this state until it receives either a maskable or non-maskable interrupt.

NMI (pin 17) $\overline{\text{INT}}$ (pin 16)

A falling edge signal on the non-maskable interrupt input initiates the following activity after the processor finishes its current instruction.

1.   The program counter is saved on the stack.

2.   The processor transfers control to memory location 0066H.

The programmer cannot disable the NMI input.

Interrupt Request ($\overline{\text{INT}}$) is an active low input that can be used by I/O devices to demand the processor's attention. $\overline{\text{INT}}$ can be disabled by software and has a lower priority than the non-maskable

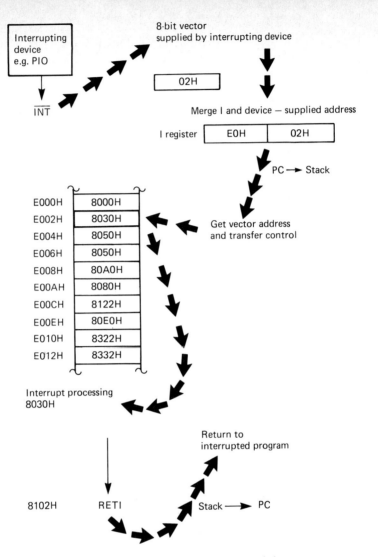

Figure 2.24 Z80 mode 2 interrupt activity

interrupt. There are three different operating modes for $\overline{\text{INT}}$ that can be selected by the programmer using the IM0, IM1 and IM2 instructions (the default after reset is mode 0). Each mode initiates a different action.

MODE 0 – The processor detects the interrupt at the end of its current instruction after which it acknowledges the interrupt by driving $\overline{\text{IORQ}}$ and $\overline{\text{M1}}$ true. The interrupting device then 'jams' a RESTART instruction on the data bus initiating an unconditional jump through one of eight possible restart locations to an interrupt routine.

MODE 1 – This mode is similar to the NMI but with the processor going instead to location 0038H to find the first instruction of its interrupt routine.

MODE 2 – This mode has been designed to utilise the capabilities of the Z80 and its family of peripheral devices, such as the Z80–PIO (Parallel Input/Output), Z80–SIO (Serial Input/Output), and the Z80–CTC (Counter Timer Circuit).

In this mode the processor makes use of a table containing 128 two byte entries, each capable of defining the start address of an interrupt service routine. The address of the selected entry in the table is obtained from two sources. The high byte of the address comes from the processor's Interrupt Vector registers and the low byte is supplied by the interrupting device, Figure 2.24. Each of these sources, of course, should have been initialised by the programmer.

On receiving the $\overline{\text{INT}}$ signal the Z80 acknowledges the interrupt using the $\overline{\text{IORQ}}$ and $\overline{\text{M1}}$ lines. The interrupting device then supplies the low order address vector. The processor then pushes the PC on the stack and continues with the above procedure to an interrupt handling routine.

$\overline{\text{RESET}}$ (pin 26)

The reset input initialises the microprocessor as follows:

1. $\overline{\text{INT}}$ interrupts are disabled.
2. The interrupt vector register is set to 00H.
3. The refresh register is set to 00H.
4. Interrupt mode 0 is selected.
5. The address and data buses go into a high impedance state.

2.4   THE INTEL 8088/8086

In 1978 Intel launched two third generation microprocessors to meet the needs of the many new microcomputer applications. The 8-bit systems of the early seventies suffered from a number of constraints:

• There was difficulty in manipulating data types greater than 8 bits, requiring operations to be split into parts with the penalty of increased execution time.

• Many applications required more memory space than the available 64 Kbytes leading to programs using overlays (i.e. only routines relevant to the immediate execution of the program are in memory at any instant. When new routines are required they are loaded from disk over the top of those not currently in use.)

• The shift away from assembly language towards code generated by compilers brought a need, not only of extra 'elbow-room' for larger programs, but also for addressing modes suited to data lying in memory rather than in processor registers.

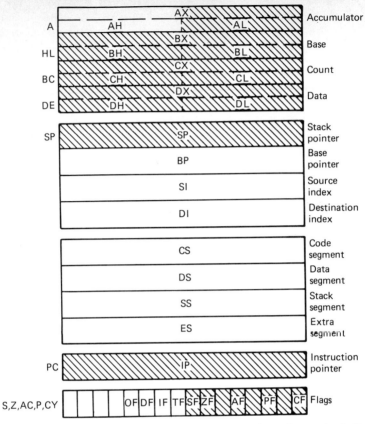

Figure 2.25 8088/8086 registers (8080, 8085 subset shown shaded)
(Reprinted by permission of Intel Corporation, copyright 1985)

- Most 8-bit processors were not designed for arithmetic, using software routines to perform the operations of multiplication and division.

The 8086 and the 8088 are closely related, both supporting 16-bit transfers within the processor and using a 20-bit address bus to access 1 Mbyte of memory. Unlike the 8086 the 8088 has an 8-bit data bus and is therefore restricted to 8-bit transfers with memory and I/O devices. In almost every other respect the two processors are identical, both capable of executing the same software instructions. The 8088 has been adopted by several manufacturers, notably IBM and VICTOR as a stepping stone to full 16-bit machines.

Both microprocessors have been designed to cover a wide spectrum of applications ranging from simple minimum memory systems where only a small number of components are required to large multi-processor systems. To support this philosophy each is capable of operating along with specialist co-processors that effectively add to the functions present on the host processor. Examples to date include the 8089 input/output processor and the 8087 numeric data processor. (At the time of writing

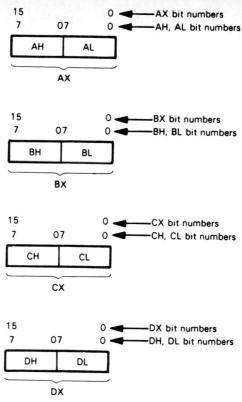

Figure 2.26 Each of the general purpose registers can be addressed as two 8-bit registers

two new co-processors are about to appear: the 82730 text co-processor and the 82586 local area network co-processor.)

Programming model

Figure 2.25 shows the register set for the 8088/8086. Each is 16 bits wide although the general purpose registers AX, BX, CX and DX can be referenced as two separate 8-bit registers, Figure 2.26. AX acts as the primary accumulator and is used with all input/output instructions. Other registers comprise: two pointer registers – Stack Pointer (SP) and Base Pointer (BP), two index registers – Source Index (SI) and Destination Index (DI), a 16-bit Program Counter (PC), a 16-bit Flag register and four 16-bit segment registers – Code Segment (CS), Data Segment (DS), Stack Segment (SS), Extra Segment (ES).

Segmentation – physical and logical addresses   All the internal registers, including the instruction pointer, are 16 bits wide. However, the address bus uses 20 bits to define *physical* addresses ranging between 0H and FFFFFH. This implies that the processor combines at least two registers to produce the final address. Figure 2.27 shows how this is

49

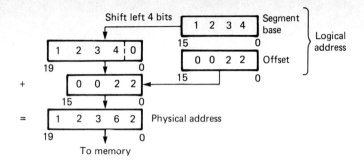

Figure 2.27 Forming a physical address from a base and offset
(Reprinted by permission of Intel Corporation, copyright 1985)

achieved. The contents of a segment register define the base of a 64 Kbyte block or segment and one of the other registers is used as an 'offset' within this block. The combination of segment and offset forms a *logical* address, e.g. 8800H:1890H refers to an offset of 1890H in a segment starting at 8800H. To obtain the actual 20-bit physical address the contents of the segment register are moved 4 bits to the left and added to the value of the offset.

For example:

Segment		8800 H
Offset	+	1890 H
Physical address		89890 H

Normally the pairing of segment and offset registers is implied by the processor instruction or operation. For example:

- the code segment is used with the instruction pointer to point to instruction codes
- the stack segment is used with the stack pointer
- the data segment is usually the default segment for data memory references although the programmer can override this assumption to access a variable in any segment

---

Addressing modes

Direct
Register indirect
Based
Indexed
Based indexed
String
Port

Figure 2.28 8088/8086 addressing modes

The concept of memory segments may at first appear complex and restrictive but it has advantages. Programs can easily be made relocatable, capable of operating in any segment. To move a program to another area of memory only requires the contents of the segment registers to be altered to point to the new base address.

Addressing modes   The 8088/8086 has various methods of accessing the data required by a program instruction. Operands may be the contents of a register, a memory location, an I/O port or perhaps part of the instruction op-code itself. Figure 2.28 summarises the different addressing modes available to the programmer.

Instruction set   The 8088/8086 instruction set includes many instructions used by their 8-bit predecessors, the 8080 and the 8085. Figure 2.29 lists the instruction mnemonics under the following headings: data transfer instructions, arithmetic instructions, bit manipulation instructions, string instructions, program transfer instructions and finally processor control instructions.

The list is more extensive (over 100 instructions) than that for the 8080/8085 with additional instructions for:

- multiplication and division of signed and unsigned binary numbers along with unpacked decimal numbers
- move, scan and compare operations for strings up to 64 Kbytes long
- non-destructive bit testing
- byte translation from one code to another
- software generated interrupts
- instructions to co-ordinate the activities in multi-processor systems

Data Transfer Instructions

General purpose	
MOV	Move byte or word
PUSH	Push word onto stack
POP	Pop word off stack
XCHG	Exchange byte or word
XLAT	Translate byte
Input/Output	
IN	Input byte or word
OUT	Output byte or word
Address object	
LEA	Load effective address
LDS	Load pointer using DS
LES	Load pointer using ES
Flag transfer	
LAHF	Load AH register from flags
SAHF	Store AH register in flags
PUSHF	Push flags onto stack
POPF	Pop flags off stack

Figure 2.29   8088/8086 instruction set

Bit Manipulation Instructions

Logicals

NOT	'Not' byte or word
AND	'And' byte or word
OR	'Inclusive or' byte or word
XOR	'Exclusive or' byte or word
TEST	'Test' byte or word

Shifts

SHL/SAL	Shift logical/arithmetic left byte or word
SHR	Shift logical right byte or word
SAR	Shift arithmetic right byte or word

Rotates

ROL	Rotate left byte or word
ROR	Rotate right byte or word
RCL	Rotate through carry left byte or word
RCR	Rotate through carry right byte or word

Arithmetic Instructions

Addition

ADD	Add byte or word
ADC	Add byte or word with carry
INC	Increment byte or word by 1
AAA	ASCII adjust for addition
DAA	Decimal adjust for addition

Subtraction

SUB	Subtract byte or word
SBB	Subtract byte or word with borrow
DEC	Decrement byte or word by 1
NEG	Negate byte or word
CMP	Compare byte or word
AAS	ASCII adjust for subtraction
DAS	Decimal adjust for subtraction

Multiplication

MUL	Multiply byte or word unsigned
IMUL	Integer multiply byte or word
AAM	ASCII adjust for multiply

Division

DIV	Divide byte or word unsigned
IDIV	Integer divide byte or word
AAD	ASCII adjust for division
CBW	Convert byte to word
CWD	Convert word to doubleword

Figure 2.29   Continued

Processor Control Instructions

Flag operations

STC	Set carry flag
CLC	Clear carry flag
CMC	Complement carry flag
STD	Set direction flag
CLD	Clear direction flag
STI	Set interrupt enable flag
CLI	Clear interrupt enable flag

External Synchronization

HLT	Halt until interrupt or reset
WAIT	Wait for TEST pin active
ESC	Escape to external processor
LOCK	Lock bus during next instruction

No operation

NOP	No operation

Program Transfer Instructions

Conditional transfers

JA/JNBE	Jump if above/not below nor equal
JAE/JNB	Jump if above or equal/not below
JB/JNAE	Jump if below/not above nor equal
JBE/JNA	Jump if below or equal/not above
JC	Jump if carry
JE/JZ	Jump if equal/zero
JG/JNLE	Jump if greater/not less nor equal
JGE/JNL	Jump if greater or equal/not less
JL/JNGE	Jump if less/not greater nor equal
JLE/JNG	Jump if less or equal/not greater
JNC	Jump if not carry
JNE/JNZ	Jump if not equal/not zero
JNO	Jump if not overflow
JNP/JPO	Jump if not parity/parity odd
JNS	Jump if not sign
JO	Jump if overflow
JP/JPE	Jump if parity/parity even
JS	Jump if sign

Unconditional transfers

CALL	Call procedure
RET	Return from procedure
JMP	Jump

Iteration controls

LOOP	Loop
LOOPE/LOOPZ	Loop if equal/zero
LOOPNE/ LOOPNZ	Loop if not equal/ not zero
JCXZ	Jump if register CX=0

Interrupts

INT	Interrupt
INTO	Interrupt if overflow
IRET	Interrupt return

Figure 2.29 Continued

String instructions

REP	Repeat
REPE/REPZ	Repeat while equal/zero
REPNE/REPNZ	Repeat while not equal/not zero
MOVS	Move byte or word string
MOVSB/	
MOVSW	Move byte or word string
CMPS	Compare byte or word string
SCAS	Scan byte or word string
LODS	Load byte or word string
STOS	Store byte or word string

String instructions register and flag use

SI	Index (offset) for source string
DI	Index (offset) for destination string
CX	Repetition counter
AL/AX	Scan value
	Destination for LODS
	Source for STOS
DF	0 = auto-increment SI, DI
	1 = auto-decrement SI, DI
ZF	Scan/compare terminator

Figure 2.29 Continued

Programming examples

Some of the mnemonics for the 8088/8086 are similar to those used by the 8080 and the 8085. Program 2.9 illustrates a simple routine that demonstrates immediate and direct addressing with the MOV instruction. When performing the 16-bit store operation the contents of the 16-bit register AX is placed in two memory locations: the high byte AH in location with offset 0201H and the low byte AL in location with offset 0200H.

The default segment for operands is the data segment. However, the programmer can, if he wishes, override this using a segment override instruction e.g.

```
SEG EX
MOV AX,[0200H]
```

If the ES register was set to 4000H the MOV instruction would obtain its data from locations 40200H and 40201H.

Program 2.10 gives a routine to add two 16-bit numbers. The result is placed in RESULT and RESULT+1. Notice how this program, like its predecessor, terminates with an INT 3 instruction. This is a single byte breakpoint that results in a jump through the interrupt vector table (00000H to 003FFH) back to the monitor program from which the routine was executed.

```
              3  ;ROUTINE TO LOAD SOME REGISTERS
              4  ;IMMEDIATE AND DIRECT ADDRESSING
              5
              6              ORG         10000100H
              7
              8
              9
             10  NUMBER1  EQU           1234H
             11  NUMBER2  EQU           5678H
             12
             13  STORE1   EQU           0200H
             14  STORE2   EQU           0300H
             15
0100 B83412  16           MOV          AX,NUMBER1
0103 A30002  17           MOV          [STORE1],AX   ;PLACE 1234H INTO 0200H
0106 B97856  18           MOV          CX,NUMBER2
0109 890E0003 19          MOV          [STORE2],CX   ;PLACE 5678H INTO 0300H
010D CC      20           INT          3
             21
```

Program 2.9   Immediate and direct addressing on the 8088/8086 (All mnemonics copyright of Intel Corporation, 1985)

```
              3  ;ROUTINE TO ADD TWO 16 BIT NUMBERS
              4  ;ANSWER STORED IN RESULT
              5
              6              ORG         10000100H
              7
              8
              9  RESULT   EQU           0200H
             10
             11  NUMBER1  EQU           2000H
             12  NUMBER2  EQU           5000H
             13
             14
0100 B80020  15           MOV          AX,NUMBER1
0103 050050  16           ADD          AX,NUMBER2
0106 A30002  17           MOV          [RESULT],AX
0109 CC      18           INT          3
             19
```

Program 2.10   16-bit addition on the 8088/8086 (All mnemonics copyright of Intel Corporation, 1985)

```
              3  ;ROUTINE TO MULTIPLY TWO 16 BIT NUMBERS
              4  ;ANSWER STORED IN RESULT_L,RESULT_H
              5
              6              ORG         10000100H
              7
              8
              9  RESULT_L EQU           0200H
             10  RESULT_H EQU           0202H
             11
             12  NUMBER1  EQU           2000H
             13  NUMBER2  EQU           5000H
             14
0100 B80020  15           MOV          AX,NUMBER1
0103 B90050  16           MOV          CX,NUMBER2
0106 F7E1    17           MUL          CX
0108 A30002  18           MOV          [RESULT_L],AX
010B 89160202 19          MOV          [RESULT_H],DX
010F CC      20           INT          3
             21
```

Program 2.11   16-bit multiplication on the 8088/8086 (All mnemonics copyright of Intel Corporation, 1985)

Both the 8088 and the 8086 can perform multiplication and division directly with two 16-bit numbers giving a 32-bit result. One of the numbers forming the product must be stored in the AX register and the answer is returned in the DX and AX registers. (DX contains the most significant 16 bits and AX the least significant 16 bits.)

Program 2.11 gives an example, multiplying the contents of the AX register with the CX register. When the operation is complete (in approximately 70–80 clock cycles) the answer is stored in four memory locations starting at RESULT_L.

8088/8086 processor description

Like their forerunner, the 8085, the 8088 and the 8086 use a multiplexed bus structure, squeezing a 16-bit microprocessor into a 40-pin dual in-line package. As Figure 2.30 shows many of the pins are given a dual role. The 16-bit data bus (8 bits on the 8088) shares the same pins as the first 16 address lines. An Address Latch Enable (ALE) signal from the processor defines the time during which the bus contains address information, allowing system components to capture and hold this address before the same pins assume the role of the data bus, Figure 2.31.

Both processors use an external clock generator chip (8284) that provides the critical timing required by the processor CLK input. Typically a 15 MHz crystal is divided by 3 in the 8284 to give a 5 MHz clock for the processor. Other signals processed by the 8284 include the system RESET and READY, an input that can be used to force the 8088/8086 to wait for slow memory or I/O devices.

Like the humble 6502 the 8088/8086 uses a pipelined architecture. With this structure the processor is free to fetch new instructions from

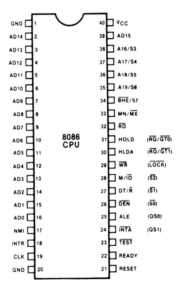

Figure 2.30 8086 processor: (a) pin configuration (Maximum mode pin functions (e.g. $\overline{\text{LOCK}}$) are shown in parenthesis) (Reprinted by permission of Intel Corporation, copyright 1985)

Common signals

Name	Function	Type
AD15–AD0	Address/Data Bus	Bidirectional, 3-state
A19/S6–A16/S3	Address/Status	Output, 3-state
$\overline{BHE}$/S7	Bus High Enable/ Status	Output, 3-state
MN/$\overline{MX}$	Minimum/Maximum Mode Control	Input
$\overline{RD}$	Read Control	Output, 3-state
$\overline{TEST}$	Wait on Test Control	Input
READY	Wait State Control	Input
RESET	System Reset	Input
NMI	Non-Maskable Interrupt Request	Input
INTR	Interrupt Request	Input
CLK	System Clock	Input
V_{CC}	+5V	Input
GND	Ground	

Minimum Mode Signals (MN/MX = V_{CC})

Name	Function	Type
HOLD	Hold Request	Input
HLDA	Hold Acknowledge	Output
$\overline{WR}$	Write Control	Output, 3-state
M/$\overline{IO}$	Memory/IO Control	Output, 3-state
DT/$\overline{R}$	Data transmit/ Receive	Output, 3-state
$\overline{DEN}$	Data Enable	Output, 3-state
ALE	Address Latch Enable	Output
$\overline{INTA}$	Interrupt Acknowledge	Output

Maximum Mode Signals (MN/MX = GND)

Name	Function	Type
$\overline{RQ/GT1, 0}$	Request/Grant Bus Access Control	Bidirectional
$\overline{LOCK}$	Bus Priority Lock Control	Output, 3-state
$\overline{S2}$–$\overline{S0}$	Bus Cycle Status	Output, 3-state
QS1, QS0	Instruction Queue Status	Output

Figure 2.30 8086 processor: (b) pin signals (Reprinted by permission of Intel Corporation, copyright 1985)

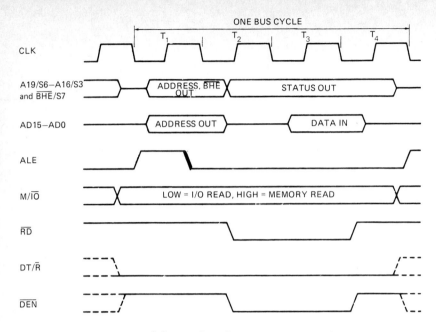

Figure 2.31 ALE defines when the processor is producing a full
20-bit address (figure shows a bus read cycle for the 8086) (Reprinted
by permission of Intel Corporation, copyright 1985)

memory while it is busy executing some instructions. This is a result of
the CPU containing two separate processing units: the Execution Unit
(EU) which executes instructions and the Bus Interface Unit (BIU) that
fetches instructions, reads operands and writes results, Figure 2.32. Both
units work independently and the processor can in most situations
overlap the instruction fetch with execution.

The execution unit contains a 16-bit Arithmetic/Logic Unit (ALU)
and handles the processor's general registers and instruction operands.
All instructions are passed to the EU from the bus interface unit via an
instruction queue.

System bus operations are performed by the BIU which uses the
segment registers, together with offsets delivered by the EU, to form 20-bit
physical addresses. During periods when the EU is busy executing
instructions, the BIU looks ahead by fetching instructions from memory
and storing them in the instruction queue (up to 6 bytes on the 8086, 4
bytes on the 8088).

58

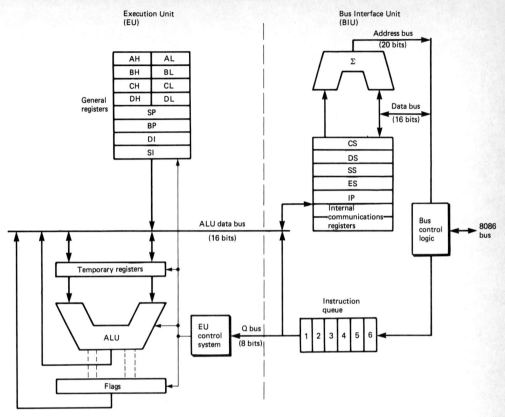

Figure 2.32 8086 internal architecture showing the Execution Unit (EU) and the Bus Interface Unit (BIU) (Reprinted by permission of Intel Corporation, copyright 1985)

Maximum/minimum mode systems To ensure that the 8088/8086 will be suitable for a wide range of applications Intel have given the user the option of configuring the processor for either a simple Minimum mode system or for a Maximum mode multi-processor system. The MN/$\overline{\text{MX}}$ input pin is tied high or low to select the required option.

Figure 2.33 gives an example of a simple minimum system. In this arrangement the 8086 provides all the control signals required to interface I/O and memory devices. Similarly to some 8085 systems, 8282 latches are often used to demultiplex the address/data bus for use with standard memory devices.

When in maximum mode the 8088/8086 can support Intel's range of co-processors which currently include the 8087 numeric data processor

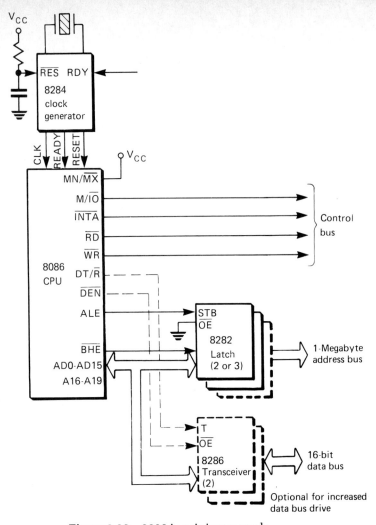

Figure 2.33   8086 in minimum mode

and the 8089 input/output processor. However, there is a price to pay for this increased computing power. To allow the host processor to communicate with its co-processor extra control signals are required. Intel have found pins for these extra signals by delegating some of the signals normally generated by the 8088/8086 to another chip, the 8288 bus controller.

Figure 2.34 illustrates a circuit using the 8086 in maximum mode.

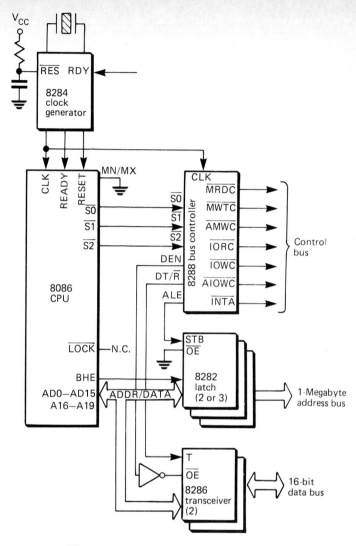

Figure 2.34   8086 in maximum mode

8088/8086 signals

1. *CPU control*

RESET (Input)
  The system reset is normally generated via the 8284 clock generator.
  On changing from high to low, the following actions occur:

a)   flag register is set to 0000H, i.e. interrupts and single
     stepping mode are disabled

b)   DS, ES, SS and PC set to 0000H

c)   CS (code segment) set to FFFFH

d)   program execution begins from location FFFF0H

READY (Input)

This input indicates that a memory or I/O device is ready to send or receive data. If READY is low, then the 8086 executes 'wait' states until READY goes true, i.e. logic 1. Again this signal is usually passed to the processor via the 8284.

HOLD (Minimum Mode–Input)

Other devices use this line to request use of the system buses. When set high, the 8086 enters a hold state after completing its current bus cycle and then acknowledges this state by setting HLDA high.

$\overline{\text{TEST}}$ (Input)

When the 8086 meets a WAIT instruction it will pause until $\overline{\text{TEST}}$ is set low.

MN/$\overline{\text{MX}}$ (Input)

This input is used to configure the processor in either:

a)   *Minimum Mode* – MN/$\overline{\text{MX}}$ pin connected to V_{cc} (+5 V) selects minimum mode and sets processor pins 24 to 31 to the following:

$\overline{\text{INTA}}$, ALE, $\overline{\text{DEN}}$, DT/$\overline{\text{R}}$, M/$\overline{\text{IO}}$, $\overline{\text{WR}}$, HLDA, HOLD

b)   *Maximum Mode* – MN/$\overline{\text{MX}}$ pin tied to V_{ss} (0 V) selects maximum mode. In this mode the 8086 is normally used along with the 8288 bus controller to operate co-processor options. In maximum mode pins 24 to 31 take on the following roles:

QS1, QS0, $\overline{\text{S0}}$, $\overline{\text{S1}}$, $\overline{\text{S2}}$, $\overline{\text{LOCK}}$, $\overline{\text{RQ/GT1}}$, $\overline{\text{RQ/GT0}}$

  2. *Data transfer controls*

$\overline{\text{RD}}$ (Output)

The read control signal.

$\overline{\text{WR}}$ (Minimum Mode–Output)

The write control signal.

ALE (Minimum Mode–Output)

A high ALE pulse signifies a valid memory address on the address/data bus. The falling edge of address latch enable is used to latch address.

$\overline{\text{DEN}}$ (Minimum Mode–Output)

Used to enable 8286/8287 transceivers on data bus.

DT/$\overline{R}$ (Minimum Mode–Output)

Controls direction of flow of data through data bus transceivers.
When:

high – data flows from processor onto system bus
low – data from buses passes to processor.

M/$\overline{IO}$ (Minimum Mode–Output)

Driven low by instructions directed at I/O devices and high for memory.

Note: on 8088 signal is inverted, i.e. ($\overline{M}$/IO) to maintain compatability with 8085.

Most of the signals described above are generated directly by the processor when in minimum mode. In a maximum mode system the 8288 bus controller uses the $\overline{S0}$, $\overline{S1}$, $\overline{S2}$ status signals to generate the following.

$\overline{MRDC}$ (Maximum Mode–Output)

Memory read command.

$\overline{MWTC}$ (Maximum Mode–Output)

Memory write command.

$\overline{AMWC}$ (Maximum Mode–Output)

Advanced memory write command. Signal gives memory an early indication of a write instruction.

$\overline{IORC}$ (Maximum Mode–Output)

I/O read command.

$\overline{IOWC}$ (Maximum Mode–Output)

I/O write command.

$\overline{AIOWC}$ (Maximum Mode–Output)

Advanced I/O write command.

Note: the 8288 also generates the following:

DEN

(Data enable) as DEN on processor but with opposite polarity.

DT/$\overline{R}$

Data transmit/receive.

ALE

Address latch enable.

$\overline{INTA}$

Interrupt acknowledge.

3. Address and data bus

8086

AD0–AD15
> Multiplexed address/data bus.

A16–A19
> Top 4 lines of the 20-bit address bus.

8088

AD0–AD7
> Multiplexed address/data bus.

A8–A19
> Top 12 lines of the 20-bit address bus.

4. CPU status

HLDA (Minimum Mode–Output)
> This processor output is set high to acknowledge a hold request made on HOLD input. When high, the processor floats its tri-state outputs.

S3, S4, S5, S6
> During the first clock period on an instruction cycle, these lines are part of the address bus. Throughout other clock cycles they provide status information.

S4	S3	
0	0	Extra segment
0	1	Stack segment
1	0	Code segment or no segment
1	1	Data segment

S5 – reflects state of interrupt enable flag

S6 – held low if 8086 is controlling the system bus

$\overline{S0}$, $\overline{S1}$, $\overline{S2}$ (Maximum Mode–Output)
> When the processor is in maximum mode, pins $\overline{S0}$, $\overline{S1}$ and $\overline{S2}$ are used to provide status information for the 8288 controller as follows:

$\overline{S2}$	$\overline{S1}$	$\overline{S0}$	
0	0	0	Interrupt Acknowledge
0	0	1	I/O Read
0	1	0	I/O Write
0	1	1	Halt
1	0	0	Instruction fetch
1	0	1	Memory Read
1	1	0	Memory Write
1	1	1	Inactive

QS0, QS1 (Outputs)
Pins QS0 and QS1 provide details of the processor's instruction queue status.

$QS0$	$QS1$	
0	0	No operation
0	1	The first byte of an instruction is being executed
1	0	The queue is being emptied
1	1	A subsequent instruction byte is being taken from the queue

$\overline{RQ/GT0}$ (Maximum Mode–Input–Output)
The request/grant is line used to obtain control of the tri-state buses. The 8088/8086 acknowledges a request by outputting a low going pulse on the same line. When the new bus master is finished it returns control by passing a second low going pulse to the 8088/8086.

$\overline{RQ/GT1}$ (Maximum Mode–Input–Output)
Same as $\overline{RQ/GT0}$ but with a lower priority (i.e. request grant sequence only carried out with this line provided that $\overline{RQ/GT0}$ is not already in progress).

$\overline{LOCK}$ (Maximum Mode–Output)
This output is used to define when the 8088/8086 is executing an instruction prefixed by a LOCK instruction. During this time external hardware should be used to ensure other bus masters do not obtain control of the system bus.

5. *Interrupt controls*

INTR(Input)
> Interrupt request input (level sensitive). If the interrupt enable bit is set (1) and INTR is high, then the 8088/8086 will first enter an interrupt acknowledge sequence before transferring control to interrupt routine.

$\overline{\text{INTA}}$ (Output)
> Output held low while 8088/8086 is performing an interrupt acknowledge sequence. For maximum mode system $\overline{\text{INTA}}$ is generated by the 8288 bus controller.

NMI (Input)
> Non-maskable interrupt input pin (edge sensitive on a low–high transition). Control is passed to a service routine starting at 00008.

6. *Supplies*

0 V, 5 V
> Single 5 V supply (±10%).

7. *Clock*

CLK
> The clock signal is usually generated by an 8284 clock generator. (The crystal frequency is 3 times the resulting CLK frequency, for example, a 15 MHz crystal gives a 5 MHz processor clock.)

The 80186 and 80286 microprocessors
The 80186 and 80286 are Intel's second generation of 16-bit micro-processors. Both are software compatible with the 8086 but include many advanced features.

One of the problems facing system designers is the high chip count, and consequently the high cost, of producing a system supporting the 8086 or the 8088 in the maximum mode. In the 80186, (there is also a version with an 8-bit data bus, the 80188) Intel have included as many as 20 additional functions in one, 68 pin, square JEDEC type A package. These include:

- on-chip clock generator, providing an 8 MHz system clock from a 16 MHz crystal
- bus controller for local bus
- two Direct Memory Access (DMA) channels
- three 16-bit timers, two of which are connected to four input/output pins to count and time external events as well as to act as pulse generators
- programmable interrupt controller
- programmable wait state generator allowing up to three wait states to be inserted for all accesses to defined memory or I/O addresses

- programmable memory and peripheral chip select logic providing six memory chip select outputs and seven peripheral device selects

Among other improvements are: ten additional instructions, including BLOCK I/O allowing a string of bytes or words to be transferred at data rates of 2 Mbytes/sec between memory and I/O devices, and the integration of 16-bit multiplication and division into hardware, giving at least a threefold speed increase over the 8086.

The 80286 is targeted at a second market, offering an increased address space and sophisticated operating system support. Like the 8088/8086, the 80286 allows the use of co-processors, e.g. the 80287, its own version of the 8087 numeric data processor.

To provide flexibility for different applications, the 80286 will operate in two modes: real and protected. In the former, the processor has an address space of 1 Mbyte and operates up to six times faster than the 8086. In the protected mode the real address space is extended to 16 Mbytes, but programmers can make use of a virtual address space of 1 gigabyte (one billion bytes).

Many modern operating systems support the concept of multi-tasking, with a single processor executing several programs apparently simultaneously (e.g. UNIX from Bell Labs, Concurrent CP/M and MP/M from Digital Research). Implementing a multi-tasking strategy can represent a considerable program overhead to many microprocessors. However, the 80286 overcomes this problem by making use of on-chip hardware performing task switching.

Figure 2.35 illustrates the increase in performance of Intel's processors from the early 8-bit 8085 to the 80286.

Processor	Performance (MIPS)
8085	0.07
8086	0.3
80186	0.7
80286	1.5

Figure 2.35 Performance comparisons of a number of Intel processors measured in MIPS (million instructions per second)

2.5 THE MOTOROLA MC 68000

The MC68000 utilises a 16-bit data bus to communicate with both memory and peripheral devices; a 24-bit address bus provides a sixteen megabyte (16 777 216 byte) address space. The 68000 is only one of a family of processors ranging from the 68008, with an 8-bit data bus, to the 68020 with full 32-bit address and data buses. To date, the latter represents the most powerful in the range, operating at 16.67 MHz and capable of processing instructions at a sustained rate of 2 to 3 million instructions per second (MIPS) and at burst rates of up to 8 MIPS.

With operating system support very much in mind, the 68000 was designed to function at two levels: *user* and *supervisor*. The latter is a higher privilege stage supporting a number of extra instructions (e.g. the system RESET instruction). As a result it is normally reserved for the operating system, leaving application programs to run in the lower privilege, *user*, state. Adopting this two level approach, and making those instructions that have important system effects illegal to application programs, gives a fair degree of security against a 'rogue' program completely crashing the system.

The 68000 has 61 instruction types, 14 addressing modes and can operate on six different data types, namely individual bits, binary coded decimal (BCD) digits, ASCII characters, 8-bit bytes, 16-bit words and 32-bit long words.

Similar to other Motorola processors, the 68000 has no special I/O instructions; consequently all input/output is memory mapped. Peripheral devices from Motorola's family of 8-bit processors can be easily interfaced, e.g. the 6854 Advanced Data Link Controller and the 6821 Peripheral Interface Adaptor. In addition, the 68000 is supported by its own range of advanced peripheral chips, Figure 2.36.

68120	Intelligent peripheral controller (IPC)
68122	Cluster terminal controller (CTC)
68540	Error detection and correction circuit (EDCC)
68451	Memory-management unit (MMU)
68450	Direct memory access controller (DMAC)
68230	Parallel interface/timer (PI/T)
68561	Multiprotocol communications controller (MPCC)
68341	Floating-point read-only memory
68340	Dual-port RAM (DPR)
68453	Bubble memory controller
68560	Serial direct memory access processor (SDMA)

Figure 2.36   68000 peripheral devices (Courtesy of Motorola Limited)

Programming model
Although externally the 68000 has a 16-bit data bus, internally it has many features of a 32-bit microprocessor. There are eight data registers (D0 through to D7), eight address registers (A0 through A7), a program counter register and a 16-bit status register, Figure 2.37.

The processor automatically makes use of address register A7 as a stack pointer. However, since the 68000 has separate stack pointers for its two operating modes, address register A7 is duplicated: in the user state it is the user stack pointer, in the supervisor state A7 is the supervisor stack pointer.

The 68000 contains a 32-bit program counter, but only the low order 24 bits are used. (The 68020 makes use of the full 32 bits in conjunction with an expanded memory space.) Bytes can be accessed using either even or odd addresses, but only even addresses are used with word (16-bit) and long word (32-bit) operands.

The 16-bit status register is split into two halves, termed the *system byte* and the *user byte*, Figure 2.38. Only the five least significant bits are employed in the user byte to hold the following flags: carry (C), overflow

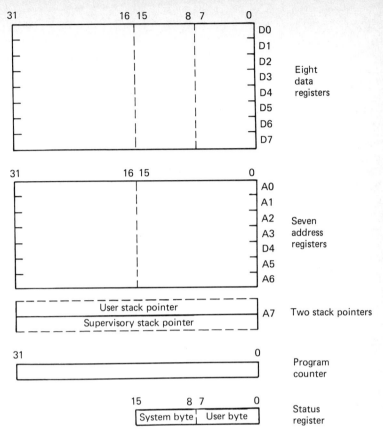

Figure 2.37 68000 registers (Courtesy of Motorola Limited)

(V), zero (Z), negative (N) and the extend flag (X), used in multiprecision arithmetic operations.

Unlike the instruction related status bits of the user byte, the system byte contains information relating to processor control. Bits in the system byte can only be altered when the 68000 is in the supervisor state. The three least significant bits form the *interrupt priority mask*. All interrupts with a numeric value greater than that specified by these bits will be serviced by the microprocessor; interrupts equal to or less than the interrupt mask will be ignored. The supervisor flag (S) is set when the 68000 is in the supervisor mode; when clear the 68000 is in user mode. Finally, setting the trace mode flag (T) enables the processor's internal debug circuitry, allowing it to single step, stopping after each program instruction to enter the supervisor mode and then jumping to a user supplied trace routine. Normally the trace routine displays the contents of the processor's registers and flags before returning to the main program.

Instruction set and addressing modes Surprisingly, the 68000 has eleven instructions fewer than the MC6800, Figure 2.39. Instruction

69

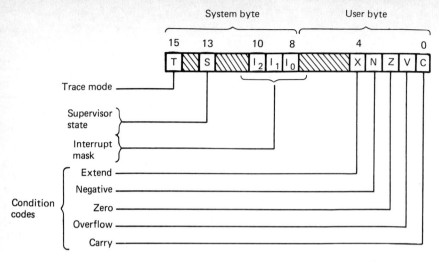

Figure 2.38 Status register (Courtesy of Motorola Limited)

mnemonics are independent of both registers and data types, leaving the programmer to select the mnemonic for the operation required and then complete the instruction with the data size, source and destination.

Instructions, which vary in length between one and five words, can be classified under the following headings:

> data movement
> arithmetic instructions
> logical operations
> shift and rotate instructions
> bit manipulation
> binary coded decimal instructions
> program control
> system control

Data movements are achieved through instructions like MOVE – transferring bytes, words or long words, SWAP – exchanging the lower half of a data register with the upper half, EXG – exchanging the contents of two registers. Arithmetic operations include ADD and SUB, performing addition and subtraction on 8-, 16- or 32-bit quantities, MUL providing 16-bit by 16-bit multiplication, giving a 32-bit answer, and DIV supporting a 32-bit by 16-bit division. Program control operations make use of a number of conditional and unconditional branches, jumps and subroutine calls. Figure 2.40 shows the variety of tests supported by the conditional branch instructions.

The 68000's fourteen addressing modes can be formed into the six basic addressing groups shown in Figure 2.41. Memory is 'byte addressable', however all accesses to words or long words must be made to an even address, reference to an odd address will result in an 'address error' trap, with the processor vectored through locations at the bottom of the

Mnemonic	Description	Mnemonic	Description
ABCD	Add decimal with extend	MOVEM	Move multiple registers
ADD	Add	MOVEP	Move peripheral data
AND	Logical and	MULS	Signed multiply
ASL	Arithmetic shift left	MULU	Unsigned multiply
ASR	Arithmetic shift right	NBCD	Negate decimal with extend
B_{CC}	Branch conditionally	NEG	Negate
BCHG	Bit test and change	NOP	No operation
BCLR	Bit test and clear	NOT	Ones complement
BRA	Branch always	OR	Logical or
BSET	Bit test and set	PEA	Push effective address
BSR	Branch to subroutine	RESET	Reset external devices
BTST	Bit test	ROL	Rotate left without extend
CHK	Check register against bounds	ROR	Rotate right without extend
CLR	Clear operand	ROXL	Rotate left with extend
CMP	Compare	ROXR	Rotate right with extend
DB_{CC}	Test cond., decrement and branch	RTE	Return from exception
DIVS	Signed divide	RTR	Return and restore
DIVU	Unsigned divide	RTS	Return from subroutine
EOR	Exclusive or	SBCD	Subtract decimal with extend
EXG	Exchange registers	S_{CC}	Set conditional
EXT	Sign extend	STOP	Stop
JMP	Jump	SUB	Subtract
JSR	Jump to subroutine	SWAP	Swap data register halves
LEA	Load effective address	TAS	Test and set operand
LINK	Link stack	TRAP	Trap
LSL	Logical shift left	TRAPV	Trap on overflow
LSR	Logical shift right	TST	Test
MOVE	Move	UNLK	Unlink

Figure 2.39   68000 instruction set (Courtesy of Motorola Limited)

T	True
F	False
HI	High
LS	Low or Same
CC	Carry Clear
CS	Carry Set
NE	Not Equal
EQ	Equal
VC	Overflow clear
VS	Overflow set
PL	Plus
MI	Minus
GE	Greater or Equal
LT	Less Than
GT	Greater Than
LE	Less or Equal

Figure 2.40 Tests supported by the conditional branch instructions
(Courtesy of Motorola Limited)

Register Direct Addressing

Data register direct	EA = Dn
Address register direct	EA = An

Address Register Indirect Addressing

Register indirect	EA = (An)
Postincrement register indirect	EA = (An), An $\leftarrow$ An + N
Predecrement register indirect	An $\leftarrow$ An − N, EA = (An)
Register indirect with offset	EA = (An) + d_{16}
Indexed register indirect with offset	EA = (An) + (Ri) + d_8

Absolute Data Addressing

Absolute short	EA = (Next word)
Absolute long	EA = (Next two words)

Program Counter Relative Addressing

Relative with offset	EA = (PC) + d_{16}
Relative with index and offset	EA = (PC) + (Ri) + d_8

Immediate Data Addressing

Immediate	DATA = Next word(s)
Quick immediate	Inherent data

Implied addressing

Implied Register	EA = SR, USP, SP, PC

EA	= effective address	USP	= user stack pointer
An	= address register	d_8	= 8-bit offset (displacement)
Dn	= data register	d_{16}	= 16-bit offset (displacement)
SR	= status register	N	= 1 for byte, 2 for words, and 4 for long words
PC	= program counter	()	= contents of
SP	= active system stack pointer	$\leftarrow$	= replaces
Ri	= address or data register used as index register		

Figure 2.41 68000 addressing modes (Courtesy of Motorola Limited)

memory map to a suitable service routine. (A number of other error conditions can also be trapped by the processor, e.g. illegal addressing mode and overflow on divide.) All addressing modes operate 'consistently', with all relevant modes available to any instruction that specifies an operand in memory. Further, all the address registers (A0–A7) can be used for the direct, register indirect and indexed addressing modes.

Programming examples

Program 2.12 illustrates the 68000's decrement and branch instruction DBcc (cc stands for condition), used to repeat a section of code a given number of times. The instruction is two words long and is made up of three parameters, namely a condition, a data register to be decremented, and a 16-bit relative displacement. If the condition is met or the contents of the selected register equals –1, then the following instruction in the code is executed. If the condition is not met then the contents of the selected register (D0 in the example) are decremented by one, and program control passed to an address evaluated using the relative displacement.

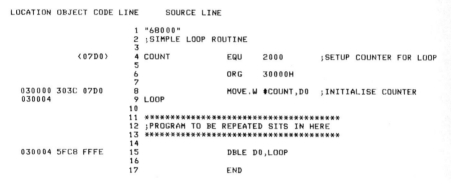

```
LOCATION OBJECT CODE LINE      SOURCE LINE

                          1  "68000"
                          2  ;SIMPLE LOOP ROUTINE
                          3
         <07D0>           4  COUNT           EQU     2000        ;SETUP COUNTER FOR LOOP
                          5
                          6                  ORG     30000H
                          7
030000 303C 07D0          8                  MOVE.W #COUNT,D0   ;INITIALISE COUNTER
030004                    9  LOOP
                         10
                         11  ****************************************
                         12  ;PROGRAM TO BE REPEATED SITS IN HERE
                         13  ****************************************
                         14
030004 5FC8 FFFE         15                  DBLE D0,LOOP
                         16
                         17                  END
```

Program 2.12 Example illustrating looping with the DBcc instruction

In the example the D0 register is first loaded with a value of COUNT equal to 2000H. Each time the DBLE instruction is executed, the contents of the D0 register is tested for the 'less than or equal to' condition and when D0 equals zero, the loop is terminated with program control passing to the next instruction.

Great care is required with the DBcc instruction, which uses reverse logic to that of the conditional branch instruction Bcc. With DBcc, branching terminates when the condition is met, while with Bcc, branching occurs when the condition is met.

The examples shown in Program 2.13 illustrate the 68000's ability to perform addition on 8-bit, 16-bit and 32-bit quantities. Notice how the assembler uses the directives .B, .W and .L appended to the operation code to specify the data size.

Finally, Program 2.14 gives an example of a 32-bit binary divide routine. The long word occupying four bytes starting at location LOCNUM1 is divided by the 16-bit word in locations LOCNUM2 and LOCNUM2+1. The

```
                        1 "68000"
                        2 ;EXAMPLES OF 8, 16, 32 BIT ADDITION
                        3
                        4 ;DEFINE SOME DATA
                        5
          (0011)        6 NUMBER1         EQU             11H     ;BYTE DATA
          (0022)        7 NUMBER2         EQU             22H
                        8
          (3333)        9 NUMBER3         EQU             3333H ;WORD DATA
          (4444)       10 NUMBER4         EQU             4444H
                       11
       (55555555)      12 NUMBER5         EQU             55555555H   ;LONG WORD DATA
       (66666666)      13 NUMBER6         EQU             66666666H
                       14
                       15 ;DEFINE LOCATIONS TO STORE ANSWERS
                       16
       (00010000)      17 ANSWER1         EQU             10000H
       (00010002)      18 ANSWER2         EQU             10002H
       (00010004)      19 ANSWER3         EQU             10004H
                       20
                       21                 ORG             30000H
                       22
                       23 ;8 BIT ADDITION
  030000 103C 0011     24                 MOVE.B          #NUMBER1,D0  ;GET FIRST NUMBER
  030004 0600 0022     25                 ADD.B           #NUMBER2,D0  ;ADD TO SECOND
  030008 13C0 0001     26                 MOVE.B          D0,ANSWER1   ;STORE RESULT
                       27
                       28 ;16 BIT ADDITION
  03000E 303C 3333     29                 MOVE.W          #NUMBER3,D0
  030012 0640 4444     30                 ADD.W           #NUMBER4,D0
  030016 33C0 0001     31                 MOVE.W          D0,ANSWER2
                       32
                       33 ;32 BIT ADDITION
  03001C 203C          34                 MOVE.L          #NUMBER5,D0
  030022 0680          35                 ADD.L           #NUMBER6,D0
  030028 23C0 0001     36                 MOVE.L          D0,ANSWER3
                       37
                       38                 END
```

Program 2.13   8-, 16- and 32-bit addition

```
                        1 "68000"
                        2 ;EXAMPLE OF 32 BIT DIVIDE
                        3
                        4 ;DEFINE MEMORY SPACE
                        5
  000000                6 LOCNUM1         DS.L 1          ;32BIT DIVIDEND
  000004                7 LOCNUM2         DS.W 1          ;16 BIT DIVISOR
  000006                8 ANSWER          DS.L 1          ;SPACE FOR 16 BIT REMAINDER
                        9                                 ;AND 16 BIT QUOTIENT
                       10
                       11                 ORG     30000H
                       12
  030000 2039          13                 MOVE.L  LOCNUM1,D0   ;DIVIDEND INTO D0
  030006 80F9          14                 DIVU    LOCNUM2,D0   ;DIVIDE _ (LOCNUM1)/(LOCNUM2)
  03000C 23C0          15                 MOVE.L  D0,ANSWER    ;RESULT (REMAINDER AND QUOTIENT)
                       16                                      ;INTO ANSWER
                       17
                       18                 END
```

Program 2.14   32-bit division

result, made up of a word quotient and a word remainder, is placed in
memory starting at ANSWER.

One special condition is worth some attention. Attempting to divide
a number by zero will result in the processor initiating a zero divide trap,
causing it to vector to an error handling routine, using pointers at
locations 000014H to 000017H (entry number 5 in the processor's vector
table).

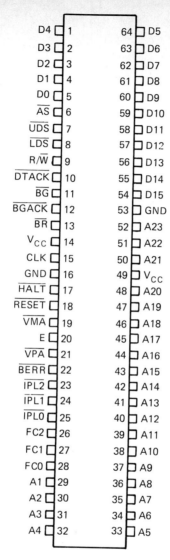

Figure 2.42 68000 microprocessor (Courtesy of Motorola Limited)

68000 pinout and signals

Unlike Intel's approach with the 8088/8086, Motorola have not utilised a multiplexed bus structure to 'shoehorn' a 16-bit processor into the standard 40-pin package. Instead, the 68000 is housed in a 'massive' 64-pin package, Figure 2.42.

The chip is provided with two V_{cc} (+5 V) and two ground pins in order to reduce noise problems at high frequencies. A processor clock input accepts a single phase TTL clock in the frequency range DC to 8 MHz.

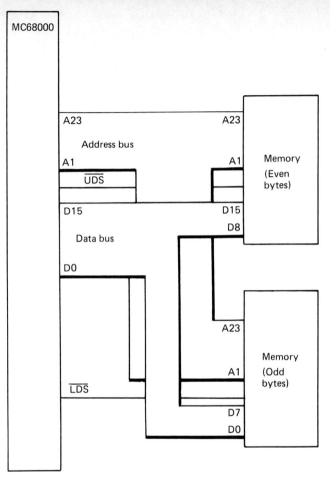

Figure 2.43   68000 byte/word addressing using LDS (Lower Data Strobe) and UDS (Upper Data Strobe)

In a similar way to the 8088/8086, the 68000 employs a pipelined architecture, pre-fetching instructions from memory while it is still busy executing the current instruction.

Close examination of the processor shows that address line A0 is missing. Instead, the 68000 makes use of two data strobe signals to select either individual bytes or complete 16-bit words, Figure 2.43. When the Upper Data Strobe (UDS) is active, data is transferred on the upper eight data lines (D8–D15) to or from memory locations with an even address. When the Lower Data Strobe (LDS) is active, data is transferred to or from odd addresses on the lower half of the data bus. To perform a word transfer, the processor activates both strobes.

68000 signals

A1–A23

Address bus: used along with UDS and LDS to provide a 16 Mbyte address space.

D0–D15

Data bus: supports 8-bit or 16-bit data transfers.

$\overline{\text{UDS}}$, $\overline{\text{LDS}}$

Data strobes: used by the processor to identify byte transfers on either the upper or lower part of the data bus. Enabling both strobes initiates a word transfer.

$\overline{\text{AS}}$

Address strobe: indicates that the address bus contains a valid address and provides a bus lock for indivisible operations.

R/$\overline{\text{W}}$

Read/not write: used by the processor to inform other circuit components of the direction of data transfer.

$\overline{\text{DTACK}}$

Data transfer acknowledge: this input is used by the processor to support asynchronous transfers with slow devices (memory or I/O chips); when a device has either accepted (in a write operation) or placed data (in a read operation) on the bus, it notifies the 68000 by asserting $\overline{\text{DTACK}}$.

$\overline{\text{BR}}$, $\overline{\text{BG}}$, $\overline{\text{BGACK}}$

Bus request, bus grant, bus grant acknowledge: if a device wishes to make use of the system buses for a DMA operation, it requests permission using $\overline{\text{BR}}$. The 68000 will then grant permission by activating $\overline{\text{BG}}$. Finally the requesting device will acknowledge that it has control by activating $\overline{\text{BGACK}}$.

$\overline{\text{IPL0}}$, $\overline{\text{IPL1}}$, $\overline{\text{IPL2}}$

Interrupt priority level: these processor inputs are used by an interrupting device to state its priority level. If the binary number reflected in these bits is greater than the value in the interrupt mask (in status register), then the interrupt will be allowed.

FC0, FC1, FC2

Function codes: these lines provide external devices with information about the current bus cycle (e.g. user program or data, supervisor program or data, interrupt acknowledge).

$\overline{\text{RES}}$

Reset: this input/output provides initialisation for the processor and peripheral devices. On reset, the 68000 comes up in the supervisor mode and immediately loads the stack pointer from entry 0 in the vector table (i.e. locations 00000–00003) and the program counter from entry 1 (i.e. locations 00004–00007). (Note: the bottom 1 Kbyte of system memory is used to hold 256, four byte vectors labelled 0 to 255.)

$\overline{\text{HALT}}$

Halt: when this bidirectional line is driven by an external device, the processor will stop after completing its current bus cycle.

$\overline{\text{BERR}}$

Bus error: this input informs the processor of any problems with the cycle currently being executed.

E

Enable: this signal is used to synchronise data transfers with 6800 peripherals.

$\overline{\text{VPA}}$

Valid peripheral address: this input tells the 68000 that a 6800 peripheral device is being addressed and that data transfers should be synchronised with the 'E' clock.

$\overline{\text{VMA}}$

Valid memory address: this output is the processor's response to VPA, informing 6800 family devices that the bus contains a valid address.

Problems

2.1 What are the principal tasks performed by the microprocessor?

2.2 Give a detailed account of the sequence of events that take place when a microprocessor performs: (a) a READ operation; (b) a WRITE operation.

2.3 An EPROM with an access time of 800 nsec has to be used with a Z80 microprocessor operating at 6 MHz. What problem will arise? How would you overcome it?

2.4 Both Intel and Zilog have a different approach from Motorola when dealing with the microprocessor interface to input/output devices. Explain this difference in approach and show how it would have to be taken into account when designing address decode circuitry.

2.5 Explain the term 'pipelining'.

FURTHER READING

For more detail on any microprocessor the obvious source is the manufacturer's data sheet and application notes. Normally these are available from a distributor and not from the chip manufacturer directly. However, not everyone likes information in this condensed form. A number of text books have been written on each of the processors described in this chapter. The following list forms a sample of the more useful.

Camp, R.C., Smay, T.A. and Triska, C.J., 1979. *Microprocessor Systems Engineering*. Portland, OR: Matrix.

Leventhal, L., 1979. *6502 Assembly Language Programming*. Berkeley, CA: Osborne/McGraw-Hill.

Ferguson, J. and Shaw, T., 1983. *Assembly Language Programming on the BBC Micro*. London: Addison-Wesley.

Barden, 1978. *The Z80 Microcomputer Handbook*. Howard Sams.

Mostek, 1977. *Z80 Programming Manual*. MK78515.

Coffron, J.W., 1983. *Z80 Applications*. Berkeley, CA: Sybex.

Rector, R. and Alexy, G., 1980. *The 8086 Book*. Berkeley, CA: Osborne/McGraw-Hill.

Kane, G., Hawkins, D. and Leventhal, L., 1984. *68000 Assembly Language Programming*. Berkeley, CA: Osborne/McGraw-Hill.

Also recommended as light reading are a number of articles in popular journals:

Routledge, J., May 1983. 'The iAPX 186 Microprocessor – Comparing Old and New' *Electronic Engineering*, p. 63.

Zingale, T., April 1983. 'Intel's 80186 – a 16-bit Computer on a Chip' *Byte*, p. 132.

Wells, P., November 1984. 'The 80286 Microprocessor' *Byte*, p. 231.

Greopler, P.F. and Kennedy, J., November 1984. 'The MC 68020 32-bit Microprocessor' *Byte*, p. 159.

Chapter 3

Software production

The objectives of this chapter are:

- to introduce machine code programming;
- to examine the use of an assembler as a means of generating machine code
- to examine a wide range of assembler directives;
- to introduce relocatable object code and the use of a linker;
- to introduce the concept of modular programming;
- to examine the integration of assembly language modules with those from a high level language.

The principal advantage of microprocessor systems over discrete logic circuitry is their ability to be programmed to perform a wide range of tasks. The list of instructions that defines the task is called a program. Many different languages are used to program computers, each presenting the programmer with its own set of features. Normally, these features are directed towards particular application areas. For example:

PASCAL BASIC FORTRAN	general purpose, educational, engineering, and scientific applications
COBOL	business applications
dBASEII	database applications
C	operating systems and communications
FORTH	control applications
LISP PROLOG	general purpose, natural language processing

However, irrespective of the language used, all computer programs are translated into the language of the microprocessor itself – *machine code*.

Machine code is the set of binary patterns used by the processor to represent its instruction set, i.e. the list of primitive operations it can perform, such as storing the contents of a register in a memory location or incrementing the contents of a register. The codes used to represent these functions, along with the nature and number of facilities, differ for different microprocessors. As a result machine code programs generated for one microprocessor cannot usually be moved easily to another.

In the following sections a number of techniques used to generate code are examined, ranging from writing programs directly in machine code to high level options that ease the task using assemblers, compilers or interpreters.

3.1 MACHINE CODE PROGRAMMING

Machine code programs are similar to other programs in that they are made up of a mixture of instructions and data. For example the following 6502 routine tells the microprocessor to store the number 41 (hex) in memory locations 7C10 (hex).

Address	Data in hex	Data in binary
2000	A9	1010 1001
2001	41	0100 0001
2002	8D	1000 1101
2003	10	0001 0000
2004	7C	0111 1100

The first code A9 (hex) tells the microprocessor to load its internal accumulator register with the next number, namely 41 (hex). The following code 8D (hex) then instructs it to transfer the contents of the accumulator to memory location 7C10 (hex). (Notice how addresses within a 6502 program are always placed low byte followed by high byte. This is a feature of many processors). The numbers representing the instructions are called operation codes or op-codes.

A question often asked by beginners to machine code programming is 'How does the microprocessor know the difference between data and op-codes?'. The answer is simple. The first number the processor finds in a program it assumes is an op-code. On reading the instruction, the microprocessor then knows where to find the next code. For example, after reading the 'load accumulator' code A9 (hex), in the program above, the processor needed one more byte to complete the current instruction and as a result the program counter is set to the location of the next op-code, namely 2002 (hex).

Programming directly in machine code usually involves a simple monitor program that allows the programmer to enter bytes into consecutive memory locations before transferring control to the first instruction.

In some machines this is the only method of programming, e.g. KIM and SDK86, and some users have become proficient at writing fairly long and complex programs. However, most people find it tedious and prone to error requiring continuous reference to op-code tables.

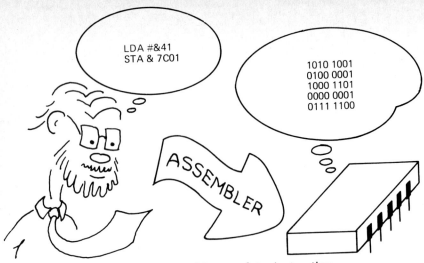

Figure 3.1 An assembler translates instruction mnemonics into machine code

3.2 ASSEMBLY LANGUAGE PROGRAMMING

In assembly language abbreviations called mnemonics are used to represent the different microprocessor instructions. A translating program, called an assembler, is then used to convert the assembly language statements into machine code, Figure 3.1.

Line assembler
The simplest form of assembler is the line assembler where each line or statement in a program is converted to code and loaded into memory. Figure 3.2 again uses the 6502 as an example illustrating the line assembler on the Rockwell Aim 65.

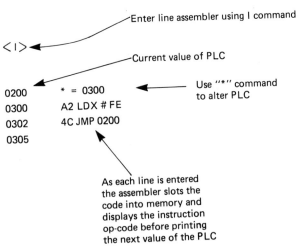

Figure 3.2 Using the line assembler on the Aim 65

Before the programmer starts entering a routine an initial value is given to the Program Location Counter (PLC). The assembler uses this pointer to position the final absolute or machine code in memory, automatically incrementing it to point to the next available location, Figure 3.3.

Line assemblers offer a gentle introduction to assembly language programming and not surprisingly are used by many universities and colleges in introductory courses. They also prove useful when writing relatively short routines for testing or making small changes (patches) to a larger program.

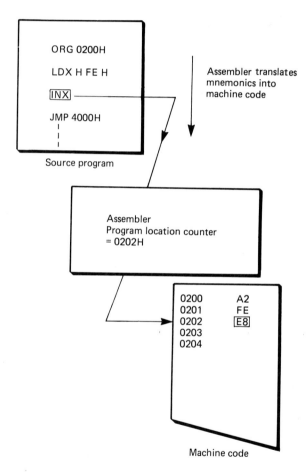

Figure 3.3 The assembler uses the Program Location Counter (PLC) to hold the address of the current instruction being translated

Two-pass assembler

Serious applications are more likely to make use of a full two-pass assembler. With this approach the programmer employs a suite of programs, Figure 3.4:

Text Editor	Can be either a simple editor or even a word processing package that allows text in the form of assembly language statements to be written into a text file. The names, source file or source program are often given to a text file containing assembly language statements stored as ASCII characters.
Assembler	The program that converts the source file into machine code. Some assemblers, like the line assembler described above, also load the code into memory ready for execution; others leave the code in a *relocatable format* ready for final positioning by the Linker/ Loader.
Linker/Loader	As the name suggests this program can be used to link together relocatable files produced by the assembler and position the final code in memory.

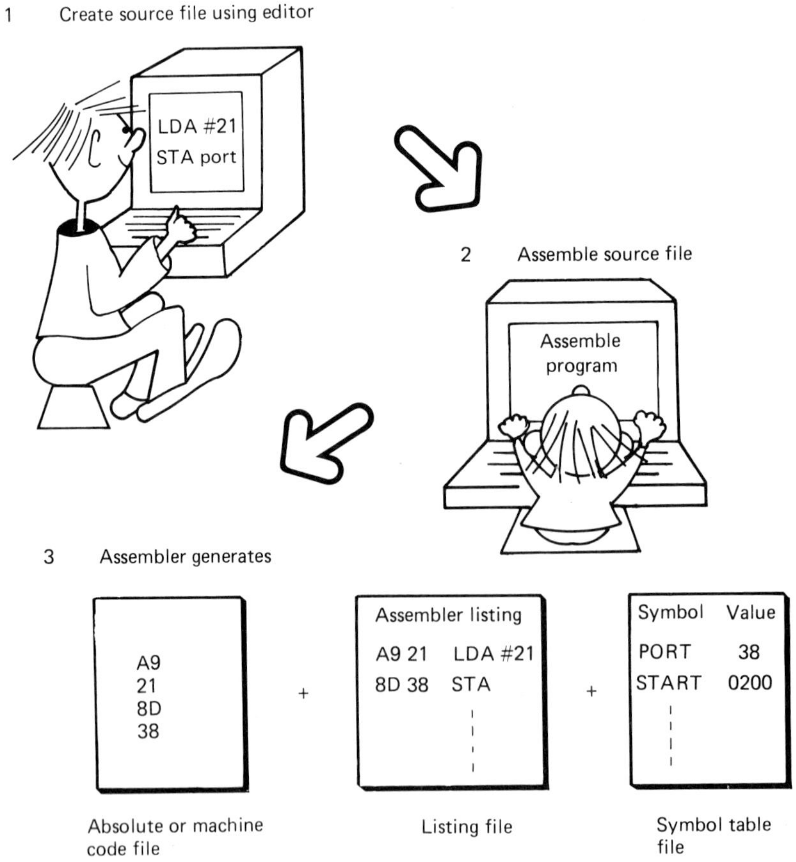

1   Create source file using editor

Figure 3.4 Program development with a full two-pass
assembler

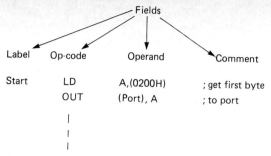

Figure 3.5 Format of assembly language statements in source file

Most assemblers expect each line in the source program to contain a single statement which is split into four fields. Each field can contain a variable number of characters and is usually separated from a neighbouring field by either a space or a TAB character that acts as a delimiter informing the assembler that a new field is about to start.

Figure 3.5 shows some typical lines of Z80 code. The *label* field can contain a sequence of letters or digits starting with a letter, that acts as an identifier for a program address.

The mnemonic for the chosen instruction is placed in the *op-code* field. Normally the list of mnemonics used by the assembler will be that specified by the manufacturer of the microprocessor, but beware, there can be differences.

The *operand* field holds any additional data required along with the instruction mnemonic e.g. register, data or address information. Any numeric information can usually be expressed in any number system, the default being decimal. To use any other system a letter is placed after the number. The common letters used are:

H – hexadecimal
C – octal
B – binary

Possible confusion between hexadecimal quantities and labels is avoided by preceding all hex numbers starting with a letter with a leading zero. Arithmetic and some logical operations are usually allowed within operands. Figure 3.6 illustrates some of the possibilities, others are given later in the chapter.

Finally, the *comments* field, although ignored by the assembler, is essential to good programming and should contain a clear description of the function of each line of code. Normally comments can be placed in any field provided they start with a semi-colon ';'. (Whenever a semi-colon is placed in a line the remainder of the line is assumed, by the assembler, to be a comment.)

As an example, Program 3.1 gives a printout of the source file of a short Z80 program used to generate a time delay. Notice how the routine makes use of a label to define the destination of the conditional jump

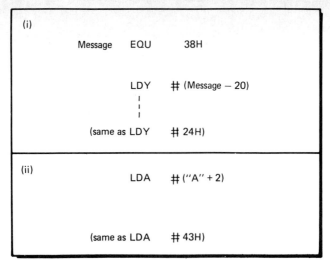

Figure 3.6 Using arithmetic expressions in the operand field

instruction and also the extensive use of comments to document not only the effect of the individual instructions but also of the whole subroutine.

As well as producing code most assemblers also give you the option of generating an *assembler listing file* and a *symbol table file*. The former contains not only the original source statements but also the code generated by the assembler, whereas the latter displays all the symbols and labels together with their values, Figures 3.7 and 3.8.

```
"Z80"
********************************
*                              *
*  SUBROUTINE TO FORM TIME DELAY *
*                              *
*  ALTERS:        A,D,E,FLAGS  *
*                              *
********************************


                LD  DE,8000H    ;LOAD DE WITH TIME CONSTANT
HERE            DEC DE          ;DECREMENT INPUT VALUE
                LD  A,D         ;INTO A WITH VALUE IN D
                OR  E           ;OR THIS WITH VALUE IN E
                JP  NZ,HERE     ;BACK TO DECREMENT IF NOT ZERO
                RET
```

Program 3.1 Z80 routine to generate a time delay

Pseudo-operations

Pseudo-operations are placed in the source code along with the assembly language mnemonics. They themselves are not translated into machine code but are used instead to give instructions to the assembler. The following outlines some of the more common and gives examples of their use:

```
                        1  "Z80"
                        2  ***********************************
                        3  *                                 *
                        4  * SUBROUTINE TO FORM TIME DELAY    *
                        5  *                                 *
                        6  * ALTERS:          A,D,E,FLAGS     *
                        7  *                                 *
                        8  ***********************************
                        9
                       10
0000 118000            11                    LD DE,8000H  ;LOAD DE WITH TIME CONSTANT
0003 1B                12  HERE              DEC DE       ;DECREMENT INPUT VALUE
0004 7A                13                    LD A,D       ;INTO A WITH VALUE IN D
0005 B3                14                    OR E         ;OR THIS WITH VALUE IN E
0006 C20003            15                    JP NZ,HERE   ;BACK TO DECREMENT IF NOT ZERO
0009 C9                16                    RET
                       17
```

Figure 3.7   Assembler listing file from delay routine
(Program 3.1)

```
Asmb_sym record:
HERE                    0003H
```

Figure 3.8   Symbol table file (Program 3.1)

ORG The origin statement is used to set the assembler's Program Location
Counter (PLC). In Program 3.2 the ORG statement has been used to
instruct the assembler to produce code that will eventually lie from
location 8000 (hex) upwards.

EQU The equate instruction allows you to assign a value to a label or
symbol. Again Program 3.2 gives an example with the symbol
TIME_CONST defined equal to A000 (hex). It would of course be
possible to write this routine without the EQU, but using it makes
programs more readable and simple to update, especially if a data
value is used several times within a routine.

DB/DEFB or FCB
The define byte or form constant byte pseudo-op is used to set a
memory location to a specific value. For example, Program 3.3
shows how it can be used to load the three memory locations 3000

```
                        1  "Z80"
                        2  ***********************************
                        3  *                                 *
                        4  * SUBROUTINE TO FORM TIME DELAY    *
                        5  *                                 *
                        6  * ALTERS:          A,D,E,FLAGS     *
                        7  *                                 *
                        8  ***********************************
                        9
                       10                    ORG 8000H
                       11
        (A000)         12  TIME_CONST        EQU 0A000H
                       13
8000 11A000            14                    LD DE,TIME_CONST
8003 1B                15  HERE              DEC DE       ;DECREMENT INPUT VALUE
8004 7A                16                    LD A,D       ;INTO A WITH VALUE IN D
8005 B3                17                    OR E         ;OR THIS WITH VALUE IN E
8006 C28003            18                    JP NZ,HERE   ;BACK TO DECREMENT IF NOT ZERO
8009 C9                19                    RET
```

Program 3.2   Delay routine using pseudo-operations

```
LOCATION OBJECT CODE LINE        SOURCE LINE

                          1  "Z80"
                          2
                          3                    ORG  3000H
     3000  010203         4                    DEFB 01,02,03
```

Program 3.3   Using the Define Byte pseudo-operation

(hex), 3001 (hex) and 3002 (hex) with the values 01, 02 and 03. Some
assemblers allow you to insert ASCII strings with **DB**. For example

```
          ORG  2000H
          DB   "ABC"
```

would insert 41 (hex), 42 (hex) and 43 (hex) into locations 2000 (hex)
to 2002 (hex). Other assemblers have a special pseudo-op for ASCII
strings, e.g. **ASC**.

DW/DEFW or FCW

Define word or form constant word assigns values to memory
locations in a similar manner to **DB**. As the name suggests, two
locations are used to store a 16-bit word. By convention the least
significant byte of the 16-bit word is stored in the first location and
the most significant byte in the following location. For example

```
          ORG  2000H
          DW   0ABCDH, 1234H
```

would place

0CDH	in 2000H
0ABH	in 2001H
34H	in 2002H
12H	in 2003H

DS or RMB

Define space or reserve memory bytes advances the PLC by the
required number of bytes leaving space. Common examples of its use
are reserving space for variables or for a system stack, Program 3.4.

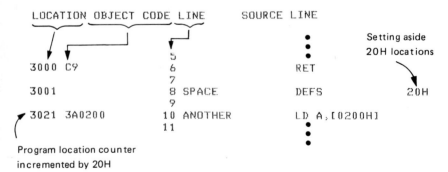

Program 3.4   Setting aside space using the DEFS pseudo-operation

88

END

Marks the end of the source code. Any lines following END will be ignored by the assembler. This pseudo-op is optional with many assemblers whereas others make use of it along with a label or value in the operand field to define a starting or transfer address for the program.

Many pseudo-operations are used to format the assembler listing, for example

TITLE

This pseudo-op allows you to place a title on the first line of each page in the assembler listing. For example

TITLE "SERIAL OUTPUT ROUTINE"

SKIP/PAGE/EJECT

Forces the assembler to start a new page in the assembler listing.

Program example The short routine shown in source and as an assembler listing in Program 3.5 generates a binary 'upcount' on a set of eight light emitting diodes (LEDs). Figure 3.9 shows the arrangement. The MEDC controller board detailed in Appendix B drives the LEDs through port B of a PIO (Parallel Input Output) chip.

After defining symbols the routine begins by loading the stack pointer and initialising the PIO, setting up port B as an output port. The routine then enters the main program loop that outputs the contents of the incrementing B register, to port B.

Since each program instruction would take only a few microseconds to perform the program makes use of a delay subroutine to slow down the count so that it can be easily observed. Subroutine DELAY wastes time decrementing the contents of the DE register pair to zero. Notice how the time constant for the delay is passed to the subroutine in the DE register pair. This technique greatly increases its flexibility allowing it to be used for a wide range of delays.

Expressions

The operand field in an assembly language statement specifies values or locations needed by the microprocessor instruction. In many assemblers the operand field can contain a combination of symbols and numbers forming an expression. The range of operators that can be used depends on the assembler. In the Hewlett Packard assemblers offered on their 64000 series development system the following arithmetic and logical operators can be used:

```
"Z80"
                    TITLE              "BINARY COUNT ROUTINE"
***********************************************************************
*                                                                     *
* ROUTINE TO OUTPUT BINARY COUNT TO LEDS CONNECTED TO PORT B          *
* OF PIO                                                              *
*                                                                     *
***********************************************************************

                    ORG  0000H

STACK_TOP           EQU  083FFH

PORT_B              EQU  01H          ;PIO PORT B ADDRESS
CONT_B              EQU  PORT_B+2     ;CONTROL REGISTER FOR PORT B

MOD3                EQU  11001111B    ;MODE 3 CONTROL BYTE
TIME_CONST          EQU  0A000H

;END OF DEFINITIONS

START               LD SP,STACK_TOP
                    LD A,MOD3         ;MODE 3 DATA BYTE IN A
                    OUT [CONT_B],A    ;MODE 3 BYTE TO PORT B
                    LD A,00           ;DATA DIR BYTE IN A (ALL BITS O/P)
                    OUT [CONT_B],A    ;DATA DIR BYTE NOW IN DDR

;PORT IS NOW SET UP

                    LD B,0FFH         ;B-REG WILL BE USED AS A COUNTER

LOOP                INC B             ;INCREMENT COUNTER
                    LD A,B            ;PUT RESULT IN A FOR OUTPUT
                    OUT [PORT_B],A    ;OUTPUT TO PORT B
                    LD DE,TIME_CONST  ;SETUP DELAY REQUIRED
                    CALL DELAY        ;OFF TO DELAY ROUTINE
                    JP LOOP           ;BACK TO INCREMENT COUNT AGAIN

***********************************
*                                 *
* SUBROUTINE TO FORM TIME DELAY   *
*                                 *
* ENTER WITH TIME CONSTANT IN     *
* DE.                             *
*                                 *
* ALTERS:        A,D,E,FLAGS      *
*                                 *
***********************************


DELAY               DEC DE            ;DECREMENT INPUT VALUE
                    LD A,D            ;INTO A WITH VALUE IN D
                    OR E              ;OR THIS WITH VALUE IN E
                    JP NZ,DELAY       ;BACK TO DECREMENT IF NOT ZERO
                    RET


                    END START
```

Program 3.5 Binary count routine: (a) source

```
                        1  "Z80"
                        3  ***********************************************************
                        4  *                                                         *
                        5  * ROUTINE TO OUTPUT BINARY COUNT TO LEDS CONNECTED TO PORT B  *
                        6  * OF PIO                                                   *
                        7  *                                                         *
                        8  ***********************************************************
                        9
                       10                    ORG 0000H
                       11
        (83FF)         12 STACK_TOP          EQU 083FFH
                       13
        (0001)         14 PORT_B             EQU 01H          ;PIO PORT B ADDRESS
        (0003)         15 CONT_B             EQU PORT_B+2     ;CONTROL REGISTER FOR PORT B
                       16
        (00CF)         17 MOD3               EQU 11001111B    ;MODE 3 CONTROL BYTE
        (A000)         18 TIME_CONST         EQU 0A000H
                       19
                       20 ;END OF DEFINITIONS
                       21
0000 3183FF            22 START              LD SP,STACK_TOP
0003 3ECF              23                    LD A,MOD3        ;MODE 3 DATA BYTE IN A
0005 D303              24                    OUT [CONT_B],A   ;MODE 3 BYTE TO PORT B
0007 3E00              25                    LD A,00          ;DATA DIR BYTE IN A (ALL BITS O/P)
0009 D303              26                    OUT [CONT_B],A   ;DATA DIR BYTE NOW IN DDR
                       27
                       28 ;PORT IS NOW SET UP
                       29
000B 06FF              30                    LD B,0FFH        ;B-REG WILL BE USED AS A COUNTER
                       31
000D 04                32 LOOP               INC B            ;INCREMENT COUNTER
000E 78                33                    LD A,B           ;PUT RESULT IN A FOR OUTPUT
000F D301              34                    OUT [PORT_B],A   ;OUTPUT TO PORT B
0011 11A000            35                    LD DE,TIME_CONST ;SETUP DELAY REQUIRED
0014 CD001A            36                    CALL DELAY       ;OFF TO DELAY ROUTINE
0017 C3000D            37                    JP LOOP          ;BACK TO INCREMENT COUNT AGAIN
                       38
                       39 ***********************************
                       40 *                                 *
                       41 * SUBROUTINE TO FORM TIME DELAY   *
                       42 *                                 *
                       43 * ENTER WITH TIME CONSTANT IN     *
                       44 * DE                              *
                       45 *                                 *
                       46 * ALTERS:        A,D,E,FLAGS      *
                       47 *                                 *
                       48 ***********************************
                       49
                       50
                       51
001A 1B                52 DELAY              DEC DE           ;DECREMENT INPUT VALUE
001B 7A                53                    LD A,D           ;INTO A WITH VALUE IN D
001C B3                54                    OR E             ;OR THIS WITH VALUE IN E
001D C2001A            55                    JP NZ,DELAY      ;BACK TO DECREMENT IF NOT ZERO
0020 C9                56                    RET
                       57
                       58
        (0000)         59                    END START
```

Program 3.5   Binary count routine: (b) assembler listing

+   addition
-      subtraction
*   multiplication
/   division
.AN   logical AND
.NT   logical one's complement
.OR   logical OR
.SL   shift left
.SR   shift right

It is important to note that these expressions are evaluated at 'assembly-time' generating unique operands for that version of the

91

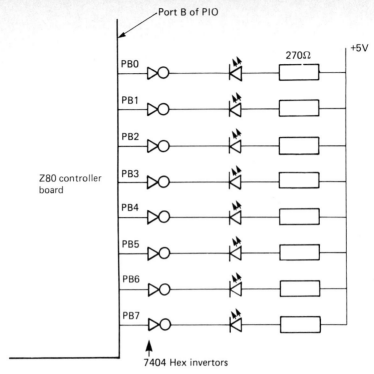

Figure 3.9 Z80 controller board driving LEDs connected to port B of PIO

machine code program, i.e. the expressions themselves are not part of the 'run-time' program.

Program 3.6a illustrates the use of expressions to evaluate delay constants for bit times in a serial character output routine. Before assembly the processor clock frequency and the desired serial transmission rate are entered as equate statements at the start of the routine. The following two lines then evaluate the delay required for each bit of the serial character BDELOUT and the slightly larger delay required for the stop bit SDELOUT. (The bit time is made up of a delay subroutine using the time constants above and the time required to execute the actual program instructions. Since the stop bit has less program overhead it requires a larger time constant in the delay subroutine to give the same overall bit time.)

Program 3.6b shows the result of assembling the source program configured for a system with a 2 MHz clock transmitting at 1200 baud. If the routine has to be used with a system operating at a different frequency or different baud rate then it would be reassembled with CLK and BAUD set to their new values leaving the two expressions to evaluate the required delays.

```
"Z80"
                    EXTERNAL  DELAY,PORTA
                    GLOBAL SEROP
;
;BAUD RATE DELAY EQUATES
;
CLK                 EQU 2           ;MHZ
BAUD                EQU 12          ;DECABAUD
;
BDELOUT             EQU ((10000*CLK)/BAUD-131)/24+1+5
SDELOUT             EQU BDELOUT*11/10
;
*********************************************************************
*NAME:              SEROP                                          *
*INPUTS:            DATA IN C-REG FOR OP                           *
*OUTPUTS:           DATA IN C-REG IN SERIAL FORMAT TO PORT A B0    *
*CALLS:             DELAY                                          *
*ALTERS:            A,FLAGS                                        *
*DESCRIPTION:                                                      *
*Z80 SERIAL O/P PROGRAM                                           *
*USES BIT 0 OF PORT 0                                             *
*IDLE STATE =1                                                    *
*CHARACTER TO BE PLACED IN C BY CALLER                            *
*LINE MUST BE SET TO 1 WHEN THIS IS CALLED                        *
*CHARACTER IS PLACED IN C-REG BY CALLER                           *
*AUTHOR L. MACARI                                                 *
*********************************************************************
SEROP:
                    DI
                    PUSH BC
                    PUSH DE         ;B,C,D,E SAVED ON STACK
;
                    LD B,08         ;BIT COUNTER IN B
                    LD A,00         ;SET BIT 0 TO START BIT
LOOP:
                    OUT [PORTA],A   ;OUTPUT BIT              :11T
                    LD DE,[BDELO]   ;BIT DELAY IN DE         :20T
                    CALL DELAY      ;WAIT BIT TIME           :17T
;
                    LD A,C          ;GET CHARACTER FROM C     :4T
                    RRCA            ;LSB INTO CARRY           :4T
                    LD C,A          ;SAVE ROTATED SEROP IN C  :4T
                    JR C,SET1                                :12T :7T
SET0:
                    LD A,00         ;SET B0 TO 0              :7T
                    JP CONT                                  :10T
SET1:
                    NOP             ;TO EQUALISE TIME IN TWO PATHS :4T
                    LD A,01         ;SET B0 TO 1              :7T
CONT:
                    DEC B           ;DECREMENT COUNTER        :4T
                    JP P,LOOP       ;IF NOT FINISHED BACK TO LOOP :10T
;
                    LD A,01         ;STOP BIT SET
                    OUT [PORTA],A   ;OUTPUT BIT
                    LD DE,[SDELO]   ;LOAD DE WITH STOP DELAY VALUE
                    CALL DELAY      ;WAIT
;
                    POP DE
                    POP BC          ;RESTORE REGISTERS
                    EI
                    RET
;
;CONSTANTS USED BY SEROP
;
BDELO               DEFW BDELOUT
SDELO               DEFW SDELOUT
;
```

Program 3.6   Serial output routine – use of expressions:
(a) source

Conditional assembly

Some assemblers offer a range of pseudo-operations that only allow
subsequent statements to be assembled if a specified condition is met.
One common use of this feature enables the programmer to use flags, at
the start of the source program, to select which of the following modules
or subroutines have to be assembled and included in the final code.

```
                    1 "Z80"
                    2                 EXTERNAL  DELAY,PORTA
                    3                 GLOBAL SEROP
                    4 ;
                    5 ;BAUD RATE DELAY EQUATES
                    6 ;
        (0002)      7 CLK            EQU 2              ;MHZ
        (000C)      8 BAUD           EQU 12             ;DECABAUD
                    9 ;
        (0045)     10 BDELOUT        EQU ((10000*CLK)/BAUD-131)/24+1+5
        (004B)     11 SDELOUT        EQU BDELOUT*11/10
                   12 ;
                   13 **********************************************************************
                   14 *NAME:          SEROP                                                *
                   15 *INPUTS:        DATA IN C-REG FOR OP                                 *
                   16 *OUTPUTS:       DATA IN C-REG IN SERIAL FORMAT TO PORT A B0          *
                   17 *CALLS:         DELAY                                                *
                   18 *ALTERS:        A,FLAGS                                              *
                   19 *DESCRIPTION:                                                        *
                   20 *Z80 SERIAL O/P PROGRAM                                              *
                   21 *USES BIT 0 OF PORT 0                                                *
                   22 *IDLE STATE =1                                                       *
                   23 *CHARACTER TO BE PLACED IN C BY CALLER                               *
                   24 *LINE MUST BE SET TO 1 WHEN THIS IS CALLED                           *
                   25 *CHARACTER IS PLACED IN C-REG BY CALLER                              *
                   26 *AUTHOR L. MACARI                                                    *
                   27 **********************************************************************
0000               28 SEROP:
0000 F3            29                 DI
0001 C5            30                 PUSH BC
0002 D5            31                 PUSH DE            ;B,C,D,E SAVED ON STACK
                   32 ;
0003 0608          33                 LD B,08            ;BIT COUNTER IN B
0005 3E00          34                 LD A,00            ;SET BIT 0 TO START BIT
0007               35 LOOP:
0007 D300          36                 OUT [PORTA],A      ;OUTPUT BIT              :11T
0009 ED5B0030      37                 LD DE,[BDELO]      ;BIT DELAY IN DE         :20T
000D CD0000        38                 CALL DELAY         ;WAIT BIT TIME           :17T
                   39 ;
0010 79            40                 LD A,C             ;GET CHARACTER FROM C    :4T
0011 0F            41                 RRCA               ;LSB INTO CARRY          :4T
0012 4F            42                 LD C,A             ;SAVE ROTATED SEROP IN C :4T
0013 3805          43                 JR C,SET1          :12T :7T
0015               44 SET0:
0015 3E00          45                 LD A,00            ;SET B0 TO 0             :7T
0017 C3001D        46                 JP CONT            :10T
001A               47 SET1:
001A 00            48                 NOP                ;TO EQUALISE TIME IN TWO PATHS :4T
001B 3E01          49                 LD A,01            ;SET B0 TO 1             :7T
001D               50 CONT:
001D 05            51                 DEC B              ;DECREMENT COUNTER       :4T
001E F20007        52                 JP P,LOOP          ;IF NOT FINISHED BACK TO LOOP :10T
                   53 ;
0021 3E01          54                 LD A,01            ;STOP BIT SET
0023 D300          55                 OUT [PORTA],A      ;OUTPUT BIT
0025 ED5B0032      56                 LD DE,[SDELO]      ;LOAD DE WITH STOP DELAY VALUE
0029 CD0000        57                 CALL DELAY         ;WAIT
                   58 ;
002C D1            59                 POP DE
002D C1            60                 POP BC             ;RESTORE REGISTERS
002E FB            61                 EI
002F C9            62                 RET
                   63 ;
                   64 ;CONSTANTS USED BY SEROP
                   65 ;
0030 0045          66 BDELO          DEFW BDELOUT
0032 004B          67 SDELO          DEFW SDELOUT
```

Program 3.6 Serial output routine – use of expressions:
(b) assembler listing

Program 3.7 gives an example using the IF, ELSE, ENDIF pseudo-ops.
The source listing contains two delay routines: a long routine using a
16-bit time constant and a short routine with an 8-bit constant. To select
the required routine the programmer sets the variable LONG TRUE for the
long routine and FALSE for the short routine. At assembly time only the
selected subroutine is assembled and included in the final code.

```
                        1   "Z80"
                        2   **********************************
                        3   *                                *
                        4   *  SUBROUTINE TO FORM TIME DELAY  *
                        5   *   USES EITHER 16 OR 8 BIT       *
                        6   *    DELAY ROUTINE                *
                        7   *                                 *
                        8   *  ON ENTRY DE OR D CONTAINS      *
                        9   *  THE TIME CONSTANT              *
                       10   *                                 *
                       11   *  ALTERS:         A,D,E,FLAGS    *
                       12   *                                 *
                       13   **********************************
                       14
                       15
                       16                      PROG
                       17
    (FFFFFFFF)         18   TRUE              EQU -1
       (0000)          19   FALSE             EQU 0
                       20
                       21   ; SET "LONG" TRUE FOR LARGE DELAY AND FALSE FOR SHORT DELAY
                       22
    (FFFFFFFF)         23   LONG              EQU TRUE
                       24
                       25                     IF LONG
                       26
                       27
    0000 1B            28   DELAY             DEC DE      ;DECREMENT INPUT VALUE
    0001 7A            29                     LD A,D      ;INTO A WITH VALUE IN D
    0002 B3            30                     OR E        ;OR THIS WITH VALUE IN E
    0003 C20000        31                     JP NZ,DELAY ;BACK TO DECREMENT IF NOT ZERO
    0006 C9            32                     RET
                       33
                       34
                       35                     ELSE
                       36
                       37
                       38
                       39   DELAY             DEC D       ;DECREMENT SHORT TIME CONSTANT
                       40                     JP NZ,DELAY ;BACK IF NOT ZERO
                       41                     RET
                       42
                       43                     ENDIF
```

Program 3.7   Using pseudo-ops for conditional assembly:
(a) condition TRUE assemble 16-bit delay routine

Macros

If a sequence of instructions has to be repeated at several points within a program an efficient technique is to form the instructions into a subroutine which only appears once in the final code and is called whenever required. An alternative strategy, supported by some assemblers, is to group the instructions as a macro.

The example below shows the basic format of a macro, namely a header statement specifying its name together with an optional list of parameters that can be passed to it, the source statements themselves, and finally the trailer statement MEND (macro end).

Label	Op-code	Operand	Comment
OUTPUT	MACRO	P1,P2	; header statement defining name and any parameters
	LD	A,(P1)	; source statements
	OUT	(P2),A	
	MEND		; end of macro definition

```
                    1  "Z80"
                    2  ***********************************
                    3  *                                 *
                    4  *  SUBROUTINE TO FORM TIME DELAY  *
                    5  *   USES EITHER 16 OR 8 BIT       *
                    6  *   DELAY ROUTINE                 *
                    7  *                                 *
                    8  *  ON ENTRY DE OR D CONTAINS      *
                    9  *  THE TIME CONSTANT              *
                   10  *                                 *
                   11  *  ALTERS:       A,D,E,FLAGS      *
                   12  *                                 *
                   13  ***********************************
                   14
                   15
                   16                   PROG
                   17
     (FFFFFFFF)    18  TRUE            EQU  -1
         (0000)    19  FALSE           EQU  0
                   20
                   21  ; SET "LONG" TRUE FOR LARGE DELAY AND FALSE FOR SHORT DELAY
                   22
         (0000)    23  LONG            EQU FALSE
                   24
                   25                   IF LONG
                   26
                   27
                   28  DELAY           DEC DE      ;DECREMENT INPUT VALUE
                   29                  LD A,D      ;INTO A WITH VALUE IN D
                   30                  OR E        ;OR THIS WITH VALUE IN E
                   31                  JP NZ,DELAY ;BACK TO DECREMENT IF NOT ZERO
                   32                  RET
                   33
                   34
                   35                   ELSE
                   36
                   37
                   38
0000 15            39  DELAY           DEC D       ;DECREMENT SHORT TIME CONSTANT
0001 C20000        40                  JP NZ,DELAY ;BACK IF NOT ZERO
0004 C9            41                  RET
                   42
                   43                   ENDIF
```

Program 3.7   Using pseudo-ops for conditional assembly:
(b) condition FALSE assemble 8-bit delay routine

After declaring the macro at the start of a program it can be made use of as many times as required. For example:

```
        .
        .
        .

LD          (BYTE),B

OUTPUT      BYTE,PORT
        .
        .
        .
etc.
```

An important difference between macros and subroutines is that the assembler does not produce code during a macro definition. Instead the machine code for the macro is generated and placed within the program each time the macro is called, the opposite strategy from a subroutine where the machine code only appears once in the program. Program 3.8 illustrates this using the binary count example. In this version the time delay is written as a macro and the time constant passed as a parameter.

Two assembler listings are shown. In the first the code generated by the macro is not displayed. In the second the EXPAND pseudo-op forces the assembler to display the source statements and the resulting code from the macro.

The use of macro definitions simplifies programs by eliminating repetitive writing of identical instruction sequences. They offer an advan-

```
LOCATION OBJECT CODE LINE      SOURCE LINE

                     1  "Z80"
                     2  ****************************************************************
                     3  *                                                              *
                     4  * ROUTINE TO OUTPUT BINARY COUNT TO LEDS CONNECTED TO PORT B   *
                     5  * OF PIO                                                        *
                     6  *                                                              *
                     7  ****************************************************************
                     8
                     9                  ORG  0000H
                    10
        (83FF)      11  STACK_TOP       EQU  083FFH
                    12
        (0001)      13  PORT_B          EQU  01H        ;PIO PORT B ADDRESS
        (0003)      14  CONT_B          EQU  PORT_B+2   ;CONTROL REGISTER FOR PORT B
                    15
        (00CF)      16  MOD3            EQU  11001111B  ;MODE 3 CONTROL BYTE
        (A000)      17  TIME_CONST      EQU  0A000H
                    18
                    19
                    20  *********************************
                    21  *                               *
                    22  * MACRO TO FORM TIME DELAY       *
                    23  * TIME CONSTANT PASSED AS        *
                    24  * PARAMETER                      *
                    25  *                               *
                    26  * ALTERS:       A,D,E,FLAGS      *
                    27  *                               *
                    28  *********************************
                    29
                    30
                    31  DELAY           MACRO &PARAM
                    32                  LD DE,&PARAM    ;LOAD DE WITH TIME CONSTANT
                    33  HERE            DEC DE          ;DECREMENT INPUT VALUE
                    34                  LD A,D          ;INTO A WITH VALUE IN D
                    35                  OR E            ;OR THIS WITH VALUE IN E
                    36                  JP NZ,HERE      ;BACK TO DECREMENT IF NOT ZERO
                    37                  MEND
                    38
                    39  ;END OF DEFINITIONS
                    40
                    41
0000 3183FF         42                  LD SP,STACK_TOP
0003 3ECF           43                  LD A,MOD3       ;MODE 3 DATA BYTE IN A
0005 D303           44                  OUT [CONT_B],A  ;MODE 3 BYTE TO PORT B
0007 3E00           45                  LD A,00         ;DATA DIR BYTE IN A (ALL BITS O/P)
0009 D303           46                  OUT [CONT_B],A  ;DATA DIR BYTE NOW IN DDR
                    47
                    48  ;PORT IS NOW SET UP
                    49
000B 06FF           50                  LD B,0FFH       ;B-REG WILL BE USED AS A COUNTER
                    51
000D 04             52  LOOP            INC B           ;INCREMENT COUNTER
000E 78             53                  LD A,B          ;PUT RESULT IN A FOR OUTPUT
000F D301           54                  OUT [PORT_B],A  ;OUTPUT TO PORT B
0011                55                  DELAY TIME_CONST ;OFF TO DELAY ROUTINE
001A C3000D         56                  JP LOOP         ;BACK TO INCREMENT COUNT AGAIN
```

Program 3.8 Binary count routine with the time delay written as a macro: (a) assembler listing with code within macro suppressed for clarity;

```
              23 * TIME CONSTANT PASSED AS        *
              24 * PARAMETER                      *
              25 *                                *
              26 * ALTERS:         A,D,E,FLAGS    *
              27 *                                *
              28 *********************************
              29
              30
              31 DELAY          MACRO &PARAM
              32              LD DE,&PARAM       ;LOAD DE WITH TIME CONSTANT
              33 HERE         DEC DE            ;DECREMENT INPUT VALUE
              34              LD A,D            ;INTO A WITH VALUE IN D
              35              OR E              ;OR THIS WITH VALUE IN E
              36              JP NZ,HERE        ;BACK TO DECREMENT IF NOT ZERO
              37              MEND
              38
              39 ;END OF DEFINITIONS
              40
              41              EXPAND
              42
0000 3183FF    43              LD SP,STACK_TOP
0003 3ECF      44              LD A,MOD3          ;MODE 3 DATA BYTE IN A
0005 D303      45              OUT [CONT_B],A     ;MODE 3 BYTE TO PORT B
0007 3E00      46              LD A,00            ;DATA DIR BYTE IN A (ALL BITS O/P)
0009 D303      47              OUT [CONT_B],A     ;DATA DIR BYTE NOW IN DDR
              48
              49 ;PORT IS NOW SET UP
              50
000B 06FF      51              LD B,0FFH          ;B-REG WILL BE USED AS A COUNTER
              52
000D 04        53 LOOP         INC B             ;INCREMENT COUNTER
000E 78        54              LD A,B            ;PUT RESULT IN A FOR OUTPUT
000F D301      55              OUT [PORT_B],A    ;OUTPUT TO PORT B
0011          56              DELAY TIME_CONST ;OFF TO DELAY ROUTINE
0011 11A000    +              LD DE,TIME_CONST   ;LOAD DE WITH TIME CONSTANT
0014 1B        + HERE         DEC DE            ;DECREMENT INPUT VALUE
0015 7A        +              LD A,D            ;INTO A WITH VALUE IN D
0016 B3        +              OR E              ;OR THIS WITH VALUE IN E
0017 C20014    +              JP NZ,HERE        ;BACK TO DECREMENT IF NOT ZERO
001A C3000D    57              JP LOOP           ;BACK TO INCREMENT COUNT AGAIN
```

Program 3.8   Binary count routine with the time delay written as a macro: (b) using the EXPAND pseudo-op to display machine code and source statement within macro

tage over subroutines of not requiring branching within a program or the use of a stack to store the return address. As a result programs using macros can run faster as well as operate in situations where RAM space is restricted or perhaps does not exist. (The latter is an important consideration when developing routines for small minimum systems or when designing diagnostic routines that make no assumption as to whether the RAM is working or not.)

Against these advantages, macros have the obvious disadvantage of increasing the overall program size with perhaps several copies of identical machine code appearing in the final firmware.

3.3   LINKERS AND PROGRAM MODULES

The programs examined so far have all made use of the ORG pseudo-op to give them a final position within a system's memory map. With some assemblers, it is possible to omit this pseudo-op leaving the position of the final code undefined at assembly time and allowing the load address to be added at a later stage. As a result the output from a relocating assembler is not the final machine code but an intermediate module called a relocatable file. Conversion of relocatable files to an absolute or machine code file is carried out by the linker.

The linker performs two important functions on the relocatable files produced by the assembler:

1. It allocates memory space, converting *relocatable files* to *absolute code*, and fixing them in the system memory map.

2. It allows the programmer to link together relocatable modules to produce a single machine code program.

Working with a relocating assembler/linker package has definite advantages in a large programming project. By splitting the problem down into a number of smaller problems each member of a team can be assigned to develop solutions in a relocatable format. It then remains a relatively simple task to link the relocatable modules together to form one continuous machine code program, Figure 3.10a.

In addition individual modules can be easily moved to different memory areas without having to edit and re-assemble the original source program. As a result program libraries normally store programs in relocatable format.

Figure 3.10b shows an example of two short routines that are assembled and then linked together starting at address 8000H. The source files for each start with the pseudo-operation PROG declaring that the code that follows has to be placed under the PROGRAM memory area and that a value for PROG will be assigned in the LINKER. (The example uses the relocating assembler and linker on the HP64000. It supports two other relocatable program areas defined by the pseudo-ops DATA and COMN. Each program module can contain code destined for each of these areas. During the linking operation values will be assigned to each of these program location counters and the resulting code assigned to the three program areas, Figure 3.11.

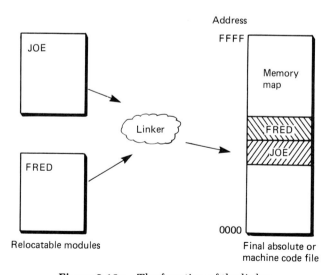

Figure 3.10a   The function of the linker

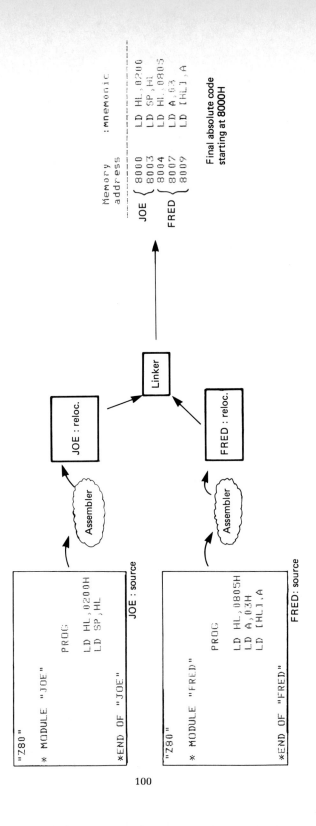

Figure 3.10b Example link on the HP64000

100

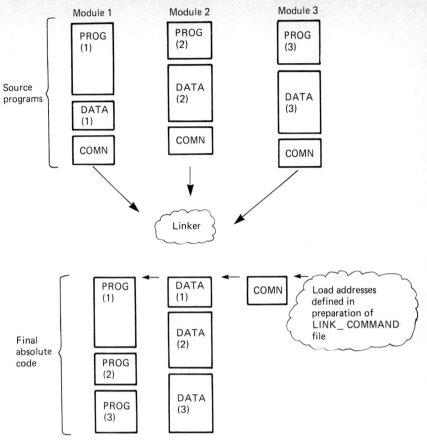

Figure 3.11 Three program counters PROG, DATA and COMN can be used to partition code on the HP64000

To help keep track of the position of different modules the linker can produce a *load map* showing the memory areas allocated to each relocatable file, Figure 3.12. The map begins by showing details of the first file linked followed by information on the other modules in the order that they were linked.

FILE/PROG NAME	PROGRAM	DATA	COMMON	ABSOLUTE
JOE:JDFM next address	8000 8004	Start and end address + 1 of module JOE		
FRED:JDFM next address	8004 800A	Start and end address + 1 of module FRED		

Figure 3.12 Load map produced by the linker for modules in Fig. 3.10b

External and global references

Problems can arise during assembly if a symbol is referenced in one program module, but defined in another module: for example, if the delay routine used in the binary count example, Program 3.5, is removed and treated as a separate module. On assembling the new count routine the assembler will report an error due to the undefined symbol DELAY.

To overcome this problem any modules referencing undefined symbols should include the EXTERNAL pseudo-op followed by a list of all symbols used but not defined within the module, e.g. the main COUNT routine should include the statement

EXTERNAL DELAY

The assembler will now happily assemble the routine, filling any references to the label DELAY with zeros in the assembler listing and noting in the relocatable file that a value for DELAY has to be obtained from another program module during linking.

Not all labels defined within a module need be made available to other modules. Any symbols that are needed should be declared global within the module they are defined using the GLB pseudo-op. Declaring a symbol global results in it being included in a global symbol table generated by the linker.

An example To help illustrate some of these points the binary count routine is shown again but restructured as a set of three program modules:

1. ZSETUP   A short code sequence that configures port B of the PIO as an output port and initialises the stack pointer. The symbol PORT_B that is used by the next module is declared global, Program 3.9.

```
LOCATION OBJECT CODE LINE    SOURCE LINE

                        1  "Z80"
                        2  *****************************************************
                        3  *                                                   *
                        4  * ROUTINE TO SET_UP PORT B AND POSITION             *
                        5  * THE STACK POINTER                                 *
                        6  *                                                   *
                        7  *****************************************************
                        8
                        9              GLOBAL PORT_B
                       10
          <0001>       11  PORT_B      EQU 01H
          <0003>       12  CONT_B      EQU 03H
          <00CF>       13  MOD3        EQU 11001111B
                       14
          <83FF>       15  STACK_TOP   EQU 83FFH        ;STACK POINTER INITIAL VALUE
                       16
                       17              PROG
                       18
0000 3183FF            19              LD SP,STACK_TOP  ;STACK POINTER INITIALISED
0003 3ECF              20              LD A,MOD3        ;MODE WORD IN A-REG
0005 D303              21              OUT [CONT_B],A   ;TO PORT CONTROL REGISTER
0007 3E00              22              LD A,00H         ;DATA BITS O/PS
0009 D303              23              OUT [CONT_B],A   ;TO CONTROL REGISTER
                       24
                       25  ;PORT B NOW SET_UP READY FOR USE.
```

Program 3.9 ZSETUP: program module to initialise the stack pointer
and configure port B

2. **ZMAIN** This is the main routine that performs the binary count using the Z80's B register as the counter. Both the symbols **PORT_B** and **DELAY** are declared external at the start of the routine, Program 3.10. Note: the assembler inserts 0s for both labels in the assembler listing.

```
LOCATION OBJECT CODE LINE     SOURCE LINE

                    1  "Z80"
                    2                       EXTERNAL PORT_B,DELAY
                    3
                    4  ;ZSETUP WILL BE LINKED IN HERE
                    5  ;THIS SETS PORTS AND STACK
                    6
                    7  ************************************************************
                    8  *                                                          *
                    9  * ROUTINE TO OUTPUT BINARY COUNT TO LEDS CONNECTED TO PORT B *
                   10  * OF PIO                                                    *
                   11  *                                                          *
                   12  ************************************************************
                   13
        (A000)     14  TIME_CONST        EQU 0A000H       ;CONSTANT USED IN DELAY ROUTINE
                   15
                   16                    PROG
                   17
0000 06FF          18                    LD B,0FFH        ;B-REG WILL BE USED AS A COUNTER
                   19
0002 04            20  LOOP              INC B            ;INCREMENT COUNTER
0003 78            21                    LD A,B           ;PUT RESULT IN A FOR OUTPUT
0004 D300          22                    OUT [PORT_B],A   ;OUTPUT TO PORT B
0006 11A000        23                    LD DE,TIME_CONST ;SELECT DELAY REQUIRED
0009 CD0000        24                    CALL DELAY       ;OFF TO DELAY ROUTINE
000C C30002        25                    JP LOOP          ;BACK TO INCREMENT COUNT AGAIN
                   26
                   27  ;END OF ROUTINE
```

Program 3.10 **ZMAIN**: main counting routine

3. **DELAY** The time delay routine produces a delay based on the time constant passed in the DE register pair. The label **DELAY** is declared global for use in other modules, Program 3.11.

```
LOCATION OBJECT CODE LINE      SOURCE LINE

                    1  "Z80"
                    2  ************************************
                    3  *                                  *
                    4  * SUBROUTINE TO FORM TIME DELAY     *
                    5  * ON ENTRY DE CONTAINS THE          *
                    6  * TIME CONSTANT                     *
                    7  *                                  *
                    8  * ALTERS:         A,D,E,FLAGS       *
                    9  *                                  *
                   10  ************************************
                   11
                   12                    GLOBAL DELAY
                   13
                   14                    PROG
                   15
                   16
0000 1B            17  DELAY             DEC DE           ;DECREMENT INPUT VALUE
0001 7A            18                    LD A,D           ;INTO A WITH VALUE IN D
0002 B3            19                    OR E             ;OR THIS WITH VALUE IN E
0003 C20000        20                    JP NZ,DELAY      ;BACK TO DECREMENT IF NOT ZERO
0006 C9            21                    RET
```

Program 3.11 **DELAY**: a 16-bit value for magnitude of delay is passed in DE register pair

Figure 3.13 shows the resulting code generated by the linker after linking the modules, in the order given above with a load address of 0000H.

```
Memory        :mnemonic
address
---------------------------------------------
      0000     LD SP,83FF
      0003     LD A,CF
      0005     OUT [03],A
      0007     LD A,00
      0009     OUT [03],A
      000B     LD B,FF
      000D     INC B
      000E     LD A,B
      000F     OUT [01],A
      0011     LD DE,A000
      0014     CALL 001A
      0017     JP 000D
      001A     DEC DE
      001B     LD A,D
      001C     OR  E
      001D     JP NZ,001A
      0020     RET
```

Figure 3.13   Disassembled listing of machine code produced by
linking program modules

One of the disadvantages of working with a set of program modules, as opposed to a single source file, is the lack of a continuous assembler listing showing all the code assembled to the correct load address and including definitions of all program labels. Without doubt a simple listing in this form proves extremely useful during program debugging. However, the linker produces two documents that help the programmer to interpret the final code. The load map, Figure 3.14, gives the position of each program module and the cross-reference table, Figure 3.15, lists all the global symbols and their values.

FILE/PROG NAME	PROGRAM	DATA	COMMON	ABSOLUTE	COMMENTS
ZSETUP:JDFM	0000				
next address	000B				
ZMAIN:JDFM	000B				
next address	001A				
DELAY:JDFM	001A				
next address	0021				

Figure 3.14   Load map for binary count example

SYMBOL	R	VALUE	DEF BY	REFERENCES
DELAY	P	001A	DELAY:JDFM	ZMAIN:JDFM
PORT_B	A	0001	ZSETUP:JDFM	ZMAIN:JDFM

Figure 3.15   Cross-reference table for binary count example

104

3.4   HIGH LEVEL LANGUAGES

Although assemblers greatly ease the task of producing machine code, assembly language suffers from a number of limitations:

1. Being a low level language it is intimately related to the registers and structure of the individual processor. As a result much of the programmer's time is concerned with processor details rather than finding a solution to the problem at hand.

2. Programs generated for one microprocessor are not usually easily transferred to another. There are exceptions to this. For example most 8080 and 8085 machine code routines will run on the Z80, the former's instruction set being for the most part a subset of the latter. The 8080 and the 8088/8086 are not code compatible but share a large number of instructions at the source code level. To gain access to the vast 8080 software base several translating routines have been developed that convert 8080 to 8088/8086 code.

3. Most common microprocessors are not equipped to perform arithmetic. Hence, arithmetic, trigonometric and scientific functions all have to be written and integrated into any assembly language program.

High level languages overcome these problems: programs are no longer processor dependent and most languages support a range of functions pertinent to the application area. Further, routines are more easily read, making use of English-like statements instead of terse mnemonics, and consequently are cheaper to write and maintain.

With all these advantages there would appear to be no position left for assembly language. However, it still retains a place in situations where speed or memory space is important as well as providing the low level driver routines that interface with system hardware.

Compilers

Like assembly language, statements in a high level language must first be converted into machine code before thay can be executed by the microprocessor. One technique achieves this using a program called a compiler. Some compilers produce machine code directly from the source statements. Others generate either assembly language statements that must then be assembled or relocatable code that can be linked to other compiled or assembled modules.

Most high level language statements will probably result in between five to ten machine code instructions and the overall code size could easily be up to three times the size of an equivalent assembly language program. However, the reduced development costs combined with compact and easily read source programs can often make a compiled solution more attractive. Further, memory size is no longer a major constraint: the low cost of memory devices coupled to the memory space of 1 MByte or more that can be addressed directly by 16-bit processors has resulted in many new machines with ample room to house compiled software.

```
 1 0000   1    "Z80"
 2 0000   1    $EXTENSIONS$
 3 0000   1    PROGRAM MAIN ;
 4 0000   1    $GLOBVAR ON$
 5 0000   1       VAR COUNT:BYTE ;
 6 0001   1    $GLOBVAR OFF$
 7 0001   1    PROCEDURE ZSETUP;EXTERNAL ;
 8 0000   1    PROCEDURE OUTPUT ;EXTERNAL ;
 9 0000   1    PROCEDURE ZDELAY;EXTERNAL ;
10 0000   1
11 0000   1    BEGIN
12 0000   1          ZSETUP ;
13 0006   1          COUNT:=0 ;
14 000B   1          REPEAT
15 000B   1                OUTPUT ;
16 000E   1                ZDELAY ;
17 0011   1                COUNT:=COUNT+1 ;
18 0019   1          UNTIL FALSE ;
19 001C   1    END .
```

Program 3.12 PMAIN: main module of binary count routine written
in Pascal

Program 3.12 gives the binary count routine described earlier written
in Pascal. Pascal is a general purpose language that has a widespread use
on both mainframe and microcomputers in educational, business and
scientific applications. Its major appeal lies with it readily supporting a
structured programming style, where large complex problems can be
broken down into a set of simple tasks and represented in a form that is
easy to read yet closely following the structure of the problem. The
example given could hardly be classed as complex but it allows comparison with the earlier assembly language version, Program 3.10. Only the
main module, PMAIN, is in Pascal while the other three – ZSETUP, OUTPUT
and ZDELAY, are written in assembly language and called as external
procedures. The global byte wide variable COUNT forms the counter. The
structure of the main module is extremely simple. After setting up the
port and initialising the system stack in the ZSETUP module, Program
3.13, COUNT is set to zero prior to entering the repeat until 'forever' loop,
outputting the current value of count to the LEDs using OUTPUT, Program
3.14 and ZDELAY, Program 3.15.

Two points are worth attention:

1. The label STACK_ defined in the ZSETUP module is a system variable
    used by the compiler to define the top of the Z80 stack.

2. Declaring the byte variable COUNT results in the compiler setting
    aside a single memory location of the same name to hold the current
    value of the counter. Hence, in the OUTPUT module it is the contents
    of COUNT that is loaded into the accumulator for output to the LEDs
    attached to port B.

When producing a list file from compilation the Pascal compiler on
the HP64000, like many others, allows you to use an EXPAND option that
displays the Z80 mnemonics produced, Figure 3.16.

```
                          1  "Z80"
                          2  ***********************************************
                          3  *
                          4  *  MODULE SETS UP PORT B AS OUTPUT
                          5  *  AND POSITION STACK
                          6  *
                          7  ***********************************************
                          8
                          9                    GLOBAL ZSETUP,PORTB,STACK_
                         10
                         11 ;PORT EQUATES
                         12
          <0001>         13 PORTB          EQU 1
          <0003>         14 CNTRLB         EQU 3
          <00CF>         15 MODE3          EQU 0CFH
          <0000>         16 DDRB           EQU 00000000B    ;ALL BITS OUTPUT
                         17
                         18 ;SETUP STACK
                         19
          <FFFF>         20 STACK_         EQU 0FFFFH
                         21
                         22                PROG
                         23
0000 3ECF                24 ZSETUP         LD  A,MODE3      ;MODE WORD IN A-REG
0002 D303                25                OUT [CNTRLB],A   ;TO PORT B CONTROL REGISTER
0004 3E00                26                LD  A,DDRB       ;DATA BITS O/PS
0006 D303                27                OUT [CNTRLB],A   ;TO CONTROL REGISTER
0008 C9                  28                RET
                         29 ;
                         30 ;PORT SET UP SUITABLE FOR OUTPUT
                         31 ;
```

Program 3.13 ZSETUP: sets up stack and configures port B as output

To form the final executable code all the relocatable files in an application are linked together. Included in the linkage is a program library containing many of the functions offered in the high level language.

The HP system provides two libraries:

LIBZ80:CZ80 the standard library containing routines for the operations, multiplication, division, comparison etc.

DLIBZ80:CZ80 this is the debug library containing the routines in the standard library plus error detection routines

All the routines in both libraries are held in a relocatable format and only those routines needed to satisfy an external reference not found in other program modules are included.

Figures 3.17 and 3.18 show the resulting load map and cross-reference table after linking the four program modules to a load address of 0000 and including the debug library. Finally Figure 3.19 gives a disassembled listing of the final executable code.

Interpreters
High level languages are implemented in most popular microcomputers using a program called an interpreter. Unlike a compiler an interpreter must remain resident in memory while the program is being executed. Further, an interpreter does not produce a separate executable machine code program. Instead it takes each high level statement, converts it to some intermediate form and then executes it before returning to the next

```
                                 1 "Z80"
                                 2
                                 3 ******************************************
                                 4 *
                                 5 * MODULE TO OUTPUT BYTE TO PORT B
                                 6 *
                                 7 ******************************************
                                 8
                                 9            GLOBAL    OUTPUT
                                10            EXTERNAL  PORTB,COUNT
                                11
                                12            PROG
                                13            NAME      "PORT B DRIVER ROUTINE."
                                14
      0000 3A0000               15 OUTPUT     LD        A,[COUNT] ;GET BYTE
      0003 D300                 16            OUT       [PORTB],A ;ONTO PORT
      0005 C9                   17            RET
```

Program 3.14   OUTPUT: subroutine to output current value of COUNT
to port B

```
                                 1 "Z80"
                                 2            GLOBAL ZDELAY
                                 3 *****************************************************************
                                 4 *NAME:       DELAY                                             *
                                 5 *OUTPUTS:    NOTHING                                           *
                                 6 *CALLS:      NOTHING                                           *
                                 7 *ALTERS:     A,D,E,FLAGS                                       *
                                 8 *DESCRIPTION:                                                  *
                                 9 *DELAY PROGRAM                                                 *
                                10 *DECREMENTS DE TILL ZERO                                       *
                                11 *****************************************************************
                                12            PROG
                                13            NAME "DELAY ROUTINE"
                                14            PROG
      0000                      15 ZDELAY
      0000 111000               16            LD DE,1000H
      0003 1B                   17 HERE       DEC DE     ;DECREMENT INPUT VALUE      ;6T
      0004 7A                   18            LD A,D     ;INTO A WITH VALUE IN D      ;4T
      0005 B3                   19            OR E       ;OR THIS WITH VALUE IN E     ;4T
      0006 C20003               20            JP NZ,HERE ;BACK TO DECREMENT IF NOT ZERO ;10T ;10T
      0009 C9                   21            RET
                                22 ;
```

Program 3.15   ZDELAY: delay routine

program statement.

The major advantage of interpreters is their ease of use: after writing a program it can be executed immediately and if any errors are detected it is a simple task to make corrections and try again. With a compiler the programmer must follow the lengthy sequence of edit, compile, link, before any updates can be tested.

Interpreters have two principle disadvantages. Every time a program is run, each statement has to be coded before it is executed with a resulting loss in speed. Secondly, interpreters cannot be used to develop software for stand alone applications, unless the interpreter itself is included in the system software.

BASIC is by far the most popular interpreted high level language with many microcomputer manufacturers including it in ROM as a resident system program. Chapter 7 includes many examples written in BBC BASIC.

```
 1  0000   1    "Z80"
 2  0000   1    $EXTENSIONS$
 3  0000   1    PROGRAM MAIN ;
            0000                         NAME      "MAIN Pascal"

 4  0000   1    $GLOBVAR ON$
 5  0000   1      VAR COUNT:BYTE;
 6  0001   1    $GLOBVAR OFF$
 7  0001   1    PROCEDURE ZSETUP;EXTERNAL;
            0000                         EXT       ZSETUP

 8  0000   1    PROCEDURE OUTPUT;EXTERNAL;
            0000                         EXT       OUTPUT

 9  0000   1    PROCEDURE ZDELAY;EXTERNAL;
            0000                         EXT       ZDELAY

10  0000   1
11  0000   1    BEGIN
            0000               MAIN:

12  0000   1        ZSETUP ;
            0000   31  ????         LD        SP,STACK_
            0003   CD  ????         CALL      ZSETUP

13  0006   1        COUNT:=0;
            0006   21  ????         LD        HL,MAIN_D
            0009   36  00           LD        [HL],0

14  000B   1        REPEAT
            000B               MAIN_L1:

15  000B   1            OUTPUT;
            000B   CD  ????         CALL      OUTPUT

16  000E   1            ZDELAY;
            000E   CD  ????         CALL      ZDELAY

17  0011   1            COUNT:=COUNT+1;
            0011   3A  ????         LD        A,[MAIN_D]
            0014   C6  01           ADD       A,1
            0016   32  ????         LD        [MAIN_D],A

18  0019   1        UNTIL FALSE;
            0019   C3  ????         JP        MAIN_L1

19  001C   1    END.
            001C   C3  ????         JP        Z_END_PROGRAM
            001F               MAIN_C:
            001F               MAIN_E:
            001F               MAIN_D:
            001F                         DEFS      1
            0020                         GLB       MAIN
            0020                         GLB       COUNT
                              COUNT EQU MAIN_D
            0020                         EXT       STACK_
            0020                         EXT       Z_END_PROGRAM
            0020                         END       MAIN
```

Figure 3.16   Expanded listing produced by compiler showing Z80
mnemonics for module PMAIN

FILE/PROG NAME	PROGRAM	DATA	COMMON	ABSOLUTE	COMMENTS
PMAIN:NAP_FG	0000				MAIN Pascal
ZSETUP:NAP_FG	0020				
OUTPUT:NAP_FG	0029				PORT B DRIVER ROUTI
ZDELAY:NAP_FG	002F				DELAY ROUTINE
next address	0039				

```
Libraries
DLIBZ80:CZ80
     Derrors:CZ80   0039
       PARAM_:CZ80   00D2
next address          0136
```

Figure 3.17   Load map for Pascal example

SYMBOL	R VALUE	DEF BY	REFERENCES
CASEERROR_	P 0084	Derrors:CZ80	
COUNT	P 001F	PMAIN:NAP_FG	OUTPUT:NAP_FG
ERR_DIVBY0	P 003F	Derrors:CZ80	
ERR_OVERFLOW	P 0039	Derrors:CZ80	
ERR_SET	P 0042	Derrors:CZ80	
ERR_UNDERFLOW	P 003C	Derrors:CZ80	
MAIN	P 0000	PMAIN:NAP_FG	
MEMERR	P 008C	Derrors:CZ80	PMAIN:NAP_FG
OUTPUT	P 0029	OUTPUT:NAP_FG	Derrors:CZ80
PARAM_	P 00D2	PARAM_:CZ80	OUTPUT:NAP_FG
PORTB	A 0001	ZSETUP:NAP_FG	PMAIN:NAP_FG
STACK_	A FFFF	ZSETUP:NAP_FG	PMAIN:NAP_FG
ZDELAY	P 002F	ZDELAY:NAP_FG	PMAIN:NAP_FG
ZSETUP	P 0020	ZSETUP:NAP_FG	PMAIN:NAP_FG
Z_END_PROGRAM	P 00A1	Derrors:CZ80	

Figure 3.18   Cross-reference table for Pascal example

```
Memory        :mnemonic
address
------------------------------
0000    LD SP,FFFF
0003    CALL 0020
0006    LD HL,001F
0009    LD [HL],00
000B    CALL 0029
000E    CALL 002F
0011    LD A,[001F]
0014    ADD A,01
0016    LD [001F],A
0019    JP 000B
001C    JP 00A1
001F    AND 3E
0021    RST 08
0022    OUT [03],A
0024    LD A,00
0026    OUT [03],A
0028    RET
0029    LD A,[001F]
```

Figure 3.19   Disassembled listing of code produced for binary count
routine (Pascal version)

Problems

3.1 Write a short routine to output a message string terminated by a control Z. Your routine should make use of a display subroutine OUTPUT that transmits an ASCII character in the accumulator to the current output device. Employ either the DB or the ASC directive to hold the message string. (Assume OUTPUT does not affect the processor registers or status flags.)

3.2 Restructure the answer to Problem 3.1 as a macro that requires a single parameter, namely the starting address of the message string.

3.3 Summarise the advantages and disadvantages of working with a relocatable assembler and linker package.

FURTHER READING

A number of good books give guidelines on program design and documentation. The following is just a selection.

Wakerly, 1981. *Microcomputer Architecture and Programming*. London: Wiley.

Kernighan, B.W. and Plauger, P., 1978. *The Elements of Programming Style*. New York, NY: McGraw-Hill.

Sommerville, I., 1985. 2nd edn. *Software Engineering*. Wokingham: Addison-Wesley.

Chapter 4

Testing and debugging

The objectives of this chapter are:

- to outline the development cycle of a typical microprocessor based product;
- to examine the range of facilities available on software debugging packages;
- to highlight the problems associated with debugging hardware and software in real-time;
- to introduce the role of the logic state analyser and the logic timing analyser;
- to introduce the use of in-circuit emulation as a powerful technique in the development process.

As all designers are aware, prototypes seldom work first time. Testing to detect the presence of errors, and debugging to locate their source and form a repair are essential ingredients in the development process.

Figure 4.1 illustrates a typical development cycle of a microprocessor based product. It often comes as a surprise to novice programmers to learn that translating their ideas into program statements, i.e. coding, takes up a relatively small percentage of the overall development time. By far the largest part of the development process is taken by testing and debugging.

This chapter concentrates on the development tools that help ease the task of system debugging. Broadly speaking these tools fall into two categories:

- software debugging packages ranging from simple monitor programs to the more powerful, purpose designed debuggers e.g. Digital Research's Z80 Symbolic Instruction Debugger (ZSID) or Dynamic Debugging Tool (DDT)
- hardware aids including logic analysers (state and timing) and in-circuit emulators

4.1 SOFTWARE TOOLS

The basic software development tools offered on most debugging packages usually include the following facilities:

- memory examine and alter

- register examine and alter
- run program from address/set breakpoints
- single step program from address

On a development kit, for example the SDK85 or 86, these features are part of the monitor program, i.e. the resident routine that allows the operator to enter and test applications programs. Software packages such as ZSID, designed to run under the CP/M operating system, offer a number of enhanced features, for example:

- a line assembler to write short routines and 'patch' errors
- a disassembler to view machine code in mnemonics
- a move memory command to relocate a block of code
- load and save files to disk
- a trace utility displaying processor activity up to a given address

The operation of each of these tools is best illustrated with the help of some simple examples.

Memory examine/alter   Two versions of this facility are commonly used. In a memory dump the operator enters the command followed by the start

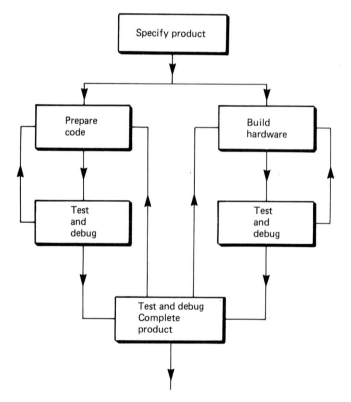

Figure 4.1   Typical development cycle of a microprocessor based product

and end address of the memory block to be examined. The debugger then displays the memory contents in hexadecimal and ASCII, Figure 4.2a. Using a substitute memory command, Figure 4.2b, the contents of a single memory location is first displayed before inviting a change.

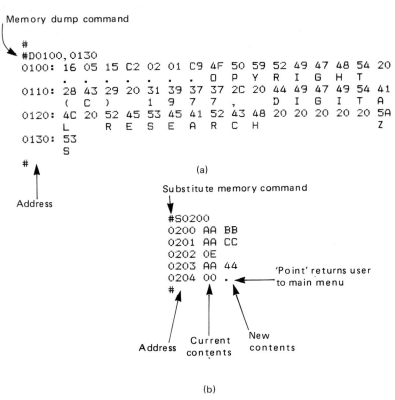

Memory dump command

```
#
#D0100,0130
0100:  16  05  15  C2  02  01  C9  4F  50  59  52  49  47  48  54  20
       .   .   .   .   .   .   .   O   P   Y   R   I   G   H   T
0110:  28  43  29  20  31  39  37  37  2C  20  44  49  47  49  54  41
       (   C   )       1   9   7   7   ,       D   I   G   I   T   A
0120:  4C  20  52  45  53  45  41  52  43  48  20  20  20  20  20  5A
       L       R   E   S   E   A   R   C   H                       Z
0130:  53
       S
#
```

Address

(a)

Substitute memory command

```
#S0200
0200  AA  BB
0201  AA  CC
0202  OE
0203  AA  44
0204  00  .
#
```

'Point' returns user to main menu

Address   Current contents   New contents

(b)

Figure 4.2 Examining and altering memory locations: (a) DUMP in ASCII and Hex; (b) the substitute memory command (from Digital Research's ZSID)

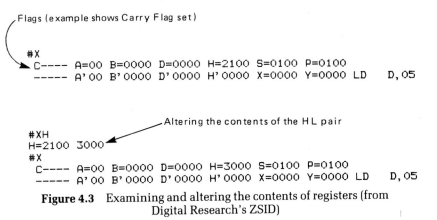

Flags (example shows Carry Flag set)

```
#X
C----  A=00  B=0000  D=0000  H=2100  S=0100  P=0100
-----  A'00  B'0000  D'0000  H'0000  X=0000  Y=0000  LD    D,05
```

Altering the contents of the HL pair

```
#XH
H=2100  3000
#X
C----  A=00  B=0000  D=0000  H=3000  S=0100  P=0100
-----  A'00  B'0000  D'0000  H'0000  X=0000  Y=0000  LD    D,05
```

Figure 4.3 Examining and altering the contents of registers (from Digital Research's ZSID)

Register examine/alter   Examining or altering the processor registers is similar to viewing or altering memory. The first example in Figure 4.3 gives a display of all the registers including the condition of the processor flags. In the second example the same command is used to display and then alter the contents of a specified register pair, namely the HL pair.

It is worth noting that the display does not show the contents of the registers at the instant the command is given. Instead it shows the values the registers will be set to before the program under development is executed.

Assemble/disassemble   A line assembler embedded within the debugger can save time when writing short test routines as well as making additions or patches to a larger program. Figure 4.4a gives an example using the line assembler to enter a short delay subroutine at 0100 (hex).

The ability to view memory contents in mnemonics, i.e. inverse assembly or disassembly, often proves useful allowing a check to be made on the actual program in memory as opposed to what is supposed to be there, Figure 4.4b.

```
#                             #
#A0100                        #L0100
0100   LD D,5                   0100   LD    D,05
0102   DEC D                    0102   DEC   D
0103   JP NZ,0102               0103   JP    NZ,0102
0106   RET                      0106   RET
0107                            0107   LD    C,A
#                              0108   LD    D,B
                                0109   LD    E,C
                                010A   LD    D,D
                                010B   LD    C,C
                                010C   LD    B,A
                                010D   LD    C,B
```

         (a)   (b)

Figure 4.4   Line assembly/disassembly: (a) inserting a short delay routine using a line assembler; (b) inverse assembly or disassembly, displaying the contents of memory in mnemonics (from Digital Research's ZSID)

```
(a)      #G0100


(b)      #
         #G0100,0106

         *0106
         #X
         -Z--- A=00 B=0079 D=0000 H=FF00 S=0202 P=0106
         ----- A'00 B'0000 D'0000 H'0000 X=0000 Y=0000 RET
```

Figure 4.5   The run command: (a) executing a program starting at 0100H; (b) as (a) but with the addition of a breakpoint at 0106H, returning control to the debugger, assuming the processor reaches 0106H (from Digital Research's ZSID)

115

Run program/set breakpoint The run or go command allows the processor to transfer from the debugger program to the program under test. Normally it is followed by the starting address of the test routine, Figure 4.5a.

Often the run command will support one or more breakpoint addresses, i.e. an address at which program execution is halted and control passed back to the debugger program. Figure 4.5b illustrates the principle with the delay routine, Figure 4.4a, returning control to the debugger before the execution of the RET instruction at 0106 (hex).

Breakpoints are extremely useful when debugging a program, allowing the user to execute a routine up to, or perhaps just past, the suspected problem area. If the breakpoint is reached, the examine registers or memory commands can then be used to examine variables,

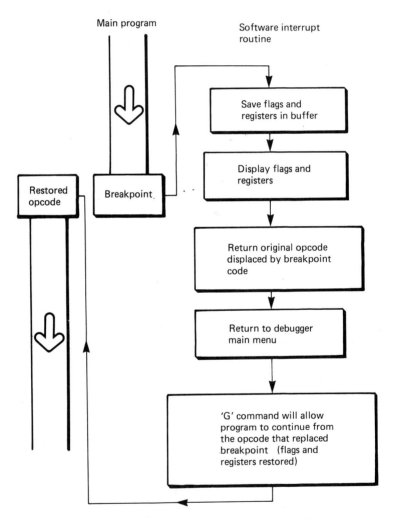

Figure 4.6   Debugger activity on meeting a breakpoint

116

flags or stack to ensure they have the correct values. In the example notice how the D register has been decremented to zero and the processor zero flag has been set.

Breakpoints are implemented in a debugging package using a software interrupt or break instruction, e.g. BRK on the 6502 or RST 38 on the Z80 and INT 3 on the 8088/8086. On setting a breakpoint the code at that address is removed by the debugger and replaced by the software interrupt code. If after executing the program the processor reaches the break code it is diverted to an interrupt routine that either displays or stores the contents of the registers before replacing the breakpoint with the original code, and returning to the debugger's main menu, Figure 4.6.

Single step/program trace   The single step facility lets the user follow a program one step at a time, stopping the program after each instruction to examine processor details before returning to the next instruction.

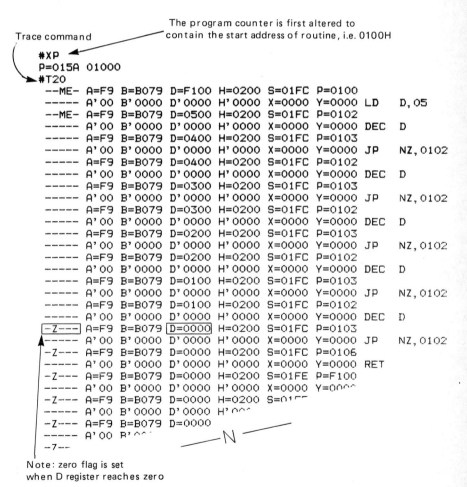

The program counter is first altered to
contain the start address of routine, i.e. 0100H

Trace command

```
#XP
P=015A 01000
#T20
  --ME- A=F9 B=B079 D=F100 H=0200 S=01FC P=0100
  ----- A'00 B'0000 D'0000 H'0000 X=0000 Y=0000 LD    D,05
  --ME- A=F9 B=B079 D=0500 H=0200 S=01FC P=0102
  ----- A'00 B'0000 D'0000 H'0000 X=0000 Y=0000 DEC   D
  ----- A=F9 B=B079 D=0400 H=0200 S=01FC P=0103
  ----- A'00 B'0000 D'0000 H'0000 X=0000 Y=0000 JP    NZ,0102
  ----- A=F9 B=B079 D=0400 H=0200 S=01FC P=0102
  ----- A'00 B'0000 D'0000 H'0000 X=0000 Y=0000 DEC   D
  ----- A=F9 B=B079 D=0300 H=0200 S=01FC P=0103
  ----- A'00 B'0000 D'0000 H'0000 X=0000 Y=0000 JP    NZ,0102
  ----- A=F9 B=B079 D=0300 H=0200 S=01FC P=0102
  ----- A'00 B'0000 D'0000 H'0000 X=0000 Y=0000 DEC   D
  ----- A=F9 B=B079 D=0200 H=0200 S=01FC P=0103
  ----- A'00 B'0000 D'0000 H'0000 X=0000 Y=0000 JP    NZ,0102
  ----- A=F9 B=B079 D=0200 H=0200 S=01FC P=0102
  ----- A'00 B'0000 D'0000 H'0000 X=0000 Y=0000 DEC   D
  ----- A=F9 B=B079 D=0100 H=0200 S=01FC P=0103
  ----- A'00 B'0000 D'0000 H'0000 X=0000 Y=0000 JP    NZ,0102
  ----- A=F9 B=B079 D=0100 H=0200 S=01FC P=0102
  ----- A'00 B'0000 D'0000 H'0000 X=0000 Y=0000 DEC   D
 -Z--- A=F9 B=B079 D=0000 H=0200 S=01FC P=0103
  ----- A'00 B'0000 D'0000 H'0000 X=0000 Y=0000 JP    NZ,0102
 -Z--- A=F9 B=B079 D=0000 H=0200 S=01FC P=0106
  ----- A'00 B'0000 D'0000 H'0000 X=0000 Y=0000 RET
 -Z--- A=F9 B=B079 D=0000 H=0200 S=01FE P=F100
  ----- A'00 B'0000 D'0000 H'0000 X=0000 Y=0000
 -Z--- A=F9 B=B079 D=0000 H=0200 S=01
  ----- A'00 B'0000 D'0000 H'0000
 -Z--- A=F9 B=B079 D=0000
  ----- A'00 B'
 -Z--
```

—N—

Note: zero flag is set
when D register reaches zero

Figure 4.7 Performing a program trace on the delay routine, Figure 4.4a, (from Digital Research's ZSID)

In a program trace the processor is allowed to execute a given number of steps of the routine under test, displaying at each step the contents of the registers along with details of the instruction just completed. Figure 4.7 shows the trace command following the delay routine. Notice how the D register is decremented five times until it reaches zero and sets the zero flag.

Obtaining a program trace using a purely software debugger has two major limitations:

1. To perform the trace the debugger must insert breakpoints into the program under test, making it impossible to test a routine that lies within ROM.

2. A second problem arises when testing programs that must be performed in real-time, e.g. software generated serial transmission, interaction with a floppy disk system. Constantly stopping and starting a real-time application to display trace information will probably disturb the routine so much that the details obtained are meaningless.

Finding the source of a problem using a debugger requires the same common sense approach needed to fault find any system. Various tests are used to stimulate the suspected problem area and the debugger is employed to gather evidence that, hopefully, leads to the source of the problem.

Two basic strategies are often used to test large programs. In the first, each low level routine is tested separately prior to being used in any high level modules – a bottom-up approach. The second uses a top-down strategy, either testing the complete program or just the high level routines with many of the primitive modules replaced by dummy routines.

Both approaches have advantages and disadvantages. In the former, routines can appear to operate satisfactorily when tested individually but may still contain unsuspected problems (e.g. the execution time, the condition of a flag etc.) that do not come to light until the routine is used in the main program. The latter approach has the advantage of testing the program as a whole but with the obvious difficulty of trying to locate problem areas in a large piece of code. In practice it would seem sensible to adopt both techniques, devoting approximately half the time ensuring that individual modules perform satisfactorily and the other half testing the overall performance of the entire program.

4.2 HARDWARE TOOLS

For many applications the only thorough way to test software is to run it in real-time in the final hardware. This can cause problems when using purely software tools that rely on interrupting the program under test to obtain information about the processor and the contents of the system buses.

Fortunately, there are two hardware tools that help overcome these limitations, namely the *logic analyser* and the *in-circuit emulator*. The usefulness of these instruments is not restricted to testing software. Both have a role to play in evaluating a prototype's hardware specification as well as the overall performance of the final hardware/software package.

Logic analysis

The logic analyser is a multi-channel recording device, with typically 32 or even more inputs that can be used to follow the time behaviour of the signals found in a digital sytem. When used to trace program flow in a microcomputer, the inputs are attached to the system buses allowing the analyser to capture address, data and control signals in its own separate buffer memory. This ability to capture program information, at full speed and without interfering with the software under test, is the analyser's main advantage over the program trace offered on software debuggers.

Most analysers are stand alone instruments, but some form part of a larger system. For example, logic analysis cards are found in micro-processor development systems and also as part of in-circuit emulators (described later in this chapter).

Figure 4.8 shows an example of a stand alone instrument. Connection to the system under test is made using a ribbon cable attached to a data pod which contains a set of input buffers to reduce loading of the system under test. Small individual probes or an Integrated Circuit (IC) test clip form the final connection. Hooking-up probes to a system's buses is both finicky and time consuming and once experienced, acts as a good incentive to purchase a personalised lead with a test clip configured for the processor in use. (Some manufacturers have moved away from test clips that rely on pressure contact with the IC's legs, and have adopted a

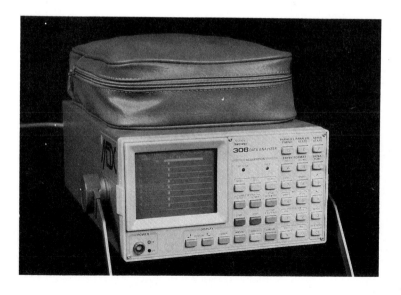

Figure 4.8 Logic analyser

more positive system where the microprocessor is removed and the analyser connection made directly into its socket. The processor is then replaced piggy-back on top. This is a good idea provided that the processor is not soldered to the board!)

A number of different display modes are offered with most analysers. Figure 4.9 shows three of the most common formats. In (a) the display shows the time behaviour at the inputs in a form similar to a multi-channel oscilloscope trace, whereas in (b) it takes the form of a state-table with the data given in either hexadecimal, octal or binary. Some analysers, especially those forming part of a development system, contain a disassembler program for one or more microprocessor families. Using this option, information captured from a microcomputer's address and data buses can be presented in the easy to follow mnemonic form shown in (c).

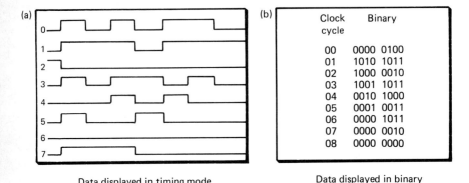

Data displayed in timing mode

Data displayed in binary

(c)   ADDRESS, DATA, STATUS

AFTER	0006H INC	HL
+001	0007H CP	L
+002	0008H JP	NZ,****
+003	0005H LD	[HL],B
+004	0006H INC	HL
+005	0007H CP	L
+006	0008H JP	NZ,****
+007	0005H LD	[HL],B
+008	0006H INC	HL
+009	0007H CP	L
+010	0008H JP	NZ,****
+011	0005H LD	[HL],B
+012	0006H INC	HL
+013	0007H CP	L
+014	0008H JP	NZ,****
+015	0005H LD	[HL],B

Data display in mnemonics

Figure 4.9   Typical logic analyser displays: (a) timing format; (b) state table; (c) disassembled or mnemonic format

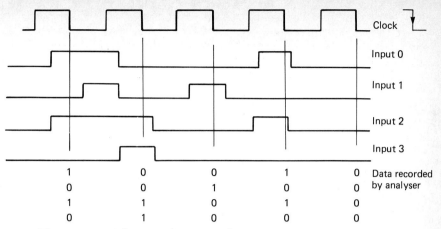

1	0	0	1	0	Data recorded
0	0	1	0	0	by analyser
1	1	0	1	0	
0	1	0	0	0	

Figure 4.10 A logic analyser samples its inputs using a clock signal

Clocks, state and timing analysers Unlike an oscilloscope, the logic analyser does not continuously monitor its inputs. Instead it samples them only when it receives a clock signal. Figure 4.10 illustrates the principle using a falling edge clock signal to strobe data into the analyser's memory.

Analysers fall into two groups based on the origin of the sampling clock, namely *state* and *timing*.

A timing analyser generates its own clock employing an internal oscillator operating at a much higher frequency than the system signals (typically 50 MHz). The use of a high speed clock allows the timing analyser to monitor detailed timing relationships between signals within the microcomputer (e.g. propagation delays through logic gates, data set-up times and the effect of loading on a system bus) and, as a result, makes it primarily a hardware debugging tool, Figure 4.11.

State analysers employ a different approach when capturing data. Instead of using an internal clock they sample data on clock edges derived from the system under test. Obtaining a clock signal is not usually difficult. All microcomputer systems make use of timing signals that define the times at which the buses hold relevant, stable information. In normal operation the analyser would employ these signals to sample bus contents at the same time as the microprocessor.

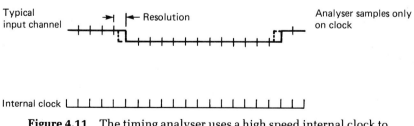

Figure 4.11 The timing analyser uses a high speed internal clock to monitor the time relationships between signals

For example, looking back at the timing diagrams for the 6502 given in Chapter 2, the falling edge of the phase 2 clock defines a time at which the data bus contains stable data and the rising edge of the phase 2 clock defines a time of stable address.

With some microprocessors, such as the 8088/8086 that use a multiplexed bus structure, the analyser has to use two separate clock signals to capture both address and data in the same machine cycle. Many of the more expensive analysers support dual clocking, with one clock to capture address and another to catch data (e.g. on the 8088/8086 the

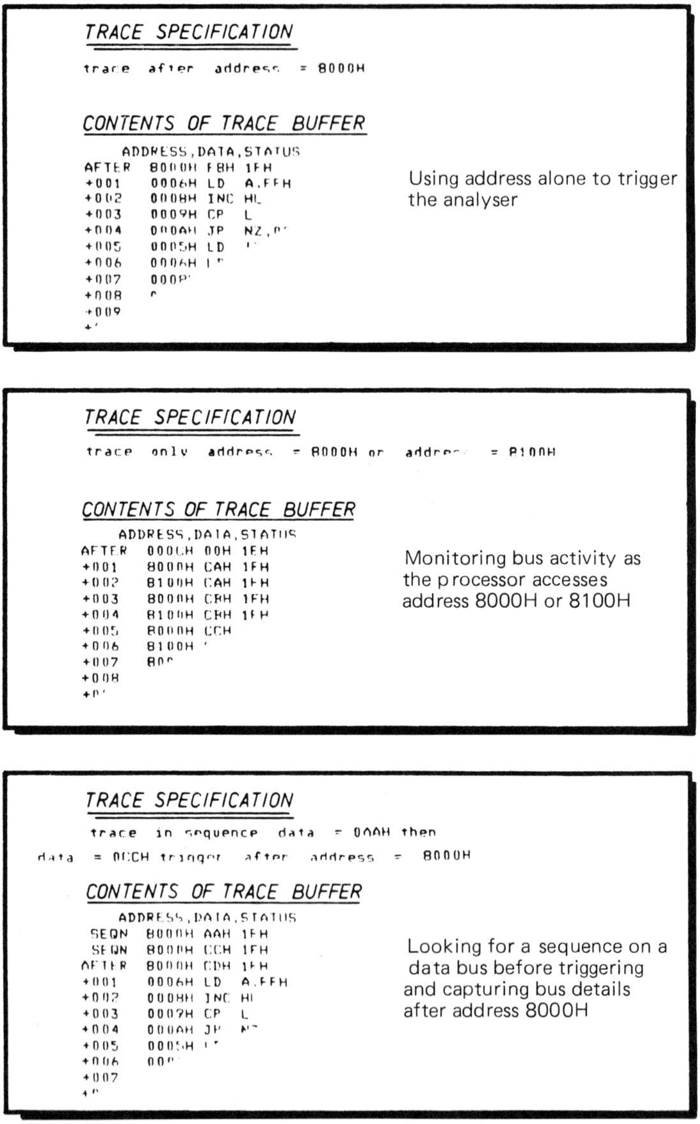

```
TRACE  SPECIFICATION

trace  after  address  = 8000H


CONTENTS OF TRACE  BUFFER

       ADDRESS,DATA,STATUS
AFTER  8000H FBH 1FH                    Using address alone to trigger
+001   0006H LD   A,FFH                 the analyser
+002   000BH INC  HL
+003   0009H CP   L
+004   000AH JP   NZ,P
+005   0005H LD
+006   0006H I
+007   000P
+008
+009
```

```
TRACE  SPECIFICATION

trace  only  address  = 8000H or  address  = 8100H


CONTENTS OF TRACE  BUFFER

       ADDRESS,DATA,STATUS
AFTER  000CH 00H 1FH
+001   8000H CAH 1FH                    Monitoring bus activity as
+002   8100H CAH 1FH                    the processor accesses
+003   8000H CBH 1FH                    address 8000H or 8100H
+004   8100H CBH 1FH
+005   8000H CCH
+006   8100H
+007   80
+008
+0
```

```
TRACE  SPECIFICATION

trace  in  sequence  data  = 0AAH then
data  = 0CCH trigger  after  address  = 8000H

CONTENTS OF TRACE  BUFFER

       ADDRESS,DATA,STATUS
SEQN   8000H AAH 1FH
SEQN   8000H CCH 1FH                    Looking for a sequence on a
AFTER  8000H CDH 1FH                    data bus before triggering
+001   0006H LD   A,FFH                 and capturing bus details
+002   000BH INC  HL                    after address 8000H
+003   0009H CP   L
+004   000AH JP
+005   0005H
+006   00C
+007
+
```

Figure 4.12   Some example trace specifications on the HP64000

falling edge of ALE defines a time of stable address and the rising edge of $\overline{RD}$ or $\overline{WR}$ defines stable data).

Triggering To give an analyser flexibility and enable it to monitor particular areas in a program or data sequence, all analysers contain trigger, or event selection, circuitry. When armed, the analyser continuously monitors its input channels and triggers when a previously defined trigger event occurs. For example the analyser could be configured to trigger and capture information after the address 8000H appears or after the byte 3AH appears on the data bus.

Depending on the sophistication of the analyser, various extra conditions can be placed on the trigger event, or more completely the *trigger specification*. Here are some possibilities:

1. **TRIGGER AFTER ADDRESS = 8000H AND DATA = 3AH**
    With this specification the analyser would wait until 8000H appeared on the address bus in the same machine cycle that 3AH appeared on the data bus.

2. **TRIGGER AFTER DATA = 60H AND STATUS = OPCODE READ**
    This time the analyser would trigger when the processor reads the op-code 60H.

3. **TRIGGER AFTER ADDRESS = 8XXXH OR ADDRESS 2000H**
    In the specification the 'X' stands for don't care. Hence the above specification would trigger the analyser on any address beginning with an 8 or address 2000H.

The exact syntax of the specification would of course depend on the analyser. Figure 4.12 gives some examples obtained from the state analyser in the HP64000.

Buffer memory At the heart of the analyser, high speed RAM acts as the recording medium, saving the logic levels at the inputs and allowing them to be replayed later for analysis. In a 32-channel device the memory would be organised as 32 bits wide by typically 256 words deep, allowing the analyser to record for 256 clock cycles, Figure 4.13.

In all the examples given so far the analyser has used its buffer memory to capture information *after* a trigger event. However, in some debugging situations it might be useful to trace the events that lead up to a known error condition. This facility is called *negative time recording*.

The idea of capturing information prior to the trigger event might at first appear strange. Figure 4.14 should help explain the concept. It displays all the 256 memory locations in the buffer memory laid out in a circle. Once armed, the analyser records data on each clock signal, as well as keeping a lookout for the trigger event. If the trigger condition is not seen after 256 clock pulses the analyser continues recording writing over the information stored previously. As soon as the trigger occurs, recording stops with the buffer holding up to 255 states *before* the trigger event.

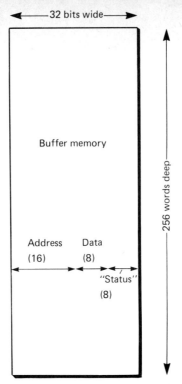

Figure 4.13 Typical layout of logic analyser buffer

A number of other strategies can be used to fill the buffer, namely, trace *about* a trigger event where the buffer holds 128 events before and after the trigger, and trace *only* a particular event where only those events that meet a specified condition are entered into the buffer, Figure 4.15.

Figure 4.16 highlights these four strategies with some examples from the Hewlett Packard analyser.

In-circuit emulation
The dedicated single board computer used to control a washing machine or a micro based cash register is unlikely to be capable of supporting the software packages required for their development. As a result software for many microprocessor based applications is generated on larger more flexible systems (e.g. a microprocessor development system (MDS) or a machine with an operating system, such as CP/M, FLEX or UNIX, providing a range of development tools).

A certain amount of debugging can be carried out within the system used to generate the code, but to test effectively both the hardware and software it is necessary to commit the final code to EPROM and transfer it to the dedicated system. Any further debugging is now carried out using a logic analyser. If faults are discovered the engineer returns to the development system to update the software and program a new EPROM.

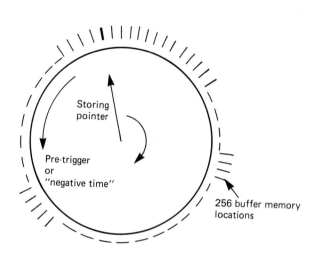

If the <u>trigger</u> event occurs here, then this location is marked as location zero and the analyser stops capturing with 255 states leading up to the trigger event in its memory

Storing pointer

Pre-trigger or "negative time"

256 buffer memory locations

"Storing pointer" stores current voltage pattern on inputs before moving on to next location

Figure 4.14   Negative time recording

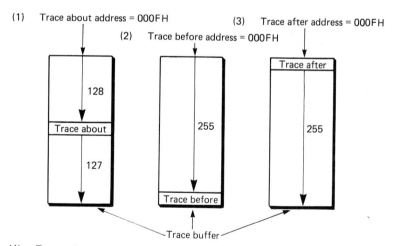

(1)   Trace about address = 000FH

(2)   Trace before address = 000FH

(3)   Trace after address = 000FH

128

Trace about

127

255

Trace before

Trace after

255

Trace buffer

(4)   Trace only

With trace only the trigger position defaults to "after". Only those states that satisfy the trace specification are placed in the buffer

Figure 4.15   Different strategies used to fill the analyser's buffer

125

The technique of in-circuit emulation shortens this time consuming procedure and allows the development system to test hardware and evaluate software within the dedicated system.

The technique was first introduced by Intel on their MDS but it is now a standard feature on most development systems. Further, several manufacturers have recognised the need for a low cost approach to system development and are now producing stand alone emulators that can be driven by any popular microcomputer.

Figure 4.17 illustrates the basic principle of the technique. The microprocessor is removed from the unit under test (*target*) and connection is made to the development system (*host*) through a dual in-line plug and ribbon cable. Normally the emulator uses a similar microprocessor to that removed from the target, to imitate or emulate the original processor. At first glance it might appear pointless to remove the

Trace after address = 000FH

```
Trace:     mnemonic                              break: none        count:
line#    address opc/data mnemonic opcode or status                   time, relative
-------------------------------------------------------------------------------
after    000F       D3     OUT [01],A
+001     0010       01                  memory read                    2.      uS
+002     7301       73                  i/o write                      2.      uS
+003     0011       11     LD DE,A000                                  1.      uS
+004     0012       00                  memory read                    2.      uS
+005     0013       A0                  memory read                    1.      uS
+006     0014       CD     CALL 001A                                  1.      uS
+007     0015       1A                  memory read                    2.      uS
+008     0016       00                  memory read                    1.      uS
+009     83FE       00                  memory write                   2.
+010     83FD       17                  memory write
+011     001A       1B     DEC DE
+012     001B       7A     LD A,D
+013     001C       B3     OR  E
+014     001D       C2     JP NZ,001A
+015     001E       1A
+016     001F       00
+017     001A       1B
+018     001B
+019
```

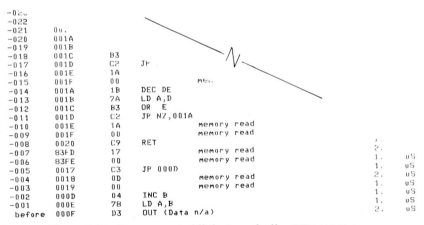

Trace before address = 000FH

```
-023
-022
-021     0u.
-020     001A
-019     001B
-018     001C       B3
-017     001D       C2     JP
-016     001E       1A
-015     001F       00            me..
-014     001A       1B     DEC DE
-013     001B       7A     LD A,D
-012     001C       B3     OR  E
-011     001D       C2     JP NZ,001A
-010     001E       1A                  memory read
-009     001F       00                  memory read
-008     0020       C9     RET
-007     83FD       17                  memory read
-006     83FE       00                  memory read
-005     0017       C3     JP 000D
-004     0018       0D                  memory read
-003     0019       00                  memory read
-002     000D       04     INC B
-001     000E       78     LD A,B
before   000F       D3     OUT (Data n/a)
```

Figure 4.16   Four ways to fill the trace buffer (HP64000): trace AFTER...; trace BEFORE...

Trace about address = 000FH

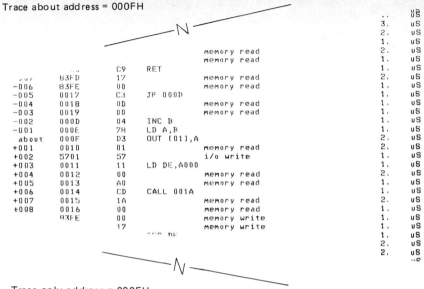

				..	uS
				3.	uS
				2.	uS
				1.	uS
			memory read	2.	uS
			memory read	1.	uS
		C9	RET	1.	uS
-007	83FD	17	memory read	2.	uS
-006	83FE	00	memory read	1.	uS
-005	0017	C3	JP 000D	1.	uS
-004	0018	0D	memory read	1.	uS
-003	0019	00	memory read	1.	uS
-002	000D	04	INC B	1.	uS
-001	000E	78	LD A,B	1.	uS
about	000F	D3	OUT [01],A	2.	uS
+001	0010	01	memory read	2.	uS
+002	5701	57	i/o write	1.	uS
+003	0011	11	LD DE,A000	1.	uS
+004	0012	00	memory read	2.	uS
+005	0013	A0	memory read	1.	uS
+006	0014	CD	CALL 001A	1.	uS
+007	0015	1A	memory read	2.	uS
+008	0016	00	memory read	1.	uS
	83FE	00	memory write	1.	uS
		17	memory write	1.	uS
			... DE	1.	uS
				2.	uS
				2.	uS
				..c	

Trace only address = 000FH

Trace:	mnemonic			break: none	count:overflow
line#	address	opc/data	mnemonic opcode or status		time, relative
after	001B	7A	LD A,D		
+001	000F	D3	OUT (Data n/a)		138.184 mS
+002	000F	D3	opcode fetch		392.922 mS
+003	000F	D3	OUT (Data n/a)		392.922 mS
+004	000F	D3	opcode fetch		392.922 mS
+005	000F	D3	OUT (Data n/a)		392.922 mS
+006	000F	D3	opcode fetch		392.922 mS
+007	000F	D3	OUT (Data n/a)		392.922 mS
+008	000F	D3	opcode fetch		392.922 mS
+009	000F	D3	OUT (Data n/a)		392 ~~
+010	000F	D3	opcode fetch		
+011	000F	D3	OUT (Data n/a)		
+012	000F	D3	opcode fe+..		
+013	000F	D3	OUT (Data n/		
+014	000F	D3			
+015	000F	..			
+016	000~				

Figure 4.16 Continued: trace ABOUT...; trace ONLY...

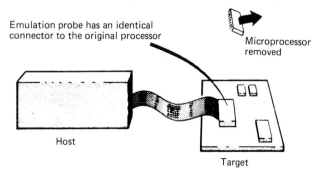

Emulation probe has an identical
connector to the original processor

Microprocessor removed

Host

Target

Figure 4.17 In-circuit emulation

127

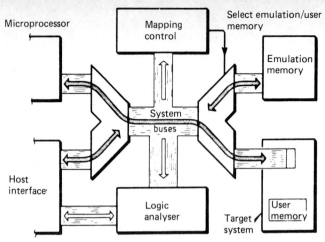

Figure 4.18 Simplified emulator architecture

original only to have it replaced by another in the emulator, but the technique allows the host to get between the target system and its microprocessor, enabling it to monitor bus activity or to inject signals into the target system.

Basic principles Figure 4.18 shows a simplified diagram of an emulator's internal architecture. Control circuitry is used to allow either the host computer or the emulation processor to gain access to the target system's buses.

Most emulators are equipped with random access memory (*emulation memory*) that can be used to add to, or take the place of memory on the target board (*user memory*). This extra RAM can prove useful during software debugging, providing workspace for the code under test before it is finally committed to ROM.

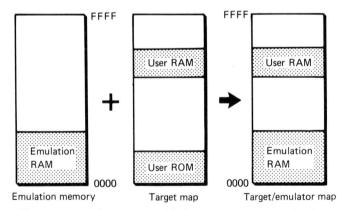

Figure 4.19 Mapping: establishing a memory map for the combination of emulator and target. (In this example 'user ROM' is overwritten by emulation RAM allowing software to be loaded and tested by the host system.)

128

The procedure of establishing a memory layout for the combination of emulator and target is called *mapping*. In microprocessor development systems this is normally accomplished from the keyboard during a configuration phase prior to emulation; some simpler systems make use of in-line switches.

An example of mapping is shown in Figure 4.19. In this arrangement the memory space normally occupied by the user ROM has been overwritten with emulation memory to allow different versions of the software to be loaded and tested. After mapping has been decided, control circuitry on the emulator ensures that all addresses established by the processor or the host system are directed at the selected memory devices, i.e. emulation or user memory.

Normally the target system's own clock circuitry would be used to run the emulator's microprocessor in *real-time*, thus ensuring that any critical timing of the target system's hardware is maintained. However, in some situations the emulator may be used purely to evaluate software, perhaps before the prototype hardware is available. To handle this possibility most emulators provide an internal clock to drive the emulator's processor.

Once configuration is complete, machine code can be loaded from the host system into either emulation or user memory and tested using the emulator's debugger.

Most emulators make use of a monitor program that allows the host to carry out tests in the target system using the software development facilities described earlier, namely:

- memory examine and modify
- emulation processor examine and modify
- single step
- software breakpoints
- trace analysis

In many emulators, trace analysis is enhanced with the addition of a logic analyser that monitors the emulation processor's activity.

ROM emulation There are cynics who maintain that the only two features common across the microcomputer spectrum are the serial data interface and the pinout of a 24-pin ROM socket. Certainly both are found on many systems, but it is the latter that has led to the popularity of the ROM emulator.

Figure 4.20 illustrates the principle. A ROM chip is removed from the target system and replaced by a dual-in-line plug and ribbon cable leading to the emulator. Within the emulator, a block of dual-ported RAM takes the place of the target system's ROM. Access to the RAM is through buffers that are controlled by the host as follows:

1. Initially the buffers are configured to give the host access to the RAM, allowing the code generated on the host to be downloaded either directly, if the emulation RAM is part of the host's memory map, or through a serial link.

2. The host then switches the buffers so that the RAM loaded with the code now appears in the target's memory map, ready for execution.

ROM emulation does not offer the powerful debugging features present in microprocessor emulators. However, it provides a simple and inexpensive method of loading code into a target system. Further, the emulator is not specific to any microprocessor family. If cross assemblers are available for the host, the emulator can be used with 8-bit, 16-bit and even single chip microcomputers, provided they all possess the standard ROM socket.

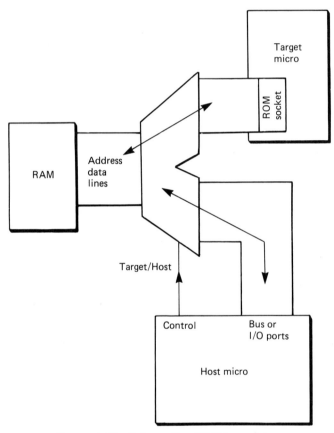

Figure 4.20 Schematic of ROM emulator

Problems

4.1 Highlight the differences between a logic state analyser and a logic timing analyser. Give examples of typical problem areas where each would be used.

4.2 Explain the term 'symbolic debugging'. In what situations would it be particularly useful?

4.3 Describe a technique used in logic analysers to capture information prior to a trigger event. Give an example of a possible microcomputer problem where this facility might be used.

4.4 Summarise the advantages of in-circuit emulation as a development technique.

FURTHER READING

A range of useful publications is available, usually free of charge, from several equipment manufacturers. The following texts also contain useful sections on system debugging.

Rafiquzzaman, M., 1984. *Microprocessors and Microcomputer Development Systems*. New York, NY: Harper and Row.

Tseng, V., 1982. *Microprocessor Development and Development Systems*. London: Granada.

Kneen, J., 1980. *Logic Analysers for Microprocessors*. Rochelle Park, NJ: Hayden.

Wakerly, J.F., 1981. *Microcomputer Architecture and Programming*. New York, NY: Wiley.

Lighter reading can be found in the following articles from popular journals:

Ferguson, J., June 1984. 'In-Circuit Emulation', *Electronics and Wireless World*, p. 53–5.

May 1983. 'Development Systems and Logic Analysers – Towards the Universal Digital Workbench', *Electronic Engineering*, p. 96.

Chapter 5

Three approaches to system development

The objectives of this chapter are:

● to examine and contrast three approaches to microprocessor system development;

● to introduce the hardware and software tools available on a commercial microprocessor development system;

● to investigate the role of a personal microcomputer with 'add-on' development tools;

● to examine a low cost approach to development and debugging using microprocessor manufacturer's evaluation kits.

For many microprocessor applications the final hardware is a simple single board, or even single chip, microcomputer with the minimum of components required to perform its dedicated function. Depending on the application, such a system may have to be built from scratch, selecting components that meet the final specification at the minimum cost. Another approach is to make use of an already built board that contains (or can easily be adapted to contain) the functions required.

Software is less likely to be obtained 'off the shelf' and in most applications has to be 'tailor made' to suit the problem in hand. The target system itself is seldom capable of supporting the program packages required to generate the software or the tools needed to test and debug the final product. What is often required is a second, probably larger system – a Microprocessor Development System (MDS).

However, not all development projects make use of a purpose designed MDS; there are a variety of approaches to the provision of development tools. This chapter examines three of the most common. The first looks at a commercial MDS. Although such a system is initially expensive, its power and ease of use should eventually lead to cost savings. In the second approach a popular microcomputer, running a widely accepted operating system, is effectively turned into an MDS by the addition of software packages and add-on development tools, e.g. EPROM programmer, in-circuit emulator, logic analyser. Finally, the third approach makes use of the relatively low cost development or evaluation kits produced by microprocessor manufacturers. These single board systems are primarily designed to give an engineer familiarity with a particular microprocessor and its family of support chips, but normally contain sufficient on-board firmware to act as a very primitive development system.

5.1 MICROPROCESSOR DEVELOPMENT SYSTEMS

Broadly speaking, development systems split into two groups, manufacturer specific and universal. Those produced by microprocessor manufacturers tend to be orientated around their own range of products (e.g. Intel's Intellec MDS and Motorola's EXORmacs), whereas general electronic instrument manufacturers (e.g. Hewlett Packard, Tektronix, Genrad, Philips) lean more towards universal systems capable of supporting a wide range of microprocessor families. In general, the former are more likely to cover a manufacturer's latest and fastest processor but are to some extent less user-friendly than the universal systems.

In this section the fundamental concepts of a microprocessor development system are described. However, the best way to grasp these concepts is to examine a typical system. The HP64000 was chosen as being representative of the currently available universal systems.

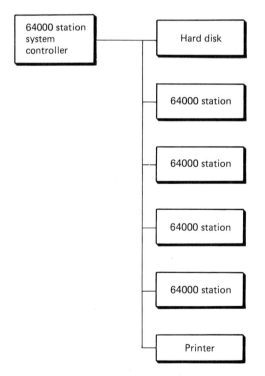

Figure 5.1　Cluster of HP64000 stations sharing a common hard disk and printer

HP64000 system overview

The HP64000 Logic Development System is a multi-station developmen system that will support up to six users. Each station is a complete microcomputer with an option of is own local storage in the form of either a miniature tape cartridge or 5¼ inch floppy disk drives. However, the system's main storage is a large Winchester disk drive which is shared by all the stations, Figure 5.1. Linking the stations together is a modified version of their own HP interface bus (HPIB), (described in Chapter 6). Each station on the bus, including the hard disk and a shared printer, has its own unique address. At boot-up or after a reset, one station (the master controller) assumes control of the cluster. However, after power-up all stations act as equals in their requests for access to the disk or printer.

Any station on a cluster can be used for software development employing the system's editor, linker and range of assemblers and compilers. Hardware development tools in the form of in-circuit emulators, logic analysers and EPROM programmers are available as additional plug-in cards. Currently HP is offering hardware support for most industry standard 8- and 16-bit microprocessors, as well as marketing a user-configurable emulator that allows a customer to 'build' an emulator for any special purpose or low volume processor not supported.

Station description

Each station is driven by HP's own microprocessor and contains 16 Kbytes of ROM and 48 Kbytes of RAM. The on-board firmware holds both diagnostic and system boot-up routines. Internally each development station contains a 13 slot card cage; three of the slots form the basic system, holding:

1. an input/output card providing an RS-232 and current loop serial interface along with the modified HPIB system bus interface

2. a display control board

3. the CPU and memory card

The remaining 10 slots are available to hold additional hardware options.

At least one station on a cluster should contain local storage in the form of a tape cartridge or floppy disk drive. Apart from acting as a means of archiving or backing up important files, it is also required for loading any new or updated versions of the system software.

Figure 5.2 shows a front view of a 64000 station. The CRT display of 25 lines by 80 columns is normally divided to give 18 lines for text entry, a single line providing status information, three lines to display system commands, and a single line at the foot of the screen holding labels for each of the eight soft keys.

The soft keys add greatly to the system's user-friendliness, providing a quick and simple method of entering commands. The display shows the current definition of each key, which changes depending on the current function of the station. For example, Figure 5.3a shows the labels

Figure 5.2 64000 station

displayed just after system boot-up. If, however, the editor is invoked using the <edit> soft key, a new menu of labels appears pertinent to the editor, Figure 5.3b. With this approach the system is guiding the operator and only offering sensible alternatives in the current mode of operation.

Figure 5.3a Soft key labels on the main system menu

Figure 5.3b   Some of the soft key labels in the editor

System software

The entire 64000 software package can be accessed using the single word commands offered in the main menu of soft keys, Figure 5.4. Most of the commands are self-evident, providing either useful file management utilities or initiating one of the development tools.

Editor   The editor is the first layer in the 64000's development package, providing the means to create new programs or revise existing ones. Special cursor and text control keys combined with on-screen editing make it straightforward and easy to use.

The editor supports three modes of operation: command mode, insert mode and revise mode. In the command mode the operator can perform various housekeeping duties such as renumbering text lines, merging files or setting tabs. The insert mode allows the entry of new lines of text to either a new or an existing file. Finally, the revise mode enables existing lines to be altered and updated.

Assemblers and compilers   Being a universal MDS, the 64000 supports both assemblers and compilers (Pascal and C) for a number of 8- and 16-bit microprocessors. Again, a station's soft keys provide a simple method of initiating assembly or compilation of a source file prepared with the editor.

For example:

`<assemble> PROG1`

would assemble the source file `PROG1`, and:

`<compile> PROG2`

136

append	log_commands
assemble	prom_programmer
<CMDFILE>	purge
compile	recover
copy	rename
date	restore
directory	store
edit	time
emulate	userid
library	verify
link	

Figure 5.4　Complete list of system commands

would compile the source file called PROG2.

The keystrokes required to assemble or compile are identical for all microprocessor families, a sensible strategy that is repeated with other development tools on the system (e.g. the linker, in-circuit emulator and trace facilities). With the code generators, the unified approach is achieved using a directive at the start of the source program that informs the operating system which of its range of assemblers or compilers is required, Figure 5.5.

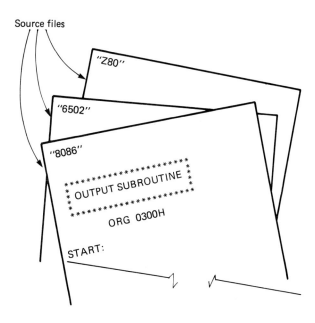

Figure 5.5　Directive at the start of a source file selects the correct assembler or compiler

137

All the assemblers perform two passes through the source code and support both macro definitions and conditional statements. Each assembler generates relocatable object code that is finally positioned and converted to absolute machine code using the system linker. Like the assemblers, the compilers also generate relocatable object code making it a simple task to integrate program modules generated from both high level and assembly language.

Normally the assembler or compiler will automatically generate both a relocatable object code file and a symbol table file. However, various command line options can be used, e.g.

    assemble PROG1 listfile printer

produces a hard copy of the assembler listing file, while

    assemble PROG1 listfile display options expand

produces an assembler listing on the display with all the source lines and codes of any macro shown.

Figure 5.6 gives a complete list of the command options available. The effect of some is shown in Chapters 2 and 3, where all the program examples were generated on the 64000.

list	Listing of source program with no macro or data expansion. All NOLIST pseudo instructions in the source program are ignored.
no list	No listing, except error messages. All LIST pseudo instructions in the source program are ignored.
expand	Listing of all source and macro generated codes. All LIST pseudo instructions in the source program are ignored.
nocode	The nocode option suppresses the generation of object code.
xref	The xref option turns on the symbol cross-reference feature of the assembler.

Figure 5.6   Assembler command line options

Linker   The prime function of the linker is to generate absolute code from the relocatable modules produced by the assembler and the compiler. The system stores this final machine code in an absolute file which can then be either programmed into an EPROM or loaded and tested under emulation, Figure 5.7. As well as producing machine code, the linker also allows several relocatable modules to be joined together to form a single absolute program. Any symbols that are declared global in one module and external in others are assigned values by the linker.

To help with modular programming the 64000 supports a simple library facility where useful relocatable files can be appended together to form one large relocatable file. The <library> soft key performs this function, adding files to a new or existing library. For example:

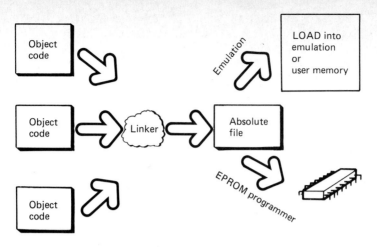

Figure 5.7 Absolute files are used by the EPROM programmer and the emulator

```
<library> PROG1 to MYLIB
```

would add the relocatable file `PROG1` to a new or existing library `MYLIB`, and

```
<library> PROG2 to MYLIB
```

adds a second module to `MYLIB`.

If any program libraries are included during linking, the linker only includes those modules that contain symbols that are not defined in any of the object files. For example, the program libraries that accompany a compiler contain routines for a number of arithmetic and trigonometric functions. If an application makes use of a particular function, only the module containing that function is included in the final code.

The 64000 linker can be initiated by one of two methods, termed interactive and simple. When linking object files for the first time, the interactive method is used to inform the system of the name and position of each object file or library that has to be included in the link. Figure 5.8 illustrates the technique (the example is taken from the set of three modules used in Chapter 3). On entry, the linker prompts for the name of an object file. After entry the linker then asks if any libraries have to be included (none is used in this example). The system then asks what initial values have to be assigned to the three program location counters, `PROG`, `DATA` and `COMN`. Since the example only makes use of one counter, namely `PROG`, the others are ignored and `PROG` is given an initial value of 0000H, placing the module `ZSETUP` at the start of the memory map. The system then prompts for another object file name and the operator enters `ZMAIN`. Again the linker asks for an initial value of the program location counter. In this example all three modules have to be laid end to end to form one piece of continuous code. As a result, `CONT` (short for continuous) is

139

entered for the PROG counter signifying that the linker has to place the second module 'hard on the heels' of the first. Finally, the module ZDELAY is added and the linker informed that a load map and a cross-reference table are required.

Before performing the link operation, the system prompts for a name for the final absolute file, in this case ZTOTAL. The same name is also assigned to a link command file that stores all the operator's replies to the linker's questions.

It is the link command file that leads to the second simple method of using the linker. To repeat all of the above procedure for updated versions of relocatable modules with the same names, the operator merely has to enter the command:

<link> ZTOTAL

The linker will report any errors that are detected during the link process. Typical errors that may occur are:

- *memory overlap* – two or more modules are attempting to use the same memory area
- *duplicate symbol* – two or more modules have declared the same symbol as global
- *undefined symbol* – the linker has found a symbol that is declared external but is not defined by a global definition
- *target processors disagree* – an attempt has been made to link together relocatable modules destined for different target microprocessors

```
                        Page #  1

File = ZTOTAL:JDFM:link_com    Fri,   7 Sep 1984, 14:32

Record #   1     size = 104
Linker is 18085_Z80:HP

Object files: ZSETUP
Library files:
PROG,DATA,COMN=0000H,0000H,0000H

Object files: ZMAIN
Library files:          '
PROG,DATA,COMN=CONT,0000H,0000H

Object files: DELAY
Library files:
PROG,DATA,COMN=CONT,0000H,0000H

Map, xref = on   on
End of file after record #   1
```

Figure 5.8 Constructing a link command file

Hardware options

To perform in-circuit emulation a 64000 station requires a minimum addition of an emulation control board and pod. Normally this is further augmented by a memory control board and memory cards, providing emulation memory that can be used to add to or overlay any memory present in a target system.

The 64000 uses the *master/slave* system for emulation, described in Chapter 4, with an emulation processor of the same type as that removed from the target located in the pod. An emulation bus, formed by a plug-on ribbon cable at the top of each card and separate from the host processor's bus, connects together the emulation subsystem, Figure 5.9. As a result, a development station is completely free to perform another task, e.g. editing or assembling a file, while the target system is left running under emulation at full speed.

Figure 5.9 Emulation cards, bus and pod

Before emulation begins, the pod is connected to the target system using the probe. After making the hardware connection, the operator presses the <emulate> soft key and enters a configuration phase in which the host asks the following set of questions about the target micro-computer to determine how much of the system has to be emulated.

141

1. Do you wish to use an internal clock (*supplied by the emulator*) or an external clock (*from the target system*)?
2. Do you always want to run the target system at full speed or can it be 'slowed down' to examine registers, user memory, etc.?
3. Do you wish to be notified if the processor meets an illegal op-code?
4. What user memory (*in target system*) do you wish to use and how much emulation memory (*in host system*) do you require?
5. Do you wish to make use of simulated I/O? (The 64000 keyboard, display, printer, RS-232 interface and hard disk can be used to simulate signals to and from actuators and transducers.)

In a similar manner to the linker, all operator replies are logged to a command file that makes subsequent entry to emulation much quicker, for example:

`<emulate> SDK85`

would initiate the emulator and configure it with the system details stored in the emulation command file SDK85.

Figure 5.10 gives an example of an emulation command file used with Intel's SDK85 single board computer. The configuration makes use of the user ROM between 0000H and 0FFFH, along with user RAM at 2000H and 2800H. In addition, emulator memory in the form of ROM and RAM has been mapped at E000H to EFFFH and F000H to FFFFH respectively.

```
                          Page #  1

    File = SDK85:NAP:emul_com    Fri,  7 Sep 1984, 14:35

    Record #   1    size = 128
              Emulation and User Memory Assignment
              -000 -400 -800 -C00          -000 -400 -800 -C00
    0---- UROM UROM UROM UROM    8----
    1----                        9----
    2---- URAM      URAM         A----
    3----                        B---
    4----                        C----
    5----                        D---
    6----                        E--- EROM EROM EROM EROM
    7----                        F--- ERAM ERAM ERAM ERAM

    Record #   2    size = 128
    Configuring 8085 processor in slot # 9. Memory slot # 7. Analysis slot # 8.
    Processor clock: external
    Clock speed greater than wait threshold: no
    Restrict processor to real time runs: no
    Stop processor on illegal opcodes: yes
    Simulate I/O: no

    End of file after record #   2
```

Figure 5.10 Example emulation command file

The above example is only one of many possible configurations. By expanding the user memory with emulation memory and retaining the on-board ROM an engineer might be using the emulator to test an application program that makes use of some of the SDK85's on-board

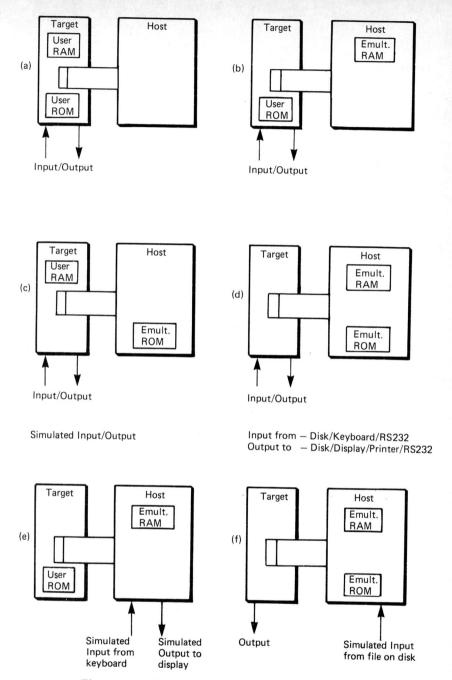

Figure 5.11 Some possible emulation configurations

routines. However, depending on the application, a number of other set-ups are possible: Figure 5.11 illustrates some.

Once configuration is complete, a new soft key menu will appear, Figure 5.12. Normally the <load> function is selected first and an absolute file loaded into either emulation or user memory. Many of the functions are similar to those found on software debugging packages, allowing the operator to examine or alter memory or registers, insert breakpoints and run or single-step the routine under test.

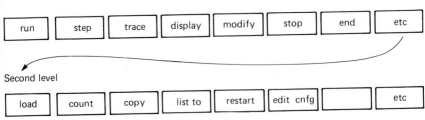

| run | step | trace | display | modify | stop | end | etc |

Second level

| load | count | copy | list to | restart | edit cnfg | | etc |

Figure 5.12 Soft key menu in emulator

Analysis The lowest cost and minimum performance analyser offered on the 64000 is a purely software package that performs non-real-time analysis. As with other debugging packages, this is achieved by constantly interrupting program execution to gather details of both the program and the state of the processor.

To perform real-time measurements an additional analyser board is required. Like the other components in the emulation system, it is located within the 64000's card cage where it is controlled and interrogated by the host processor through the main system bus. However, the analyser's inputs are connected to the emulation bus, allowing it to monitor the target system's behaviour in real-time.

Finding bugs with a logic analyser demands flexibility when defining the trigger event, or more completely the trace specification. Figures 4.15 and 4.16 show a variety of possible trace specifications, highlighting the power of the analyser.

To help simplify defining a trace specification or indeed using any of the debugging tools, the emulator and analyser both make use of the symbol table file generated by the linker. Symbolic debugging, where the operator refers to program locations using labels defined in the source code, greatly eases use, especially when tracing routines generated by compiling a high level language routine, e.g.

- "run from START"
- "trace about address = OUTPUT"
- "display memory BUFFER"

A number of other hardware/software analyser options are available for the 64000.

- *Software Performance Analyser* – provides statistical information on the efficiency and execution time of either high level or assembly language routines.

144

- *Logic State/Software Analyser* – allows the operator to trace program flow displaying the trace in terms of high level statements and their associated comment lines.

- *Logic Timing/Hardware Analyser* – a set of up to 16 probes can be used to obtain critical timing relationships between signals. The analyser uses its own clock, sampling at data rates up to 400 MHz. A range of trigger specifications allows the analyser to trigger on bus glitches or even, using a dual level threshold, on signals of a specified rise time.

5.2 GENERAL PURPOSE MICROCOMPUTER WITH 'ADD-ON TOOLS'

Undoubtedly an MDS is the ideal tool for system development, but often the initial capital expenditure is well outside the budgets of most educational establishments or small companies. An alternative approach is to make use of a general purpose microcomputer for which a useful set of development tools is available.

The software packages for any microcomputer depend for the most part on the degree of standardisation and commercial acceptance of its operating system (the program that performs housekeeping duties, providing commands to give directories, erase or copy files, run programs, etc.). Several systems are widely supported, including South West Technical's FLEX and Digital Research's CP/M80 for 8-bit systems, along with CP/M86 and Microsoft's MSDOS for 16-bit machines.

Working under CP/M

CP/M has become the standard operating system for many 8080, 8085 and Z80 based microcomputers, including the Comart Communicator, Cromemco, Rair, Research Machines, North Star, etc. Software support under CP/M is also extensive, with a number of languages including BASIC, PASCAL, FORTRAN, and business packages offering database management, word processing, and even spelling and grammar checking.

Included in the standard CP/M program package from Digital Research is an editor, ED; an assembler, ASM; and a debugging tool, DDT. However, a number of independent companies also produce software development packages, some with enhanced features, including:

- on-screen editing
- macro and conditional assembly
- symbolic debugging

Further, software development is not limited under CP/M to Z80 or 8080 microprocessors. Cross-assemblers are available that support virtually any microprocessor. Figure 5.13 illustrates the range available from one company, Avocet Systems of Delaware.

Of the many packages available for the Z80, Microsoft's Macro-80 provides a number of attractive features. The distribution diskette contains the following programs:

145

Avocet Cross-assembler	Target Microprocessor
XASMZ80	Z-80
XASM85	8085
XASM05	6805
XASM09	6809
XASM18	1802
XASM48	8048/8041
XASM51	8051
XASM65	6502
XASM68	6800/01
XASMZ8	Z8
XASMF8	F8/3870
XASM400	COP400
XASM75	NEC 7500
XMAC68K...68000	

Figure 5.13 CP/M supports assemblers and cross-assemblers for a wide range of processors (The list shows those available from one company: Avocet Systems)

M80.COM   The relocatable macro assembler with pseudo-operations supporting conditional assembly

L80.COM   The Link-80 linking loader

CREF80.COM The CREF-80 cross-reference facility

LIB.COM   The LIB-80 library manager

No text editor is contained in the package but the assembler will accept text files generated by any simple text editor, including CP/M's ED, MicroPro's WordStar in non-document mode, and WordMaster, another MicroPro product.

Program 5.1a gives an example of a source program written in a suitable format for M80. Several points are worth attention.

- The routine begins with .Z80 informing the assembler that the source code is written in Z80 mnemonics as opposed to 8080.
- All numeric constants begin with 0.
- Labels are terminated with a :

The assembler is initiated with the command:

`M80 = filename`

Like most assemblers, a set of options or software switches can be included in the command line. Figure 5.14 provides a summary of those used by Macro-80, while Program 5.1b shows the result of using the "L" option to force generation of an assembler listing.

```
.z80
;a subroutine to provide a few seconds delay
;
;registers used
;                b,c,d
;
;parameters passed
;                none
;
;declare externals and globals
;
           global   delay
;
;set up equates
;
count1    equ     09h
count2    equ     00ffh
count3    equ     00ffh
;
;main program
;
delay:    push bc
          push de
          ld b,count1
loop1:    ld c,count2           ;outer loop
loop2:    ld d,count3           ;middle loop
loop3:    dec d                 ;inner loop
          jr nz,loop3           ;inner loop
          dec c
          jr nz,loop2           ;middle loop
          djnz loop1            ;outer loop
          pop de
          pop bc
          ret
          end
```

Program 5.1a ′ Sample source program for Macro-80

Macro-80 supports two useful programming utilities: CREF-80 and LIB-80. The former generates a cross-reference listing file in which each source statement is numbered with a cross-reference number, along with a

---

Assembly command format:

M 80 = Program/n/m....

where / n / m.... are:

O	Octal listing
H	Hexadecimal listing
R	Force generation of an object file
L	Force generation of a listing file
C	Force generation of a cross reference file
Z	Z80 assembly (alternative to .Z80 in source)
I	8080 assembly
P	Each /P allocates 256 additional stack bytes
M	Initialise block data areas as defined by DS (Define Storage) to 0s
X	Suppress listing of false conditionals

Figure 5.14   Software switches used by Macro-80's assembler

```
                        .z80
                        ;a subroutine to provide a few seconds delay

                        ;registers used
                        ;                    b,c,d
                        ;
                        ;parameters passed
                        ;                    none
                        ;
                        ;declare externals and globals
                        ;
                                global   delay
                        ;
                        ;set up equates
                        ;
0009                    count1   equ      09h
00FF                    count2   equ      00ffh
00FF                    count3   equ      00ffh
                        ;
                        ;main program
                        ;
0000'   C5             delay:   push bc
0001'   D5                      push de
0002'   06 09                   ld b,count1
0004'   0E FF          loop1:   ld c,count2      ;outer loop
0006'   16 FF          loop2:   ld d,count3      ;middle loop
0008'   15             loop3:   dec d            ;inner loop
0009'   20 FD                   jr nz,loop3      ;inner loop
000B'   0D                      dec c
000C'   20 F8                   jr nz,loop2      ;middle loop
000E'   10 F4                   djnz loop1       ;outer loop
0010'   D1                      pop de
0011'   C1                      pop bc
0012'   C9                      ret
                                end


Macros:

Symbols:
0009     COUNT1        00FF     COUNT2           00FF     COUNT3
00001'   DELAY         0004'    LOOP1            0006'    LOOP2
0008'    LOOP3
```

Program 5.1b   Assembler listing produced by Macro-80

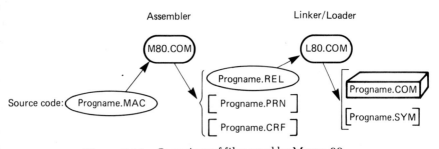

Figure 5.15   Overview of files used by Macro-80

symbol table showing variable names in alphabetical order, together with the line numbers on which they were referenced or defined (definitions are flagged with a # symbol). LIB-80 allows the programmer to support a library of useful relocatable modules that can be easily included in the final absolute code using the linker. The main function of LIB-80 is to concatenate relocatable files to form a new library. However, powerful commands allow modules to be extracted from both existing libraries and from within individual relocatable files.

Object files, including those in program libraries, can be linked and loaded using Link-80. The command format is:

```
L80 objfile1,objfile2,. . . . . . .
```

The final absolute machine code file is given the same name as the first object file but with the extension .COM signifying that it is an executable CP/M command file. (A point worth noting is that the linker automatically assumes a CP/M load address of 0100H. If a source file contains the statement ORG 0100H, the linker will load the resulting code at 0200H – beware!)

Figure 5.15 summarises the files used and generated by Macro-80.

Add-on tools

If the final product employs the same microprocessor as the host system then some debugging can be carried within the host micro. ZSID (Z80 Symbolic Instruction Debugger) described in Chapter 4, is an example of one of the many debugging packages that are available under CP/M. However, to test the combination of target hardware and software effectively, or to debug code produced for a different microprocessor family, would require some form of in-circuit emulation facility.

Several manufacturers are now meeting this need, producing in-circuit emulators that can operate either as stand alone instruments or as part of a microcomputer system. MICE (Micro-In-Circuit Emulator), produced by the Taiwan Company Microtek, is an example, Figure 5.16.

Internally, MICE contains three boards: a 32 Kbyte emulation memory card, a logic analyser card, and an emulation/control card. The latter is chosen to match the system under development from a range including many industry standard microprocessors, e.g. 8088/8086, 68000, 8085, 6809, along with the popular 'domestic' processor, the 6502.

Communication with MICE is via an RS-232 interface that can be configured to any of the standard baud rates using small internal switches. Either a display terminal or a computer system with a serial port can control MICE. When using a host system, a driver routine is required, so that the micro behaves like a VDU in full duplex mode, sending commands to MICE and receiving its reply, Figure 5.17.

Figure 5.18 lists the commands which include a line assembler, helpful for short routines or when patching a larger piece of software. A two-pass disassembler that generates labels for all subroutine, branch and jump instructions is a useful feature not even found in expensive systems Figure 5.19.

Figure 5.16 Microtek's MICE

Code generated using assemblers or compilers on the host system can be downloaded, in either Intel or Tektronix format, into the target system/emulator memory. In the opposite direction the upload command allows the operator to transfer defined memory areas into a file on the host system.

MICE's on-board logic analyser gives it the ability to follow program flow in real-time, capturing address data and some processor status signals in its massive 2048 word buffer. Forward and backward trace commands give the operator a choice of either filling the buffer with events after or events before a trigger event. However, there are limitations on the sophistication of the trace specification, which is limited primarily to address and status, Figure 5.20.

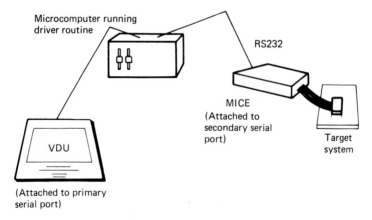

Figure 5.17 Driving MICE from a microcomputer with a serial port

150

```
>2
ASSEMBLY            A   loc
BACKWARD TRACE      B   [R] addx[c[q]]
CYCLE STEP          C
DISABLE             D   N[I|H|C
ENABLE              E   N[I|H|C
FORWARD TRACE       F   [R] addx[c[q]]
EXECUTION           G   [a|[:a2]]
BREAKPOINT          H   [0[|I|2]|I addx[c[q]]|2 addr]
INPUT               I   port[c[time]]
JUMP                J   a|[:a2]
LIST TRACE          L   |step[a|[a2[q]]]]|S[step]
MEMORY              M   [CS|DS|SS|ES] a|[a2[d]]
OUTPUT              O   port d1[d2[d3[d4]]]
REGISTER            R   [AX|BX|CX|DX|SP|BP|SI|DI|DS|ES|SS|CS|IP|FS]
INSTRUCTION STEP    S   [S|[c]
TRANSFER/TEST       T   [CS|DS|SS|ES] a1 a2 S|M|a3
UPLOAD              U   a1 a2 [T|I]
RESET               X   [a|[:a2]]
DISASSEMBLY         Z   a| [a2]
DOWNLOAD            :   (INT),/(TEK)
HELP                ?
ATTENTION           !
>
```

Figure 5.18   MICE command set

```
)Z 8000 8010

LOC       OBJ            LINE      LABEL      SOURCE CODE

8000      200680         0001      B8000      JSR   8006
8003      4C0080         0002                 JMP   8000
8006      A904           0003      S8006      LDA   #04
8008      8D1180         0004                 STA   8011
800B      CE1180         0005      B800B      DEC   8011
800E      D0FB           0006                 BNE   800B
8010      60             0007                 RTS

          DISASSEMBLY COMPLETED
```

Figure 5.19   The 'Z' command disassembles code generating
program labels

5.3   SINGLE BOARD DEVELOPMENT KITS

A number of microprocessor manufacturers, as well as independent companies, market single board microcomputers that are specially designed for control applications. Most of these systems come with sufficient software tools to allow program development for projects that either make use of the board itself or, in some cases, an even smaller, more primitive system.

A recent innovation is the 'limited BASIC' development system/ single board controller that allows a user, with little experience of programming, to develop routines in BASIC for a dedicated application. Most systems also contain an EPROM programmer along with the necessary software to transfer the BASIC program into firmware and run it automatically when the system is switched on.

Figure 5.21 shows one of the first of these systems, the Transwave (K8073) Tiny BASIC microcomputer. The board is driven by a National Semiconductor single chip microcomputer (INS 8073) with its 'on-chip' Tiny BASIC interpreter. Also included on the card is an RS-232 interface to allow communication with a VDU, an EPROM programmer, a real-time clock, a peripheral interface chip (Intel 8255) and a sophisticated communications chip (NSC ART/RC 54240) that allows up to 128 slave stations to be controlled from one master K8073 board.

151

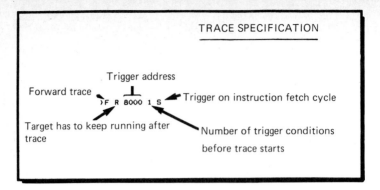

TRACE SPECIFICATION

Trigger address

Forward trace

)F R 8000 1 S ← Trigger on instruction fetch cycle

Target has to keep running after trace

Number of trigger conditions before trace starts

```
)L
 FRAME IFADDR ADDRESS DATA STATUS SPARE(8 BITS)
  0000   8000    8000    20    S    11111111
  0001           8001    06    R    11111111
  0002           01BA    80    R    11111111
  0003           01BA    80    W    11111111
  0004           01B9    02    W    11111111
  0005           8002    80    R    11111111
  0006   8006    8006    A9    S    11111111
  0007           8007    04    R    11111111
  0008   8008    8008    8D    S    11111111
  0009           8009    11    R    1111111'
  000A           800A    80    R    ' '
  000B           8011    04    ' '
  000C   800B    800B    -
  000D           -
  000E
```

The 'L' command displays the contents of the trace buffer in Hex

DISPLAY TRACE IN HEX

Adding an 'S' to the 'L' command displays the trace buffer in mnemonic form

```
)LS
 FRAME      ADDRESS DATA    MNEMONIC-CODE
  0000       8000    20      JSR   8006
  0006       8006    A9      LDA   #04
  0008       8008    8D      STA   8011
  000C       800B    CE      DEC   8011
  0012       800E    D0      BNE   800B
  0015       800B    CE      DEC   8011
  001B       800E    D0      BNE   800B
  001E       800B    CE      DEC   8011
  0024       800E    D0      BNE   800B
  0027       800B    CE      DEC   8011
  002D       800E    D0      BNE   800B
  002F       8010    60      RTS
  0035       8003    4C      JMP   8r '
  0038       8000    20
  003B       8000    20
  003E       0--
  00?? -
```

DISPLAY TRACE IN MNEMONICS

Figure 5.20 Example trace specification with MICE

In the following section two evaluation kits are examined: Rockwell's AIM 65 and the Intel SDK86. Although starting to show its age, the former is still found in many control applications and as a teaching machine for elementary interfacing courses in colleges and universities. The SDK86 is only one of a number of single board computers produced by Intel to familiarise customers with a microprocessor and its peripheral devices.

Rockwell AIM 65

The AIM 65 is one of the more sophisticated evaluation kits containing a full QWERTY keyboard, an LED display and thermal printer, along with

Figure 5.21   Transwave (K8073) Tiny BASIC microcomputer

software tools in firmware that include an editor, assembler and a choice of high level languages.

Hardware   Figure 5.22 shows the major components found on the board, namely:

- 6502 processor and associated clock circuitry
- up to 20 Kbytes of ROM
- up to 4 Kbytes of static RAM
- printer interface and 20 column thermal printer
- interface to 54 key ASCII keyboard
- interface to 20 column 16 segment LED display
- audio cassette recorder interface
- TTY and serial interface
- chip select circuitry
- user parallel port interface

The 6502 microprocessor operates at 1 MHz using a clock derived from a 4 MHz crystal oscillator divided by four. Sockets on the board support up to 4 Kbytes of static RAM (2114) with each chip holding 1 K × 4 bits of data. Five ROM sockets, each capable of holding 2 K × 8 or 4 K × 8 devices, normally contain:

- 8 Kbytes of debug/monitor
- 4 Kbytes of assembler/text editor
- 8 Kbytes of BASIC interpreter

153

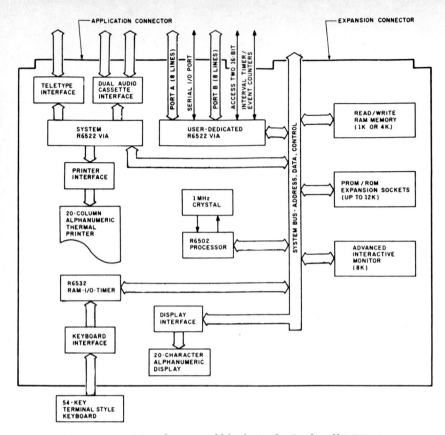

Figure 5.22 Main functional blocks in the Rockwell AIM 65

Figure 5.23 shows a memory map of the system, giving the position of both memory and the input/output devices. In common with other 6502 systems, ROM is positioned at the top of the map to hold the reset vectors and RAM at the bottom, providing workspace for zero page instructions and the processor's stack on page one.

1. *Printer*   The printer uses heat-sensitive paper and a printing head made up of 10 thermal elements, each capable of printing two 5 × 7 dot matrix characters. During operation the print head is driven from side to side as the thermal needles are turned on and off to form a single row of dots 20 characters wide. When the needles reach the end of their horizontal travel, the printer motor advances the paper by one dot row. It takes seven rows of dots to complete a full height row of characters. The entire printing operation is controlled by the AIM 65 monitor program that makes use of part of a 6522 VIA to drive the thermal needles and the printer motor.

2. *Display*   The LED display is made up of five modules, each containing a four digit 16 segment alphanumerical display with its own memory,

154

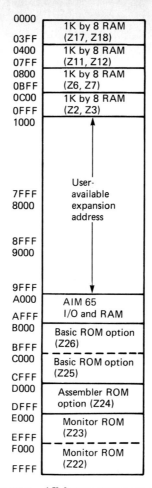

	1K by 8 RAM
0000	
03FF	(Z17, Z18)
0400	1K by 8 RAM
07FF	(Z11, Z12)
0800	1K by 8 RAM
0BFF	(Z6, Z7)
0C00	1K by 8 RAM
0FFF	(Z2, Z3)
1000	
7FFF	User-available
8000	expansion address
8FFF	
9000	
9FFF	
A000	AIM 65
AFFF	I/O and RAM
B000	Basic ROM option
BFFF	(Z26)
C000	Basic ROM option
CFFF	(Z25)
D000	Assembler ROM
DFFF	option (Z24)
E000	Monitor ROM
EFFF	(Z23)
F000	Monitor ROM
FFFF	(Z22)

Figure 5.23 AIM 65 memory map

decoder and driver circuitry, Figure 8.5. A 6520 PIA (Peripheral Interface Adaptor) interfaces the display to the AIM's address and data bus. One port of the PIA selects the module along with the required character within the module and the other port sends the ASCII code for the chosen character to the display.

3. *Keyboard* A 6532 RIOT (a combination chip containing RAM, Input/Output capability in the form of 2 parallel ports and a Timer) interfaces the keyboard to the microprocessor, Figure 8.6. The monitor software contains many fairly complex keyboard routines that provide the following features:

- detects that a key has been depressed
- performs a 'debounce' operation on keyswitches closing and opening

155

- detects the position of the depressed key in the key matrix
- detects 2-key combinations (i.e. those that use SHIFT or CNTRL along with another key)
- provides 2-key rollover, allowing a second key to be detected if it is depressed before the first one is released

At power-up, port A of the RIOT is configured as an input and monitors the state of the key-matrix columns. Port B is then used as an output, placing a logic 0 on only one of the key-matrix rows at any instant. If any key is depressed a logic 0 is transmitted across to the input on Port A containing the key. Using this 'walking ones' scanning routine, the keyboard software can detect the location of a depressed key from the position in which it has placed the logic zero in the rows and the position in which it detects the zero in the columns.

4. *User ports* To support a number of applications the AIM 65 contains an extra 6522 VIA that is left completely free. Connections for this device appear at an application connector at the rear of the board. Alongside is a similar edge connector containing all the system buses, providing a convenient method of attaching any memory or input/output expansions to the system.

Software The 8 Kbytes of monitor ROM contain a number of routines that perform the general system housekeeping, e.g. driving the display, printer, keyboard and I/O interfaces. Also contained in the ROM is a useful system debugger that allows the user to:

- display and alter the contents of memory locations and registers
- transfer the contents of blocks of memory to tape or to any serial device
- assemble short routines using a line assembler
- disassemble the contents of memory locations
- trace or single-step routines
- run machine code programs

An additional 4 Kbyte ROM holds a two-pass assembler and text editor package. When using the assembler, source code prepared by the editor can be assembled direct from memory into memory or onto tape. Working to and from tape has definite advantages with larger programs where it is very easy to run out of memory space.

A number of high level languages are available for the remaining two ROM sockets. The most popular is BASIC but other options include PASCAL, FORTH and PL/65.

Intel SDK86

The SDK86 has the appearance of a larger version of its predecessor, the SDK85. Both systems are single board microcomputers with on-board keypad and display along with a useful wire wrap prototyping area, Figure 5.24. An 8086 microprocessor, configured in minimum mode (i.e.

Figure 5.24   Intel's SDK86

for use in a system that does not support co-processors) lies at the heart of the SDK86. Also included on the board are 8 Kbytes of monitor program in 2716 EPROMs or 2316 ROMs, 2 Kbytes of RAM, a serial interface (8251A USART), a keypad and display driven by an 8279 keyboard/ display controller, two 8255A programmable peripheral interface chips, each containing three 8-bit ports, and bus expansion logic using 8286 transceivers and 74 LS244 drivers to produce a demultiplexed bus, Figure 5.25.

The memory and port maps are shown in Figure 5.26. Again, similar to the previous system, the ROM is placed at the top of the memory map to hold the processor's first instruction on reset at FFFF0H. The board also contains circuitry for a wait state generator that allows a variable number (0 through to 7) of extra clock states to be inserted into the CPU's bus cycle to compensate for any slow I/O or memory devices. As no on-board components require wait states, the generator is configured on arrival for zero wait states.

System monitor   The system firmware is in two parts: one supports operation using the built-in display and keypad, whereas the other is designed for communication with a VDU. Both programs offer a similar set of commands but only the latter is described here.

Figure 5.27 lists the monitor commands. The ten commands contain the usual functions present on most debuggers, but omit both a line assembler and a disassembler. However, the software does supply a serial loader routine (using the R command) that allows a hex file prepared on another machine to be downloaded into memory.

The SDK86 is even less of a development system than the AIM 65 and users would find it a struggle trying to develop 8086 programs in machine

157

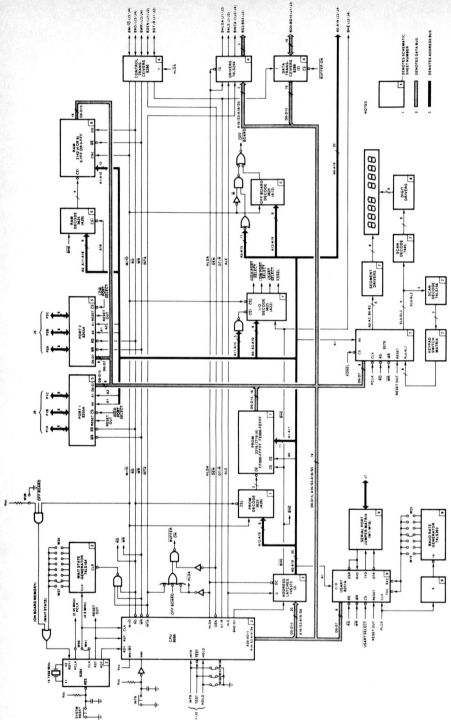

Figure 5.25 Block diagram of SDK86 (Reprinted by permission of
Intel Corporation, copyright 1985)

158

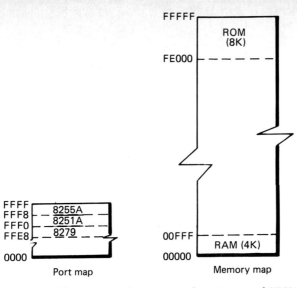

Figure 5.26 Memory and port maps of SDK86

Command	Function/Syntax
S (Substitute Memory)	Displays/modifies memory locations S[W]<addr>,[[<new contents>],]*<cr>
X (Examine/Modify Register)	Displays/modifies 8086 registers X[<reg>][[<new contents>],]*<cr>
D (Display Memory)	Displays block of memory data D[W]<start addr>[,<end addr>]<cr>
M (Move)	Moves block of memory data M<start addr>,<end addr>, <destination addr><cr>
I (Port Input)	Accepts and displays data at input port I[W]<port addr>,[,]*<cr>
O (Port Output)	Outputs data to output port O[W]<port addr>,<data>[,<data>]*<cr>
G (Go)	Transfers 8086 control from monitor to user program G[<start addr>][,<breakpoint addr>]<cr>
N (Single Step)	Executes single user program instruction N[<start addr>],[[<start addr>],]*<cr>
R (Read Hex File)	Reads hexadecimal object file from paper tape into memory R[<bias number>]<cr>
W (Write Hex File)	Outputs block of memory data to paper tape punch W[X]<start addr>,<end addr>[,<exec addr>]<cr>

Figure 5.27 Serial monitor commands (Reprinted by permission of
Intel Corporation, copyright 1985)

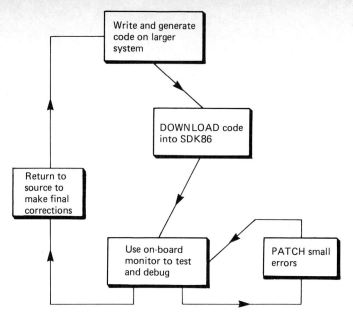

Figure 5.28 Development with the SDK86

code. Undoubtedly its principal function lies in providing a target board that accepts software prepared on a larger machine (e.g. any CP/M system with an 8086 cross-assembler) for evaluation, Figure 5.28.

FURTHER READING

For further reading on microprocessor development systems and other approaches to system development:

Tseng, V., 1982. *Microprocessor Development and Development Systems.* London: Granada.

Rafiquzzaman, M., 1984. *Microprocessors and Microcomputer Development Systems.* New York, NY: Harper and Row.

Camp, R.C., Smay, T.A. and Triska, C.J., 1979. *Microprocessor Systems Engineering.* Portland, OR: Matrix.

May 1983. 'Development Systems and Logic Analysers – Towards a Universal Digital Workbench', *Electronic Engineering*, p. 96.

Details of the HP64000 MDS can be obtained from Measurement Systems Group, Hewlett Packard, South Queensferry, West Lothian, Scotland.

The Microtek 'MICE' is marketed in the UK by ARS, Doman Road, Camberley, Surrey.

Chapter 6

Interfaces and peripherals

The objectives of this chapter are:

- to examine a wide range of communications standards including RS232, RS423, RS422 and IEEE488;
- to describe interfaces to a number of common microcomputer peripheral devices;
- to examine a number of memory devices and their interface to the system buses.

A microprocessor must be capable of communicating with memory, along with a number of external devices, e.g. a keyboard, a modem, a printer and disk drives. All of these external devices are peripherals and the micro requires specialist hardware that provides the peripheral interface. This chapter looks first at two well-defined standard interfaces before examining some of the more common memory and peripheral devices that form part of most microcomputer systems.

6.1 SERIAL INTERFACING

Serial data links are now well established as a means of communication between computers or between computers and peripherals, Figure 6.1. The original, and still pertinent, incentive for using serial transmission was its low cost, providing two-way communication on only three conductors compared with over 16 in some parallel systems. However, with most microcomputer installations the popularity of serial transmission is not based purely on low cabling costs, but more on the wide acceptance of a serial interface standard that is now found on many peripheral devices, including printers, plotters, VDUs, etc.

Serial data
Inside a computer, data is transmitted from one device to another in a parallel format, typically with all 8 bits lying side by side on the system data bus. With serial communication, a pair of conductors transport data in the form of a bit stream with each bit of information given its own time slot. Figure 6.2 illustrates a typical serial packet containing 8 bits of data framed with a START bit and a STOP bit. Normally a serial line will idle in the logic 1 state with a start bit signalling a receiver that a data packet

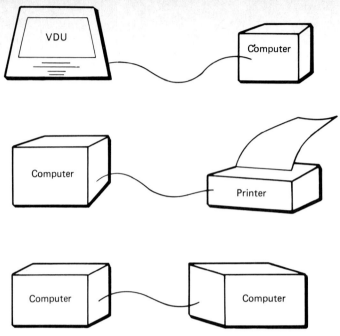

Figure 6.1   Serial data links have a wide range of applications

follows. The least significant bit of data is usually transmitted first and the packet terminated by 1, 1½ or 2 stop bits, leaving sufficient time to recover before the arrival of the next packet.

The majority of serial links are asynchronous (i.e. a common clock signal is not transmitted with the data), with the result that both the transmitter and the receiver must run at one within a range of standard frequencies. These standard frequencies are known as baud rates and indicate the number of bits transmitted per second when the line is carrying data. (Strictly speaking, baud rate is defined as the number of discrete conditions or events transmitted per second which can in some situations differ from the number of bits/sec.) Figure 6.3 shows the common baud rates that range from 50 through to 19 200, i.e. 19.2K baud. The lower speeds are used with electromechanical devices, such as teleprinters, and the higher speeds with VDUs or data links between systems.

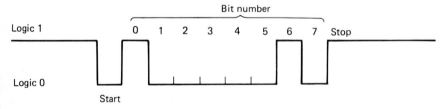

Figure 6.2   Typical serial data packet

Baud rate	Typical application
50	
75	Teletypes and
110	similar devices
150	
300	Medium speed
600	printers
1200	and VDUs
1800	
2400	High speed
3600	printers
4800	and VDUs
9600	
19200	Data links

Figure 6.3 Common baud rates and their uses

Parity Many serial links pass through regions subject to noise from sources such as the electric mains or switching of inductive loads. Any interference can lead to data errors with a resulting requirement for some mechanism for their detection. One simple technique involves transmitting an extra bit, called a parity bit, with each data item.

There are two strategies that can be followed when evaluating the parity of a data packet. In one, the even parity scheme, the parity bit is chosen so that the total number of logic ones in the data bits plus the parity bit is even. Alternatively, the odd parity scheme selects the parity bit so that the total number of bits is odd, Figure 6.4.

The parity bit can be determined such that the number of logic 1s (including the parity bit) is even or odd.

e.g.

Data	Parity bit	
	Even	Odd
0000 0000	0	1
0100 0001	0	1
0000 0010	1	0

Figure 6.4 Evaluating the parity bit with an *even* and *odd* parity scheme

Before transmission, both the source and destination must agree on the scheme in operation. The transmitter then evaluates and appends the relative parity bit onto the data packet. At the destination the receiver then independently evaluates the parity of the packet, using the same scheme, and compares it with the parity transmitted by the source, Figure 6.5.

It is worth noting that a single parity bit error detection scheme is far from foolproof: only an odd number of bit errors will be detected, with an even error count resulting in the parity bit fallaciously reporting correct

Hardware or software can be used to check the parity bit on received characters and to generate the parity bit for transmitted characters.

e.g.   Even parity strategy

Transmitted	Received	Error?
00001000 (Parity 1)	00001000 (Parity 1)	No
10000000 (Parity 1)	00000000 (Parity 1)	Yes

Figure 6.5   Using the parity bit to detect errors

data. Not all serial links bother to evaluate a parity bit. Some always transmit the parity bit set (MARK parity), whereas others leave it clear (SPACE parity), or miss it out completely (NO parity). Figure 6.6 shows examples of all these possibilities.

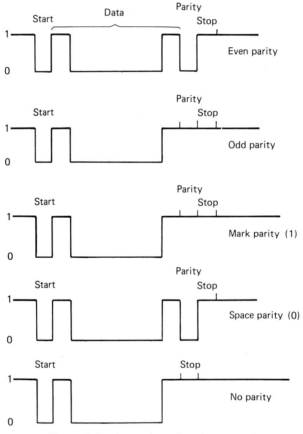

Figure 6.6   A number of parity strategies

Parallel to serial conversion   A number of specialised single chip LSI packages are now marketed to perform the conversion from the parallel data format found inside a computer system, to serial data. The common mnemonics used for these devices are:

UART   Universal Asynchronous Receiver Transmitter

ACIA   Asynchronous Communications Interface Adaptor

USART   Universal Synchronous/Asynchronous Receiver Transmitter

SIO   Serial Input Output device

At the heart of all these devices a shift register or a multiplexer feeds parallel data, sent to an output buffer, out as a serial stream of bits, or collects bits from a serial stream to form a single byte at an input buffer, Figure 6.7. A number of other on-board registers perform functions including:

- selecting the required baud rate, number of data bits and stop bits
- selecting the parity scheme in operation
- selecting the action to be performed if an error is detected
- flagging the system that the output buffer is empty or the input buffer is full

Along with these basic features, most UARTs support a number of control lines that help to ensure safe transfer of data (discussed later in this chapter).

In some low-cost systems, serial to parallel conversion is carried out in software, making use of two pins (an input and an output) on a parallel interface. Program 3.6 is an example of a typical conversion routine. After generating the start bit, the byte to be serialised is shifted, one bit at a time, across the selected output pin on the parallel port chip (bit 0 on port A of a Z80 PIO). A delay routine provides the individual bit times, setting the baud rate. The example shown does not make use of any parity scheme, but if desired this too can be included in a software parallel to serial conversion.

Data transfers

A *simplex* data link only supports data transfers in the one direction, Figure 6.8a. The connection between a microcomputer and a simple printer would be a suitable candidate for a simplex link, with the micro acting solely as the transmitter and the printer as the receiver.

If data transmission is required in both directions (e.g. between a microcomputer and a VDU), then there are two other common modes of operation. A *full duplex* link allows simultaneous transmission in both directions, Figure 6.8b. Clearly, to operate this strategy both devices require to have completely independent transmit and receive circuitry. When implemented using a VDU and micro system, normally any characters selected on the keyboard go directly to the micro system which then echoes them back, along with any reply, to the VDU's screen.

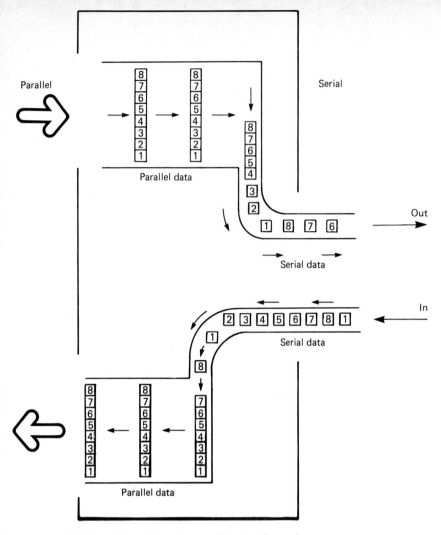

UART — Universal Asynchronous Receiver - Transmitter

Figure 6.7 UARTs perform parallel to serial and serial to parallel conversions

With a *half duplex* link, two-way communication is possible only on an alternate basis, with one device talking and then the other, Figure 6.8c. If this type of link is established between a micro and a VDU, then an internal switch is made within the VDU that echoes all keyboard characters directly to the screen. (A common mistake made when configuring a new system is to use a VDU in half duplex with a computer working in full duplex. With this situation double characters appear on the screen: one echoed directly from the keyboard and the other from the micro.)

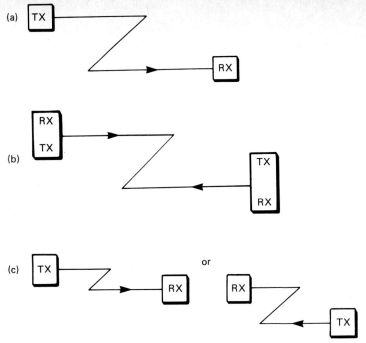

Figure 6.8 (a) Simplex data link; (b) Full duplex link; (c) Half duplex link.

Flow control Having decided on the type of serial link, there remains the problem of ensuring that data exchanges take place in a safe and efficient manner. Without some mechanism for controlling transfer, data could be lost due to a transmitter sending before a receiver was ready and time could be wasted with a transmitter waiting to send data even though the receiver was available.

There are two commonly used techniques for obtaining flow control: XON–XOFF and ETX–ACK. Both employ ASCII control characters to toggle transmission on or off. The XON–XOFF protocol requires a full duplex link along with the following codes:

XON	Transmit on	–	ASCII character DC1. i.e. 11H
XOFF	Transmit off	–	ASCII character DC3. i.e. 13H

Figure 6.9 illustrates the technique with a serial link between a computer and a printer with its own print buffer. As the buffer begins to fill, it transmits an XOFF command back to the computer. The computer then stops and waits until it receives an XON command, signalling that the printer has managed to almost empty its buffer.

The ETX–ACK protocol again uses ASCII control characters to perform flow control, but does not require the sophistication of a full duplex link. Figure 6.10 outlines the procedure. The transmitter sends a predetermined fixed length block of characters (80 in the example) to the

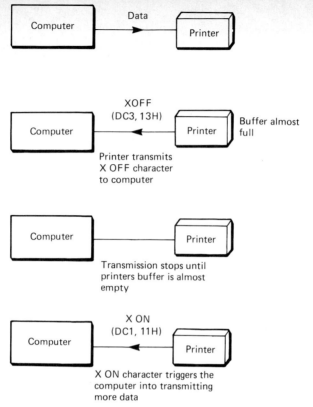

Figure 6.9 Flow control with the XON–XOFF control codes

receiver, followed by an ASCII ETX character (End of Text – code 03H). After performing whatever operations are necessary on the block just arrived, the receiver then signals the transmitter that it is ready for another block by sending an ACK character (ACKnowledge – code 06H).

RS-232 and other standards

There are several standards, established by a number of American and European organisations, that define the electrical characteristics and the mechanisms for transfer of serial data. One of the most popular is RS-232C (the C indicates the current revision), published by the Electronic Industries Association (EIA), an organisation of American manufacturers of electronic equipment. A second standard, V24, produced by the Consultative Committee in International Telegraphy and Telephoning (CCITT – a committee of the International Telcommunication Union, which is itself an agency of the United Nations) is almost, but not quite, identical to RS-232C, defining procedures for interchanging information and leaving the V28 standard to define pin allocations on connectors together with voltage levels. However, for most purposes RS-232C and V24 can be regarded as being synonymous.

ETX = "End of TeXt" = 03H

ACK = "ACKnowledge" = 06H

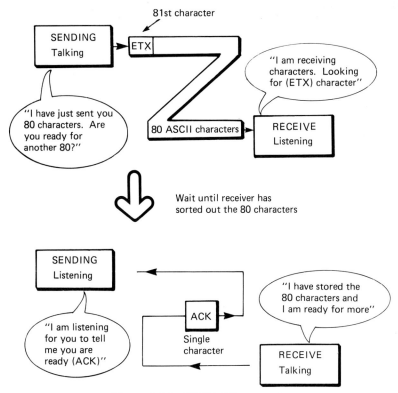

Figure 6.10   ETX/ACK protocol

The RS-232C standard is made up of four parts: definition of electrical signal levels, physical characteristics of connectors etc., a functional description of the signals, and finally details of how these signals are used with different types of modem.

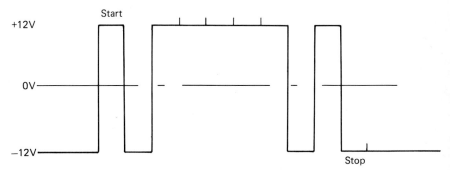

Figure 6.11   Voltage levels on an RS-232 signal

Unlike the voltage levels found inside the computer, RS-232 uses +12V and −12V to represent logic 0 and logic 1 (a problem for some microcomputer manufacturers who need to install additional power supplies). Figure 6.11 shows the voltage levels for a typical serial packet; note how the line idles at −12V, i.e. logic 1.

The pin assignments of the 21 signals found on the popular 25 pin 'D' type connector (not itself part of the standard) are shown in Figure 6.12. A number of the signals betray the origin of the standard, namely as a means of connecting terminals to computers using modems and the telephone network. The terminology labels the ultimate source or destination of data as DTEs (Data Terminal Equipment) and any devices that are used to convey data from source to destination as DCEs (Data Communication Equipment), Figure 6.13. However the terminology breaks down when peripherals are interfaced directly to systems with some microcomputers configured as DCEs (i.e. they transmit data on pin 3 and receive data on pin 2) and others as DTEs (transmitting on pin 2 and receiving on pin 3). The serial ports on a Comart Communicator are both configured as DCEs, with the result that the cable to a terminal (DTE) connects pin 2 to pin 2

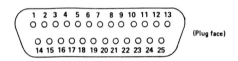

25-way connector

Name	Pin
Cable screen	1
Signal ground or common return	7
Transmitted data	2
Received data	3
Request to send	4
Ready for sending (Clear to send)	5
Data set ready	6
Connect data set to line/Data terminal ready	20
Data channel received line signal detector	8
Data signal quality detector	−
Data signalling rate selector (DTE source)	23
Transmitter signal element timing (DTE source)	24
Transmitter signal element timing (DCE source)	15
Receiver signal element timing (DCE source)	17
Select standby	(24)
Transmitted backward channel data	14
Received backward channel data	16
Transmit backward channel line signal	19
Backward channel ready	13
Backward channel received line signal detector	12
Calling indicator	22
Select transmit frequency	11
Remote loopback for point-to-point circuits	21
Local loopback	18
Test indicator	25

Figure 6.12 Pin assignments and signals on an RS-232 interface

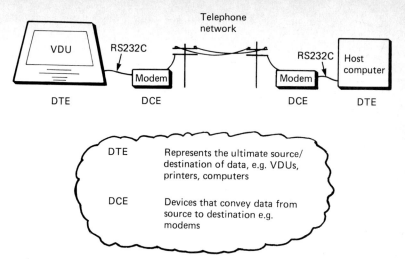

Figure 6.13 Data Terminal Equipment and Data Communication Equipment

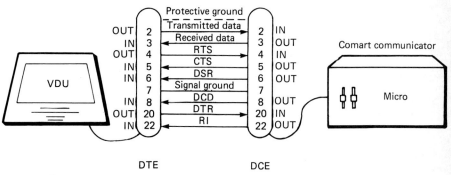

Figure 6.14 Some micros have their serial ports configured as DCEs and some as DTEs. The Comart Communicator is a DCE

and pin 3 to pin 3, Figure 6.14. If, however, a micro configured as a DTE is used with a terminal (e.g. a serial port on the TRS80) the connecting cable requires a twist, connecting pin 2 to pin 3 in both directions, Figure 6.18. This simple solution is often called a *null modem*.

Many of the pins on an RS-232 interface are not used in micro-peripheral connections. Normally a three wire link (pins 2, 3 and 7) will prove satisfactory for most applications if used with one of the flow control techniques described earlier. However, some configurations adopt a different strategy to ensure safe data transfer, making use of two groups of control signals present on the interface: the data handshake lines and the equipment readiness signals.

Figure 6.15 illustrates the operation of the two handshake lines: Request To Send ($\overline{RTS}$) and Clear To Send ($\overline{CTS}$). The terminal requests to be allowed to transmit by setting $\overline{RTS}$ true (i.e. logic 0). If the DCE device is ready to receive data it signals the terminal by setting $\overline{CTS}$ true. The

171

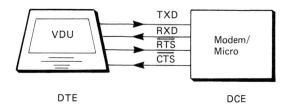

RTS and $\overline{\text{CTS}}$ control transmission of data
from terminal (DTE) to modem/micro (DCE)

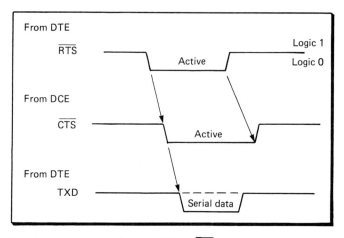

Terminal requests transmission by driving $\overline{\text{RTS}}$ low.
The DCE device replies by driving $\overline{\text{CTS}}$ low.
The terminal then transmits data.
$\overline{\text{RTS}}$ is not turned on again until $\overline{\text{CTS}}$ is turned off.

Figure 6.15 The data handshake lines $\overline{\text{CTS}}/\overline{\text{RTS}}$

terminal then transmits its data in the form of either a single character or a block, depending on the scheme in operation. Once $\overline{\text{RTS}}$ has been 'turned off' (logic 1) it cannot be turned on again until the clear to send signal has been turned off by the DCE device. This ensures that the DTE device does not restart transmission while the DCE device is still busy with the previous data.

The equipment readiness signals, Data Terminal Ready ($\overline{\text{DTR}}$) and Data Set Ready ($\overline{\text{DSR}}$) are used to declare that each device is ready to pass data if required. Therefore if $\overline{\text{DTR}}$ is on (logic 0), the terminal is ready to pass data to the DCE device. Similarly if $\overline{\text{DSR}}$ is on, the modem or micro is available to transmit to the terminal, Figure 6.16.

If all four control signals are used then the conditions shown in Figure 6.17 must be met before data can be transmitted. However, many cables between micros and peripherals only make use of some of these

172

Data Terminal Ready (DTR) — Data Set Ready (DSR)

(DTE ready)   (DCE ready)

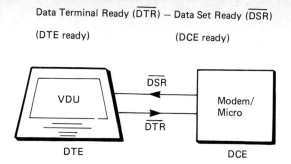

DTE   DCE

DTR and DSR are used to declare equipment ready.
DTR must be on (logic 0) before the DCE device
(modem) can declare the communication channel
open by setting DSR on (logic 0).
If DTR goes off (logic 1) the DCE device is removed
from the communication channel.

Figure 6.16   Equipment readiness signals DTR/DSR

For transmission from DTE to DCE

The following conditions must be met
(i.e. all must be TRUE 'logic 0'):

1.   Data Terminal Ready   (DTR) ⎱   Equipment
2.   Data Set Ready   (DSR) ⎰   readiness

3.   Request To Send   (RTS) ⎱   Channel
4.   Clear To Send   (CTS) ⎰   readiness

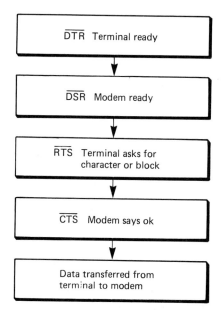

Figure 6.17   Conditions for transmission to occur

173

signals, and in roles different from their original intention. Figure 6.18 shows some examples of these special cables.

One of the great limitations of RS-232 is its maximum transmission distance of 50 feet when operating at 9600 baud; for slower speeds the

3 wire system

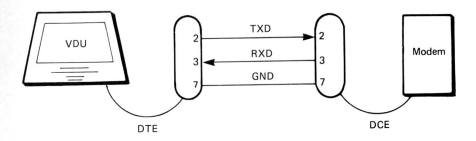

3 wire system with loop back

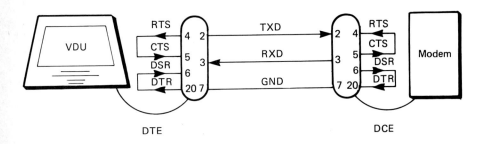

3 wire system with 2–3 twist (NULL modem)

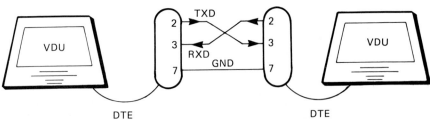

Figure 6.18 Not all peripherals use the standard RS-232 cable

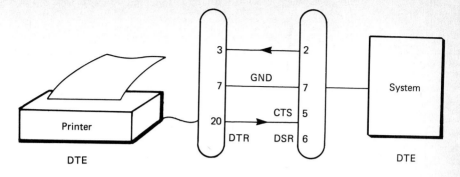

When printer 'wants' data, $\overline{\text{DTR}}$ goes low pulling either $\overline{\text{CTS}}$ or $\overline{\text{DSR}}$ low.
When printer buffer fills, printer halts system by raising DTR.

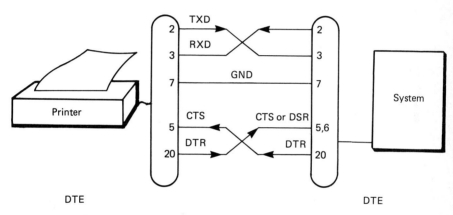

Similar to above example with additional lines allowing the system to
monitor the printer's 'status' register. Before transmitting 'status',
printer checks its $\overline{\text{CTS}}$ input

Figure 6.18 Continued

distance can be greater. In practice many cables are longer but they then
lie outside the standard and run the risk of loading problems and
increased error rates.

The maximum speed of 19 200 baud is more than adequate when
working with a VDU, where the screen can be completely filled with
characters in approximately 1 second. However when used for file
transfer between systems, even this maximum speed can appear slow,
taking over 10 seconds to transfer a 20 Kbyte file (longer if bytes are
transmitted as two ASCII characters along with checksums).

Current loop   The current loop interface, used originally with Teletype
terminals, is regaining popularity as a relatively robust method of transmitting serial data over longer distances. Two pairs of wires are used in

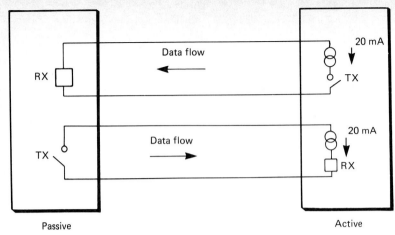

Figure 6.19   20 mA current loop serial link

which the idle state is a current of 20 mA (logic 1), with the transmitters interrupting the current flow to produce the logic 0 state, Figure 6.19.

A current loop interface can be either active or passive. If a device supplies the current for the loop it is termed active. On the other hand, a device in which the receiver merely detects the current changes and the transmitter switches the current, is termed passive. Figure 6.20 illustrates a typical active receiver and passive transmitter.

Current loop will work over distances up to 300m at 9600 baud and has a further advantage over RS-232 that the transmitter and the receiver can be electrically isolated (usually achieved using an opto-coupler in the receiver). These features, combined with its high noise immunity, have led to its wide acceptance in industrial applications.

RS-422 and 423   The Electronics Industry Association, realising the limitations of RS-232, brought out two new standards in 1978:

- EIA Standard RS-422-A 'Electrical Characteristics of Balanced Voltage Digital Interface Circuits'
- EIA Standard RS-423-A 'Electrical Characteristics of Unbalanced Voltage Digital Interface Circuits'

To support transmission at a higher data rate (up to 10 megabaud) RS-422 employs a balanced system with two wires for each signal. Using this arrangement, each interface contains a differential receiver which rejects noise common to both lines while detecting small differential signals, Figure 6.21.

Unfortunately, existing RS-232 equipment cannot be connected directly to RS-422. With this in mind, the EIA produced RS-423, an unbalanced system similar to RS-232, which gives increased performance over RS-232 (transmission rates up to 100 kilobaud) while still supporting existing equipment, Figure 6.22.

Figure 6.23 summarises the important parameters of a number of serial interfaces.

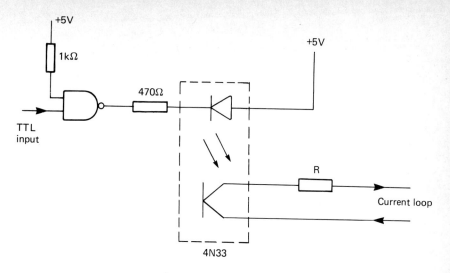

Current loop transmitter

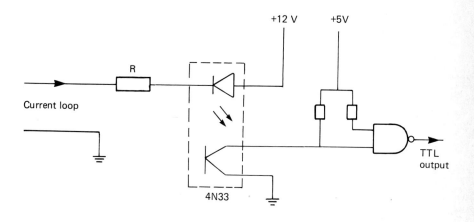

Current loop receiver

Figure 6.20 Current loop interface

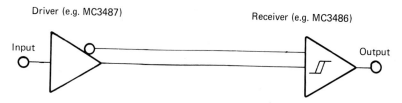

Figure 6.21 RS-422 interface uses a balanced transmission system

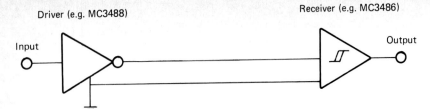

Figure 6.22 RS-423 interface: single ended voltage interface (unbalanced)

	Logical levels 0	Logical levels 1	Maximum speed (bits/s)	Maximum distance (ft)
TTL	0 to 0.8 V	2.4 V to 5 V	$\sim 25 \times 10^6$	~ 30
RS232C	5 V to 15 V	-5 V to -15 V	2×10^4	50
RS423	4 V to 6 V	-4 V to -6 V	10^5	40 at max speed 4000 at 9000 baud
RS422	2 V to 6 V	-2 V to -6 V	10^7	40 at max speed 4000 at 10^5 baud
20 mA	0 mA	20 mA	10^4	1500

Figure 6.23 Summary of limiting parameters for a number of serial interfaces

6.2 IEEE 488 – GENERAL PURPOSE INTERFACE BUS

Since its introduction in the early seventies, the General Purpose Interface Bus (GPIB, sometimes called the HPIB due to its close association with Hewlett Packard who played a major role in its development) has grown in popularity as a means of interfacing a wide range of instruments and peripherals to microcomputer systems. Many machines have been designed with interface capability on-board (e.g. Pet, Osborne, and several HP micros) while others can have it easily appended by the addition of an interface box or card (e.g. Apple, BBC micro, S100 systems).

Undoubtedly the great appeal of the GPIB lies in its ability to solve many of the traditional problems associated with interfacing computers to instrumentation, leaving the biologist, chemist or engineer free to concentrate on solving his own measurement problem.

A standard for the bus was first published by the Institution of Electrical and Electronic Engineers (IEEE) in 1975 (IEEE standard 488) and updated with minor revisions in 1978.

Overview

The GPIB uses a parallel bus structure containing 16 signal lines and eight ground lines. The bus standard allows for a maximum of 15 devices connected in parallel with a maximum cable length of 20m. Each device on the bus is given a unique identity or address.

All GPIB devices must be capable of performing at least one of the following roles:

LISTENER   Any device that can accept data from the bus is said to have listener capability. For example, a card punch, a printer, or a programmable signal generator.

TALKER   A device capable of transmitting data over the bus. Examples are a card reader, voltmeter, etc.

CONTROLLER A device capable of managing the bus, specifying which device is allowed to talk (active talker) and which device(s) is allowed to listen (active listener(s)). At any instant there can be only one active controller. If a cluster contains several controllers, only one can be configured as the master controller, ready to take control at power-up or if the bus is reset.

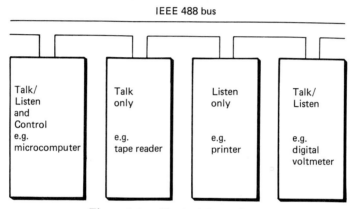

IEEE 488 bus

Talk/
Listen
and
Control
e.g.
microcomputer

Talk
only

e.g.
tape reader

Listen
only

e.g.
printer

Talk/
Listen

e.g.
digital
voltmeter

Figure 6.24 Typical GPIB cluster

A large number of devices have both talk and listen capability. For example, a programmable multimeter is a listener to accept instructions selecting the required function and range, as well as a talker, allowing it to reply with the measurement. Figure 6.24 shows a typical GPIB cluster.

The interface
The signals on the bus can be split into three groups:

   8 data lines
   3 data handshake lines
   5 general interface management lines

The remaining eight pins on the standard 24 pin connector, Figure 6.25 comprise a braided shield, a logic ground and individual grounds forming twisted pairs with each of the signals DAV, NRFD, NDAC, IFC, SRQ and ATN.
    The bidirectional data bus is used to transfer information from one device to another in a bit parallel, byte serial asynchronous form (not unlike the synchronous data transfers found inside a micro) using ASCII

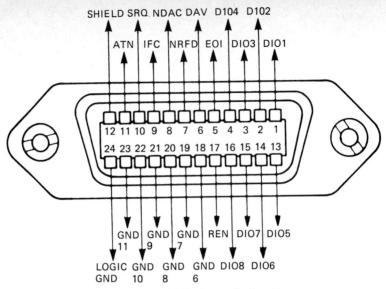

Figure 6.25 GPIB pinout designations

seven-bit coded data with the eighth bit employed as a parity check.

Information on the bus falls into two categories: data en route to and from instruments (e.g. àn ASCII text file passing from a micro to a printer) and special GPIB commands.

All exchanges on the data lines are co-ordinated using the three handshake lines DAV (Data AVailable), NRFD (Not Ready For Data) and NDAC (Not Data ACcepted). Figure 6.26 illustrates how data is transferred. (Note: the GPIB uses a logic 0 as the true condition.) The sequence begins with the talker detecting that NRFD has gone false (high), with the slowest listener. The talker then sets DAV true, informing the listeners that the data bus now contains new valid data. The first listener to respond sets NRFD true, indicating that it is not ready to accept any more new data. Following this, NDAC goes false (i.e. data accepted) with the

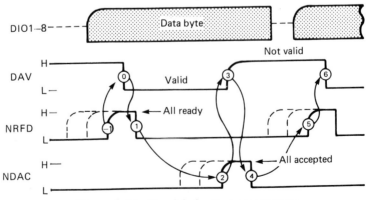

Figure 6.26 Handshake timing sequence

180

slowest listener, indicating that all the listeners have accepted the data. The talker then sets DAV false to signal that the current byte on the data lines is no longer valid. Finally, the first listener sets NDAC low, and the slowest listener sets NRFD high (i.e. ready for data) in preparation for the next exchange.

It is worth noting that both the NDAC and NRFD lines are wired-OR functions between all the listeners. Hence NDAC is only released when the slowest listener has accepted data and NRFD is released when the slowest listener is ready for new data. This simple technique ensures that data transfers occur at a speed suited to the slowest device taking part.

The five interface management lines, Figure 6.27, form a *control bus* performing a number of interface housekeeping functions.

Attention (ATN) is driven only by the controller and monitored by all other devices. When true (logic 0) the interface is in the command mode with the data lines holding interface command codes or station addresses. In the false condition (logic 1) the interface is in data mode, with the active talker passing data to the active listener(s).

Remote enable (REN) is another controller only output used to place a device under remote control.

Service request (SRQ) acts like an interrupt line, allowing instruments that have either just completed a measurement or encountered a problem (e.g. a printer that has run out of paper) to demand attention from the controller.

Talk and listen addresses

Each device on a GPIB cluster should have a unique *device address* in the range 0 to 30. Normally this address can be selected by small in-line switches, positioned either inside or on the rear panel of the device.

Name	Mnemonic	Description
Attention	ATN	Causes all devices to interpret data on the bus as a controller command and activate their acceptor handshake function (command mode) or data between addressed devices (data mode)
Interface Clear	IFC	Initializes the GPIB system to an idle state (no activity on the bus)
Service Request	SRQ	Alerts the controller to a need for communication
Remote Enable	REN	Enables devices to respond to remote program control when addressed to listen
End Or Identify	EOI	Indicates last data byte of a multibyte sequence; also used with ATN to parallel poll devices for their status bit

Figure 6.27 Bus management lines

Device Address (decimal)	Listen Address (Hex)	Talk Address (Hex)
0	20	40
1	21	41
2	22	42
3	23	43
4	24	44
5	25	45
6	26	46
7	27	47
8	28	48
9	29	49
10	2A	4A
11	2B	4B
12	2C	4C
13	2D	4D
14	2E	4E
15	2F	4F
16	30	50
17	31	51
18	32	52
19	33	53
20	34	54
21	35	55
22	36	56
23	37	57
24	38	58
25	39	59
26	3A	5A
27	3B	5B
28	3C	5C
29	3D	5D
30	3E	5E

Figure 6.28   Talk and listen addresses

Corresponding to each device address are two address codes called *the talk address* and *the listen address*. Figure 6.28 shows the relationship.

Prior to any transaction between a talker and listeners, the controller uses these address codes to enable the participants. The selection is carried out with the bus in command mode (i.e ATN true), with each device keeping a lookout for its own talk or listen address code. For example, if a controller wished to set up a transaction between a paper tape reader (talker) at device address 21, a printer (listener) at device address 16, and a video display (listener) at device address 4, it would place the following code sequence on the data lines while holding ATN true:

55H – talk address device 21
30H – listen address device 16
24H – listen address device 4

When ATN was released by the controller, each device would adopt its proper role in the subsequent data exchange.

Commands and data

From the address table given earlier it can be seen that the maximum talk and listen addresses are 5EH and 3EH respectively. The following two codes, 5FH and 3FH, are given special functions, namely as the untalk (UNT) and the unlisten (UNL) commands. The former can be used by the controller to 'unaddress' or silence the current talker. This command is not often used since addressing any device to talk automatically unaddresses all the others. The unlisten command is, however, frequently used as a means of ensuring that only those devices meant to listen, do listen, i.e. there are no eavesdroppers left from some previous transaction.

The concept of unlistening eavesdroppers is crucial to efficient operation of the bus as the data handshake, described earlier, forces transfers to take place at a speed suited to the slowest listener. Hence the need to ensure that no unnecessary slow device is enabled. For example, if a printer was left eavesdropping while a disk system transferred data into a microcomputer's memory, then all the data transfers would take place at a rate governed primarily by the printer.

In operation a GPIB alternates between the command and data modes in a manner similar to the fetch and execute cycles performed by a microprocessor, Figure 6.29. The similarity also extends to the use of mnemonics for the various bus commands, Figure 6.30. The commands can be divided into two groups: universal commands and addressed commands.

The former, as the name suggests, are directed at all instruments on the bus that contain the necessary functions to obey them, and take the form of either a special code on the data lines (a multi-line command) or activation of one or more of the bus management lines (a uni-line command). Addressed commands are similar except that they are directed at specific addressed devices. All addressed commands have a multi-line format.

When the GPIB enters the data mode (ATN false), information changes hands between a talker and listeners. The format and nature of the data depends on each instrument and lies outside the GPIB interface

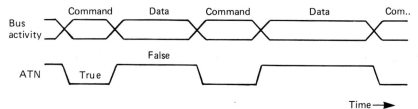

Figure 6.29 The GPIB alternates between the command and data modes

183

ATN	Attention
DCL	Device clear
GET	Group execute trigger
GTL	Go to local
LAG	Listen address group
LLO	Local lockout
MLA	My listen address
MTA	My talk address
PPC	Parallel poll configure
PPU	Parallel poll unconfigure
PPE	Parallel poll enable
PPD	Parallel poll disable
SCG	Secondary command group
SDC	Selected device clear
SPD	Serial poll disable
SPE	Serial poll enable
TCT	Take control
UNL	Unlisten
UNT	Untalk

Figure 6.30   GPIB mnemonics

standard. A simple device, such as a printer, would probably receive its data in the form of a string of ASCII characters forming a text file, whereas a digital multimeter would make use of ASCII code sequences to select function and range.

Figure 6.31 follows the bus activity when a microcomputer sends a short message to a printer. The micro is acting as the bus controller at device address 21 and the printer as a listener at device address 16. The sequence begins with the controller setting ATN true before addressing itself to talk, unlistening all devices and addressing the printer to listen. On releasing the ATN line the data transfer takes place.

Bus signal	Characters on data bus	Hex	Comments
ATN	MTA	55	Talk address (code 21)
(true)	UNL	3F	Unlisten command
	LAG	30	Listen address group (code 16)
↓			ATN set false
$\overline{\text{ATN}}$	F	46	
(false)	R	52	
	E	45	Data
	D	44	
	\<CR\>	0D	
	\<LF\>	LF	

Figure 6.31   Bus activity between a microcomputer (controller) and a printer (listener)

Polling

The service request (SRQ) management line allows devices to signal the controller that they are in need of attention. On detecting a request, the controller then carries out a polling procedure to determine who requested service and why.

The GPIB standard supports two methods of polling: *serial* and *parallel*. Only devices with talker capability can be serial polled, with the controller addressing each device in turn with an SPE command (Serial Poll Enable). The polled device replies, sending a status byte on which a logic 0 in bit 7 confirms that it was responsible for activating the SRQ line; the remaining bits normally display a device dependent code that reflects why the SRQ line was set. Performing a serial poll of the requesting device causes it to release the SRQ line.

A parallel poll is often used to provide a rapid check on the status of up to eight devices at the same time (e.g. to determine which instruments are ready to send or receive data).

Before making use of a parallel poll the controller carries out a configure procedure in which each device is assigned one of the eight data lines. The poll itself is initiated by the controller simultaneously asserting the ATN and EOI management lines. Polled devices then use their assigned bit to report their status. If more than eight devices are in use, a parallel poll can still be carried out but some data lines have to be shared.

Example – controller and listener/talker

Most low cost implementations of the GPIB make use of a microcomputer to act on the system controller. Figure 6.32 shows one example, the HP85 personal computer being used to control Solartron's locator, a multifunction digital meter with listener/talker capability. The IEEE adaptor for

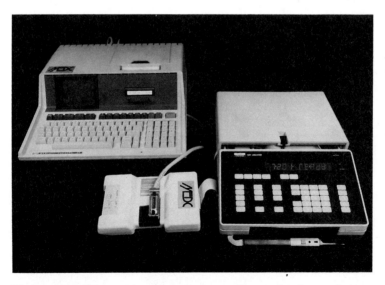

Figure 6.32   HP85 microcomputer (controller) and Solartron locator
(talker/listener)

the HP85 is in two parts: the electrical interface in the form of a plug-in card, and a set of ROMs containing a number of useful driver routines that allow the bus to be accessed using high level commands in a BASIC program. For example the BASIC statement:

```
10 OUTPUT 716;"FRED"
```

would perform the GPIB activity shown in the earlier Figure 6.31, i.e. set up the controller (device address 21) as the talker and the unit at device address 16 as the listener before transferring the ASCII string "FRED". (Note: the prefix of 7 before the device address of the listener relates to the channel number of the interface card within the HP85 personal computer.)

In a similar manner, the ENTER statement allows the controller to take on the role of a listener and accept data from some GPIB device acting as a talker, e.g.

```
50 ENTER 716;A$
```

enables the controller to set up device 16 as a talker, configure itself as a listener and assign the data received to the string variable A$, Figure 6.33.

Program statements	Bus signal	Characters on data bus	Hex	Comments
ENTER 716;A$	ATN	UNL	3F	Unlisten
	↓	MLA	35	Listen address (code 21)
		TAG	50	Talk address (code 16)
	ATN̄		X	ATN set false
			X	
			X	Data transferred from
			X	talker to listener
		<CR>	0D	
		<LF>	0A	End of data

Figure 6.33 Bus activity on performing the ENTER command

The OUTPUT and ENTER commands are only two of the many extra BASIC statements available for use with the interface. Figure 6.34 gives a complete list.

Solartron's locator is a multi-function instrument providing all the usual features found on a digital multimeter, i.e. current, voltage and resistance measurement, along with a number of functions directed at digital systems, namely signature analysis, frequency and pulse width measurement, transition and event counting. The locator connects to the GPIB by means of an external interface box which uses small in-line switches to select its device address as well as to configure it as either a listener only, a talker only, or a listener/talker. All of its functions can be selected and operated remotely over the bus using commands made up of ASCII strings. For example, the short program shown below could be used to sample the frequency of a signal at the locator's input probe.

High level statement	Actions performed
ABORTIO 7	IFC, assumes active control [IFC] MTA, leaves ATN true [ATN•MTA] Terminates I/O operation [No sequence generated]
ASSERT 7;X	Immediate write to CR2. IFC is not asserted.
CLEAR 701	Addressing performed, then send SDC to device 01 [ATN•UNL,MTA,LAG,SDC]
CLEAR 7	No addressing. Send DCL (Note: ATN remains true; user may use RESUME 7 to set ATN false) [ATN•DCL]
CONTROL 7,n;X	Writes X to CRn when interface becomes non-busy
ENABLE INTR 7;X	Writes X to CR1 when interface becomes non-busy
ENTER 705;X	Device 05 is addressed to talk, HP-85 is addressed to listen, data is input to X
ENTER 7;X	Inputs data to X [No sequence generated] Waits until addressed to listen then inputs data to X [No sequence generated]
HALT 7	Terminates I/O operation [No sequence generated]
LOCAL 7	REN is set to false (REN)
LOCAL 701	Addressing is performed, then GTL is sent (Note: ATN remains true. User may use RESUME 7 to set ATN false) [ATN•UNL,MTA,LAG,GTL]
LOCAL LOCKOUT 7	LLO is sent [ATN•LLO]
OUTPUT 705;X	HP-85 is addressed to talk, device 05 is addressed to listen, data X is sent

Figure 6.34   High level HPIB commands available on the HP85 microcomputer

High level statement	Actions performed
OUTPUT 7;X	Outputs data X [No sequence generated] Waits until addressed to talk, then outputs data X [No sequence generated]
PASS CONTROL 715	Device 15 is addressed to talk, then $\overline{TCT}$ is sent [ATN●UNL,MLA,TAG,UNL,TCT,$\overline{ATN}$]
PASS CONTROL 7	No addressing. Send TCT [ATN●UNL,TCT,$\overline{ATN}$]
PPOLL (7)	Sends IDY (Identify) [ATN●EOI(>6µs),$\overline{ATN}$●$\overline{EOI}$]
REMOTE 7	REN is set true [REN]
REMOTE 701	REN is set true, then device 01 is addressed (Note: ATN is left true) [REN,ATN●UNL,MTA,LAG]
REQUEST 7;X	If bit 6 of X is =1 then SRQ is set true. The HP-85 then SRQ if set
RESET 7	Sets the HP-IB interface to its power-on state. If system turned off and then on again
RESUME 7	Sets ATN false [$\overline{ATN}$]
SEND 7;commands	Sends specified commands with ATN true. ATN is left true
SEND 7;data	Sends specified data with ATN false. ATN is left false
SPOLL (7)	Conducts a serial poll [ATN●SPE,$\overline{ATN}$,<data>,ATN●SPD,UNT]
SPOLL (724)	Addresses device 724 to talk then conducts serial poll [ATN●UNL,MLA,TAG,SPE,ATN,<data>,ATN●SPD,UNT]
STATUS 7,n;X	Sets X to the value of SRn
TRIGGER 7	Sends GET [ATN●GET]
TRIGGER 701	Addresses device 01, sends GET (Note: ATN is left true) [ATN●UNL,MTA,LAG,GET]

Figure 6.34 Continued

```
10 REMOTE 716
20 OUTPUT 716;"01F5"
30 ENTER 716;A$
40 PRINT A$
50 END
```

The command string in line 20 is made up of two codes:

> 01 enables output from locator onto the GPIB
> F5 selects frequency measurement

(Figure 6.35 shows some of the Solartron locator's command codes.)
On execution, the program prints the measurement returned from the locator, e.g.

FREQUENCY 0 Hz

Figure 6.36 shows a logic analyser trace of the bus activity during the frequency measurement.
The second program, shown below, again employs the locator to perform a frequency measurement. However, this time the GPIB control line SRQ is used to flag the controller that the locator has just completed its measurement.

```
20 ON INR 7 GOSUB 400
30 ENABLE INR 7;8
40 OUTPUT 716;"01F5Q3"
50 DISP "WAITING"
60 GOTO 50

400 ENTER 716;A$
410 DISP A$
420 S=SPOLL (716)
430 ENABLE INTR 7;8
440 RETURN
```

The program begins by enabling interrupts from the GPIB interface and informing BASIC that program flow has to be diverted to the subroutine starting at line 400 whenever the SRQ line is actuated.
Line 40 sets up the locator to measure frequency and includes the Q3 command, enabling it to make use of the SRQ line whenever data is available.
The following program statements, lines 50 and 60, then occupy the HP85 in a time wasting loop, waiting until an interrupt is received from the locator.
The interrupt routine at line 400 begins with the controller entering and displaying the frequency measurement. Performing a serial poll at line 420 releases the SRQ line and line 430 re-enables interrupts from the interface, allowing the controller to detect the next measurement. Finally, the return statement in line 440 forces the controller to continue with its repetitive display.

———— N ————

```
F00 :  return to READY state
F01 :  event count
F02 :  transition count
F03 :  period/width
F04 :  delay
F05 :  frequency
F06 :  signatures
F07 :  line signatures
F08 :  line data, centred on line hhhh

F09 :  current probe trigger, trigger at hhhh

F10 :  volts D.C.
F11 :  current D.C.
F12 :  resistance
F13 :  temperature
F14 :  self test
F15 :  logic level
F16 :     volts A.C.
F17 :  current A.C.
F18 :  option select:

          alarm recall              F18[A?]
          alarm entry               F18[A.1202]
          alarm off                 F18[B] or F18[P]
          time  recall              F18[C?]
          time  entry               F18[C.1150]
          GPIB version recall       F18[D?]
          main version recall       F18[E?]


F?  :  outputs current function ; 00 to 18
```

———— N ————

```
Q0 :  generate no SRQ's
Q1 :  generate SRQ's on error  (see table)
Q2 :  generate SRQ's on data available
Q3 :  generate SRQ's on error & data available
Q? :  outputs current state ; 0 , 1 , 2 or 3
```

```
Rnn : run for nn seconds then abort reading
R00 : off
R?  : outputs current state ; 00 to 99
```

```
S0 :  disable short bleeps
S1 :  enable short bleeps
S2 :  generate a short bleep
S? :  outputs current state ; 0, 1 or 2
```

```
T0 :  sample one reading at a time
T1 :  track taking readings continuously
T? :  outputs current state ; 0 or 1
```

Figure 6.35 Some of the locator's command set

```
STATE LISTING←←←←←←←←←←←←←←←←←←←←←←←←←←←←←←←←←←←←←←←←←←←←←←←←←←+++++
                                              SHIFT
LABEL>  ADDR    HPIB - ATN   MNEMONIC   HEX  EOI  SRQ  REN   IFC
BASE >  [HEX]   [                       ASM                    ]


[MARK]    X     [                    INSTRUCTIONS               ]


+0000*    1          ATN     *UNL*      3F             REN
+0001*    1          ATN     TAG←21     55             REN
+0002*    1          ATN     LAG←16     30             REN
+0003*    1          ATN     *UNL*      3F             REN
+0004*    1          ATN     TAG←21     55             REN
+0005*    1          ATN     LAG←16     30             REN
+0006     1                   0         4F             REN
+0007     1                   1         31             REN
+0008     1                   F         46             REN
+0009     1                   5         35             REN
+0010     1                  SPACE      20             REN
+0011     1                  SPACE      20             REN
+0012     1                  SPACE      20             REN
+0013     1                  SPACE      20             REN
+0014     1                  SPACE      20             REN
+0015     1                  SPACE      20             REN
+0016     1                  SPACE      20             REN
+0017     1                  SPACE      20             REN
+0018     1                  SPACE      20             REN
+0019     1                  SPACE      20             REN
+0020     1                  SPACE      20             REN
+0021     1                  SPACE      20             REN
+0022     1                  SPACE      20             REN
+0023     1                  SPACE      20             REN
+0024     1                  SPACE      20             REN
+0025     1                  SPACE      20             REN
+0026     1                  SPACE      20             REN
+0027     1                  <0D>       0D             REN
+0028     1                  <0A>       0A             REN
+0029*    1          ATN     *UNL*      3F             REN
+0030*    1          ATN     LAG←21     35             REN
+0031*    1          ATN     TAG←16     50             REN
+0032     1                   F         46             REN
+0033     1                   R         52             REN
+0034     1                   E         45             REN
+0035     1                   Q         51             REN
+0036     1                   U         55             REN
+0037     1                   E         45             REN
+0038     1                   N         4E             REN
+0039     1                   C         43             REN
+0040     1                   Y         59             REN
+0041     1                  SPACE      20             REN
+0042     1                  SPACE      20             REN
+0043     1                  SPACE      20             REN
+0044     1                  SPACE      20             REN
+0045     1                  SPACE      20             REN
+0046     1                  SPACE      20             REN
```

Figure 6.36 Logic analyser trace of bus activity during simple frequency measurement

LABEL>	ADDR	HPIB - ATN	MNEMONIC	HEX	EOI	SRQ	REN	IFC
BASE >	[HEX]	[		ASM				]

[MARK]	X	[	INSTRUCTIONS					]
+0047	1		SPACE	20			REN	
+0048	1		SPACE	20			REN	
+0049	1		SPACE	20			REN	
+0050	1		SPACE	20			REN	
+0051	1		0	30			REN	
+0052	1		SPACE	20			REN	
+0053	1		SPACE	20			REN	
+0054	1		H	48			REN	
+0055	1		Z	5A			REN	
+0056	1		SPACE	20			REN	
+0057	1		SPACE	20			REN	
+0058	1		SPACE	20			REN	
+0059	1		SPACE	20			REN	
+0060	1		SPACE	20			REN	
+0061	1		SPACE	20			REN	
+0062	1		SPACE	20			REN	
+0063	1		SPACE	20			REN	
+0064	1		SPACE	20			REN	
+0065	1		SPACE	20			REN	
+0066	1		SPACE	20			REN	
+0067	1		SPACE	20			REN	
+0068	1		SPACE	20			REN	
+0069	1		SPACE	20			REN	
+0070	1		SPACE	20			REN	
+0071	1		SPACE	20			REN	
+0072	1		SPACE	20			REN	
+0073	1		<0D>	0D			REN	
+0074	1		<0A>	0A			REN	

Figure 6.36 Continued

Figure 6.37 follows the bus activity in this more complex example. Notice how the SPE command (in line 0075 of the trace) clears the active state on the SRQ line.

6.3 KEYBOARDS

Full ASCII keyboards or simple hex keypads are usually made up of a set of switches arranged in the form of a matrix. Connecting each key to its own separate input would be wasteful, requiring over five 8-bit ports for a normal keyboard. Forming the keys into a matrix and using a scanning technique allows up to 256 keys to be interfaced with only two 8-bit ports.

Like most jobs with a computer, scanning can be carried out either by hardware or in software. Hardware encoded keyboards make use of special purpose chips to perform a number of tasks including detecting and encoding a depressed key. Software encoded keyboards normally employ a simple parallel port chip to form the electrical interface, leaving the host processor to perform the keyboard functions.

```
STATE LISTING←←←←←←←←←←←←←←←←←←←←←←←←←←←←←←←←←←←←←←←←←←←←←←←←←+

LABEL>   ADDR    HPIB - ATN   MNEMONIC   HEX   EOI   SRQ   REN   IFC
BASE >   [HEX]   [                       ASM                     ]


[MARK]    X      [                 INSTRUCTIONS                   ]


+0000*    1            ATN    *UNL*       3F                REN
+0001*    1            ATN    TAG←21      55                REN
+0002*    1            ATN    LAG←16      30                REN
+0003     1                   O           4F                REN
+0004     1                   1           31                REN
+0005     1                   F           46                REN
+0006     1                   5           35                REN
+0007     1                   Q           51                REN
+0008     1                   3           33                REN
+0009     1                   SPACE       20                REN
+0010     1                   SPACE       20                REN
+0011     1                   SPACE       20                REN
+0012     1                   SPACE       20                REN
+0013     1                   SPACE       20                REN
+0014     1                   SPACE       20                REN
+0015     1                   SPACE       20                REN
+0016     1                   SPACE       20                REN
+0017     1                   SPACE       20                REN
+0018     1                   SPACE       20                REN
+0019     1                   SPACE       20                REN
+0020     1                   SPACE       20                REN
+0021     1                   SPACE       20                REN
+0022     1                   SPACE       20                REN
+0023     1                   SPACE       20                REN
+0024     1                   <0D>        0D                REN
+0025     1                   <0A>        0A                REN
+0026*    1            ATN    *UNL*       3F          SRQ   REN
+0027*    1            ATN    LAG←21      35          SRQ   REN
+0028*    1            ATN    TAG←16      50          SRQ   REN
+0029     1                   F           46          SRQ   REN
+0030     1                   R           52          SRQ   REN
+0031     1                   E           45          SRQ   REN
+0032     1                   Q           51          SRQ   REN
+0033     1                   U           55          SRQ   REN
+0034     1                   E           45          SRQ   REN
+0035     1                   N           4E          SRQ   REN
+0036     1                   C           43          SRQ   REN
+0037     1                   Y           59          SRQ   REN
+0038     1                   SPACE       20          SRQ   REN
+0039     1                   SPACE       20          SRQ   REN
+0040     1                   SPACE       20          SRQ   REN
+0041     1                   SPACE       20          SRQ   REN
+0042     1                   SPACE       20          SRQ   REN
+0043     1                   SPACE       20          SRQ   REN
+0044     1                   SPACE       20          SRQ   REN
+0045     1                   SPACE       20          SRQ   REN
+0046     1                   SPACE       20          SRQ   REN
+0047     1                   SPACE       20          SRQ   REN
+0048     1                   0           30          SRQ   REN
```

Figure 6.37 Tracing bus activity throughout a routine which makes use of a serial poll

```
STATE LISTING‹‹‹‹‹‹‹‹‹‹‹‹‹‹‹‹‹‹‹‹‹‹‹‹‹‹‹‹‹‹‹‹‹‹‹‹‹‹‹‹‹‹‹‹‹

LABEL>   ADDR    HPIB - ATN   MNEMONIC   HEX   EOI   SRQ   REN   IFC
BASE >   [HEX]   [                       ASM                     ]


[MARK]     X     [                  INSTRUCTIONS                 ]


+0049      1                  SPACE      20          SRQ   REN
+0050      1                  SPACE      20          SRQ   REN
+0051      1                    H        48          SRQ   REN
+0052      1                    Z        5A          SRQ   REN
+0053      1                  SPACE      20          SRQ   REN
+0054      1                  SPACE      20          SRQ   REN
+0055      1                  SPACE      20          SRQ   REN
+0056      1                  SPACE      20          SRQ   REN
+0057      1                  SPACE      20          SRQ   REN
+0058      1                  SPACE      20          SRQ   REN
+0059      1                  SPACE      20          SRQ   REN
+0060      1                  SPACE      20          SRQ   REN
+0061      1                  SPACE      20          SRQ   REN
+0062      1                  SPACE      20          SRQ   REN
+0063      1                  SPACE      20          SRQ   REN
+0064      1                  SPACE      20          SRQ   REN
+0065      1                  SPACE      20          SRQ   REN
+0066      1                  SPACE      20          SRQ   REN
+0067      1                  SPACE      20          SRQ   REN
+0068      1                  SPACE      20          SRQ   REN
+0069      1                  SPACE      20          SRQ   REN
+0070      1                  <0D>       0D          SRQ   REN
+0071      1                  <0A>       0A          SRQ   REN
+0072*     1        ATN       *UNL*      3F          SRQ   REN
+0073*     1        ATN       LAG←21     35          SRQ   REN
+0074*     1        ATN       TAG←16     50          SRQ   REN
+0075*     1        ATN        SPE       18          SRQ   REN
+0076      1                    H        48                REN
+0077*     1        ATN        SPD       19                REN
+0078*     1        ATN       *UNT*      5F                REN
+0079*     1        ATN       *UNL*      3F                REN
+0080*     1        ATN       LAG←21     35                REN
+0081*     1        ATN       TAG←16     50                REN
+0082      1                    F        46          SRQ   REN
+0083      1                    R        52          SRQ   REN
+0084      1                    E        45          SRQ   REN
+0085      1                    Q        51          SRQ   REN
+0086      1                    U        55          SRQ   REN
+0087      1                    E        45          SRQ   REN
+0088      1                    N        4E          SRQ   REN
+0089      1                    C        43          SRQ   REN
+0090      1                    Y        59          SRQ   REN
+0091      1                  SPACE      20
+0092      1                  SPACE
+0093      1
+0094
```

Figure 6.37 Continued

194

Key
pressed

Key
released

Figure 6.38   Key bounce on closing and opening a switch

Switch bounce   One problem found with all keyboards is switch bounce. Whenever a mechanical switch is closed or opened, the contacts will make and break several times before coming to rest, Figure 6.38. This bounce can last for several milliseconds and can mislead both scanning techniques. The solution is to wait for approximately 30 milliseconds after detecting a depressed key, before any attempt is made to determine its position in the matrix. Again, either hardware or software strategies are possible. Figure 6.39 shows a typical debounce circuit using two NAND gates. The software solution takes the form of a simple delay routine.

Rollover   Close examination of a typist's fingers will reveal that before a key is released, a second and even third key has been pressed. On a low cost keyboard these extra keystrokes will be lost, masked by the first depressed key. However, more sophisticated systems will exhibit two- or even three-key rollover, with either the hardware or the software reporting the keystrokes in their correct order.

Keyboard interface   The 'walking ones' pattern used to perform a software scan of a matrix keyboard was examined in the previous chapter

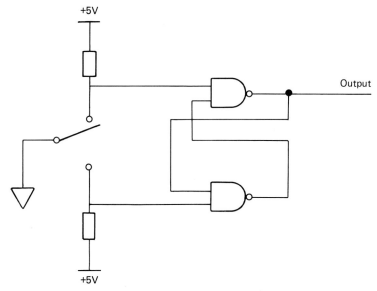

Figure 6.39   Debounce circuit using two NAND gates

195

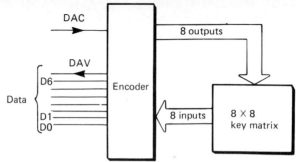

Figure 6.40   Keyboard encoder

(section 5.3). Hardware keyboard encoders have the advantage of releasing the microprocessor from time-consuming keyboard routines. In addition a good encoder chip will also solve the problems of keybounce and rollover. Figure 6.40 illustrates a typical hardware encoder. Like the software routine, the encoder uses a scanning technique to determine the position of the key in the matrix. Having found the depressed key, it loads its output register with the key code and sets its data valid (DAV) handshake line true. After the microprocessor has read the output register it replies to the encoder by transmitting a pulse to its data accepted (DAC) input.

Two strategies can be employed to service a keyboard: *polling* and *interrupt driven*. With the former the keyboard is periodically checked to see if a key is available. The example above has been configured for polling by including the data valid strobe as part of the encoder's output register. To test for data, the processor only has to read the output register and test bit 7.

Obviously, an interrupt driven keyboard is more efficient, allowing the processor to spend its time on other tasks, only giving the keyboard attention when required. If the same encoder was to be used to generate an interrupt, then the data valid line would be taken directly to the microprocessor's interrupt input. Some processors (e.g. the Z80) would also provide an interrupt acknowledge signal that would complete the data handshake.

6.4   CRT DISPLAY INTERFACE

The dramatic fall in memory costs has resulted in even the humblest personal computer offering a display of coloured text and graphics. Domestic televisions are by far the most popular form of CRT (Cathode Ray Tube) display, providing satisfactory presentation of text up to approximately 40 characters across the screen. However, most professional applications would make use of video monitors, providing higher quality displays with increased resolution, allowing more characters per line as well as finer detail in the construction of characters or graphics shapes.

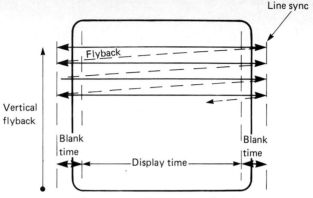

Figure 6.41 Raster scan display

The circuitry required to print characters and graphics onto a CRT can be fairly complex, especially if built from discrete logic components. Several chip manufacturers are now producing single chip CRT controllers that help simplify the task, e.g. Motorola's 6845 and 6847, or Intel's 8275.

Before examining how these controllers function it is necessary to understand the fundamentals of a CRT raster-scan display. Figure 6.41 shows the pattern swept out by the electron beam as it scans 313 lines across the screen to form one frame. In the second frame the beam fills in the gaps between the first set of lines, in a technique called interlacing, leading to a picture containing 625 lines. However, many microcomputer applications do not utilise interlace and make do with a single scan.

Two synchronisation signals control the motion of the beam on the screen. The horizontal or line sync produces the flyback at the end of each line and the vertical sync produces the vertical flyback, to the start of the first line, at the end of each frame, Figure 6.42.

Most microcomputers make use of a memory mapped screen with some of the system memory set aside to hold characters, normally in ASCII format. Screen memory is addressable by both the microprocessor and the CRT controller, with a multiplexer governing which gains access. Figure 6.43 shows one possible arrangement. With two components

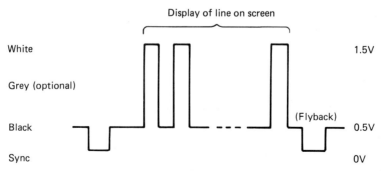

Figure 6.42 Composite video and sync

197

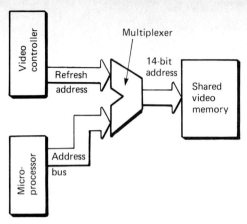

Figure 6.43 A multiplexer controls access to shared video memory

competing for the same block of memory it is important that some strategy is employed that prevents collisions. One common technique, easily implemented with the 680X/650X microprocessor families, is to allow the CRT controller access to the memory in the first half of the cycle and the processor in the second half. Since the processor normally never requires access during the first half-cycle, there is never any contention for memory and all CRT accesses are said to be *transparent*, Figure 6.44.

As well as external RAM, most CRT controllers require a character generator ROM that stores the dot patterns for the ASCII character set. Typically, characters are made up of a dot matrix 5 wide by 7 deep.

Figure 6.45 shows a typical character generator ROM. The address lines are split into two groups. One set presents the 7-bit ASCII code from the selected memory location and the other a row address provided by the CRT controller. As the electron beam moves to a new line the controller will increment the row address, releasing a row of dots making up a horizontal 'slice' through each character.

The parallel output from the character generator is converted to serial format using a shift register driven by a master video clock signal. The resulting bit stream of 1s and 0s then provides the intensity modulation of the electron beam as it scans across the CRT.

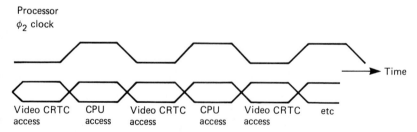

Figure 6.44 CRTC performing transparent access to video memory

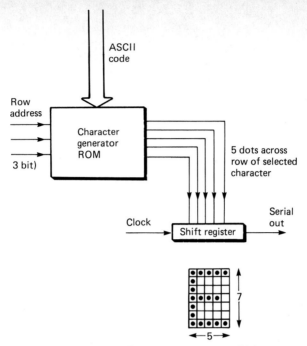

Figure 6.45 Character generator ROM

The Motorola 6845 CRT controller, shown in Figure 6.46, provides all of the signals described above as well as some extra features. The signals include:

Refresh address   14-bit address of the character that is being 'refreshed' on the screen.

Row address   five address outputs that can be used to select the row in a character generator ROM.

Cursor   This output is used to produce a moveable cursor on the display. The position of the cursor can be adjusted under program control using two internal registers in the 6845.

CRT control   The 6845 generates three CRT control signals: vertical sync, horizontal sync, and a display enable signal that indicates that the CRTC is currently supplying a refresh address in the active display area.

Light pen input   This input allows a light pen to detect the position of the spot on the screen by strobing the current contents of the refresh register into special light pen registers that can then be interrogated under program control. To the microprocessor the 6845 CRTC appears as two memory locations. One location acts as an address select, allowing the

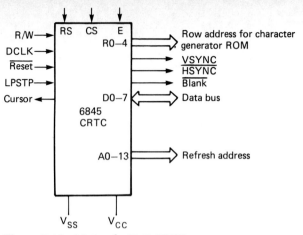

Figure 6.46 Motorola 6845 CRTC

programmer to choose one of its 18 internal registers. Communication with the chosen register then takes place through the second location, Figure 6.47.

Memory Address	Register		Function
(M)		Address register	Pointer to one of 18 on-board registers
(M+1)	R0	Horizontal total	Determines horizontal frequency of HS
	R1	Horizontal displayed	No. of displayed characters/line
	R2	Horizontal synchronised position	Determines horizontal synchronised position on line
	R3	Horizontal synchronised width	Determines width of HS pulse
	R4	Vertical total	Determines vertical frequency
	R5	Vertical total adjust	of vertical or frame sync.
	R6	Vertical displayed	Determines No. of displayed character rows
	R7	Vertical synchronised position	Determines the position of vertical synchronised pulse
	R8	Interlace mode	Selects one of two interlace modes
	R9	Max scan line address	Determines the number of scan lines/character row
	R10	Cursor start	Controls cursor form, also sets
	R11	Cursor end	cursor start and end scan line
	R12	Start address (high)	Determines first address put out
	R13	Start address (low)	as a refresh address (14 bits)
	R14	Cursor high	Stores cursor
	R15	Cursor low	location (14 bits)
	R16	Light pen high	Hold the position address register
	R17	Light pen low	when light pen strobe is received

Figure 6.47 6845 registers

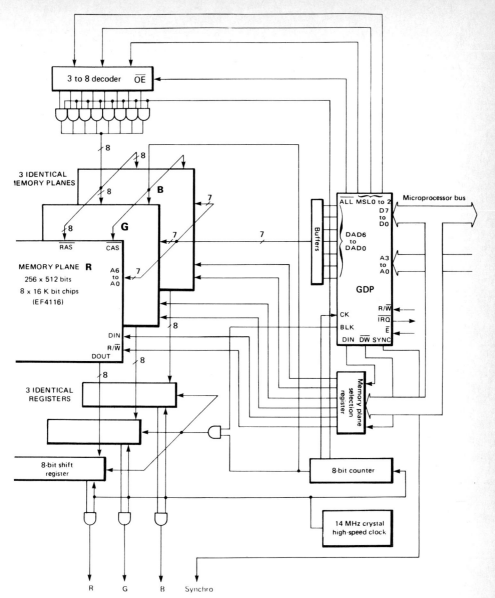

Figure 6.48 Thomson EF9365 graphics display processor

Display processors

One of the disadvantages of many CRTC shared video memory systems is that valuable microprocessor time is wasted managing the layout of text and graphics on the screen, e.g. routines are required to clear the screen, construct text other than that in the character generator ROM, draw graphics, etc. A relatively new arrival is the Graphics Display Processor (GDP), a microprocessor dedicated to graphics applications, complete with on-chip routines for fast production of line graphics as well as a number of character fonts. Working in parallel with the host system's processor, the GDP relieves the host of much of the display management overhead.

One of the first devices on the market was Thomson's EF9365, Figure 6.48. The 9365 makes use of its own display memory which is not part of the system memory map. In maximum configuration three planes of 16 Kbytes provide sufficient memory to support a display of 256 × 512 resolution in eight colours. To the host system the 9365 occupies only 16 memory locations for its 11 internal registers, Figure 6.49. Along with controlling the production of line graphics, the registers also allow the on-chip ASCII character set to be produced in a number of sizes and orientations, Figure 6.50.

6.5 MEMORY SYSTEMS

Integrated circuit, or semiconductor, memories are now the universally accepted form of memory in microprocessor systems. Some of these devices were introduced in Chapter 1, along with brief details of how they could be interfaced to a microprocessor. This section examines memory components in more detail. However, before beginning, it is of value to define some of the terms used to describe memories and their operation.

Cell   A device within a memory that can store a single bit of information, e.g. a flip-flop.

Word   A group of one or more cells that contain a single item of data. Some memories have words containing only a single bit, while others support 4- or 8-bit words. (An 8-bit word is given the special name *byte*.)

Storage Capacity   This is the term used for the total number of cells within a memory. For example, a 4096 × 1-bit memory can store 4096 words of 1-bit length. Its capacity is 4096 bits or 4 K. A 1024 × 8-bit memory can store 1024 eight-bit words, giving it a storage capacity of 8192 bits or 8 K.

Random Access   A memory for which the location of the data does not affect the time taken to write or read the data is known as random access memory.

Tri-state Logic   Tri-state logic circuits operate at normal logic levels when enabled (i.e. logic 0 and logic 1), but present a high impedance (open circuit) when disabled.

Read and Write Cycle Times   The cycle time is the minimum time that can be taken between successive memory read or memory write operations.

Access Time   This is the time from the start of a read operation to the point where the memory has produced valid data at its outputs. At first glance this might appear to be the same as the read cycle time. However,

ADDRESS REGISTER				REGISTER FUNCTIONS		Number
Binary			Hexa	Read	Write	of
A3	A2	A1	A0	R/$\overline{W}$ = 1	R/$\overline{W}$ = 0	bits
0	0	0	0	0	STATUS	CMD	8
0	0	0	1	1	CTRL 1 (Write control and interrupt control)		7
0	0	1	0	2	CTRL 2 (Vector and symbol type control)		4
0	0	1	1	3	CSIZE (Character size)		8
0	1	0	0	4	Reserved		—
0	1	0	1	5	DELTAX		8
0	1	1	0	6	Reserved		—
0	1	1	1	7	DELTAY		8
1	0	0	0	8	X MSBs		4
1	0	0	1	9	X LSBs		8
1	0	1	0	A	Y MSBs		4
1	0	1	1	B	Y LSBs		8
1	1	0	0	C	XLP (Light-pen)	Reserved	7
1	1	0	1	D	YLP (Light-pen)	Reserved	8
1	1	1	0	E	Reserved		—
1	1	1	1	F	Reserved		—

Reserved :   These addresses are reserved for future versions of the circuit. In read mode, output buffers D0-D7 force a high state on the data bus.

COMMAND REGISTER

	b7 b6 b5 b4	0 0 0 0	0 0 0 1	0 0 1 0	0 0 1 1	0 1 0 0	0 1 0 1	0 1 1 0	0 1 1 1	1 0 0 0	1 0 0 1	1 0 1 0	1 0 1 1	1 1 0 0	1 1 0 1	1 1 1 0	1 1 1 1
b3 b2 b1 b0		0	1	2	3	4	5	6	7	8	9	A	B	C	D	E	F
0 0 0 0 0	Set bit 1 of CTRL1 : Pen selection			SPACE	0	@	P	`	p								
0 0 0 1 1	Clear bit 1 of CTRL 1 : Eraser selection			!	1	A	Q	a	q								
0 0 1 0 2	Set bit 0 of CTRL1 : Pen/Eraser down selection			"	2	B	R	b	r								
0 0 1 1 3	Clear bit 0 of CTRL 1 : Pen/Eraser up selection			#	3	C	S	c	s								
0 1 0 0 4	Clear screen			$	4	D	T	d	t								
0 1 0 1 5	X and Y registers reset to 0			%	5	E	U	e	u								
0 1 1 0 6	X and Y reset to 0 and clear screen			&	6	F	V	f	v								
0 1 1 1 7	Clear screen, set CSIZE to code "minsize" All other registers reset to 0 (except XLP, YLP)			'	7	G	W	g	w								
1 0 0 0 8	Light-pen initialization (WHITE forced low)			(	8	H	X	h	x								
1 0 0 1 9	Light-pen initialization			)	9	I	Y	i	y								
1 0 1 0 A	5 x 8 block drawing (size according to CSIZE)			*	:	J	Z	j	z								
1 0 1 1 B	4 x 4 block drawing (size according to CSIZE)			+	;	K	[	k	{								
1 1 0 0 C	Screen scanning : Pen or Eraser as defined by CTRL1			,	<	L	\	l	¦								
1 1 0 1 D	X register reset to 0			−	=	M	]	m	}								
1 1 1 0 E	Y register reset to 0			.	>	N	↑	n	—								
1 1 1 1 F	Direct image memory access request for the next free cycle.			/	?	O	←	o	▨								

SMALL VECTOR DEFINITION :

b7	b6 b5	b4 b3	b2 b1 b0
1	$|\Delta X|$	$|\Delta Y|$	Direction

Dimension

ΔX or ΔY		Vector length
0	0	0 step
0	1	1 step
1	0	2 steps
1	1	3 steps

Direction

```
        010
011  ↖ ↑ ↗  001
110  ← + →  000
111  ↙ ↓ ↘  101
        100
```

Figure 6.49   Display processor's internal registers

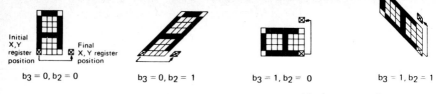

Initial X,Y register position   Final X,Y register position

b3 = 0, b2 = 0   b3 = 0, b2 = 1   b3 = 1, b2 = 0   b3 = 1, b2 = 1

Figure 6.50   ASCII character set is programmable for size and orientation

many memory devices are not capable of entering a new memory read cycle as soon as they have produced data. As a result, a memory's read cycle time is usually slightly longer than its access time.

Read and Write Cycle Timing   To help in the selection of a memory device, manufacturers' data sheets contain tables of critical parameters, detailing the memory's performance. Some of these parameters are displayed graphically in the form of a timing diagram.

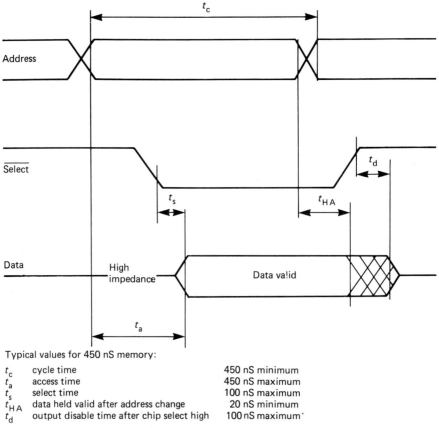

Typical values for 450 nS memory:

t_c	cycle time	450 nS minimum
t_a	access time	450 nS maximum
t_s	select time	100 nS maximum
t_{HA}	data held valid after address change	20 nS minimum
t_d	output disable time after chip select high	100 nS maximum·

Figure 6.51   Typical memory read cycle

Figure 6.51 shows a typical read cycle. The cycle begins with some device (normally the microprocessor) placing the address of the chosen data item on the memory's address pins. In order to access the data, the address must remain stable throughout the entire time the data is being read.

If the memory device has not been previously selected, by pulling its Select SEL (or Chip Select, CS) input low, this must also be done. Memories with tri-state data lines will then remain in a high impedance state for a time t_s – the select time. After this delay, valid data will appear on the data lines. The time between valid address and valid data is the access time – t_a (normally specified as a maximum value). If the address is now changed, the data lines will remain steady for a time t_{HA} – the data hold time after an address change. Removal of the select signal will result

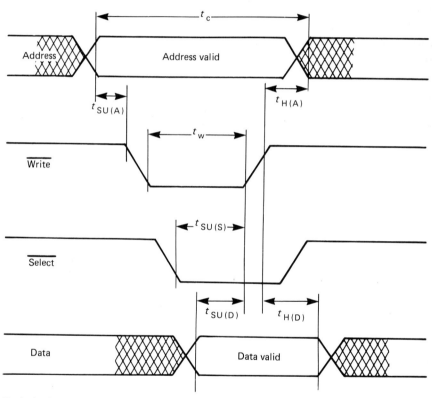

Typical values for 450 nS memory:

t_c	cycle time	450 nS minimum
t_w	write pulse width	200 nS minimum
$t_{SU(A)}$	set up time for address	0
$t_{SU(S)}$	set up time for chip select	200 nS minimum
$t_{SU(D)}$	set up time for data	200 nS minimum
$t_{H(D)}$	hold time for data	0

Hold times are not always zero but can be of the order of 10 – 20 nS

Figure 6.52 Memory write cycle

in new, and possibly changing, data appearing on the data lines for a time t_d – the disable time, before the lines return to a high impedance state.

A typical memory write cycle is shown in Figure 6.52. Again the cycle begins with the application of a binary address on the memory's address inputs. Normally a short time, known as the address set-up time – $t_{SU(A)}$, is allowed before exhorting the write enable signal WRITE. This delay gives the memory time to locate the required word in memory. (For some devices $t_{SU(A)}$ can be zero.) After $t_{SU(A)}$, the write enable line can be made active and must remain so for at least t_w – the smallest write pulse width. If the memory device is not selected, then SEL must be activated for at least $t_{SU(S)}$ – the set-up time for the chip select, before the write enable signal is removed.

To ensure a successful write operation, data has to remain valid for at least a time of $t_{SU(D)}$ – the data set-up time, before the write enable signal is removed. Further, data must continue to remain stable for a time $t_{H(D)}$ – the data hold time, after the write enable signal is removed (with some memories this time can also be as low as zero).

Finally, the address has to remain valid for a time $t_{H(A)}$ – the address hold time, after the WRITE is removed.

Although the terminology used here for the various time delays is adopted by many manufacturers, it is not a standard and some data sheets may use slightly different terms. However, the parameters described do define the important times that have to be taken into account when selecting memory to operate with a given microprocessor running at a particular clock frequency. For example, Intel's 8085A-2 microprocessor makes use of a 5 MHz internal clock and expects data to be valid two clock cycles after the address has been set up (i.e. in 400 ns). Therefore for satisfactory operation, memory with an access time less than 400 ns must be used, e.g. 350 ns memory would be satisfactory.

Read only memories

Read only memories are non-volatile, providing a means of permanently storing programs and data. Normally ROMs are programmed either by the manufacturer or the user before they are incorporated in a microprocessor system. Depending on the programming technique, ROMs can be divided into a number of categories.

1. *Fusible Link ROMs* are supplied with each cell containing an unbroken link representing the logic 0 state. In the programming procedure a suitable voltage is used to break those links that have to be set to logic 1. Figure 6.53 shows one example, the 74S288, a 32 × 8-bit ROM with tri-state outputs. Programming is carried out one bit at a time by pulling the required data line low while all the others are held at +5 V using 3K9 pull-up resistors. The V_{cc} supply to the whole chip is increased to +10.5 V and the chip select line activated for the required programming time.

2. *Mask Programmable ROMs* are programmed by the IC manufacturer using a photographic mask to establish the electrical interconnections on the chip. A special mask has to be made for each program

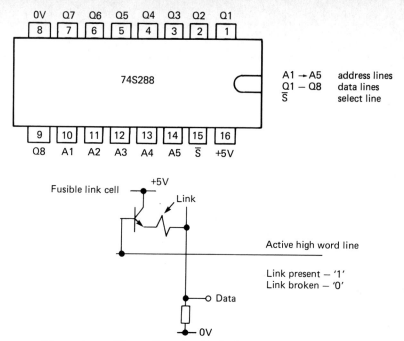

Figure 6.53   The 74S288 fusible link programmable ROM

stored in the ROM and since the set-up costs are relatively high, the whole exercise only becomes economic when producing large quantities of identical ROMs.

3. *Ultra-violet Erasable ROMs* are user-programmable, and as the name suggests, easily erased, allowing them to be reprogrammed with new information. A typical example of an EPROM is the 2716, Figure 6.54. Along with the normal address, data and select lines, the 2716 has an output enable pin and a programming supply pin. The chip enable, CE, also acts as a programming pin.

When erased, all the 2716's 2 K × 8 bits are set to 1. The programming procedure changes the required data bits to 0. (Programmed bits are stored as charges on small, low leakage capacitors. The application of UV light alters the insulation and allows the charge to escape.) Programming is carried out simultaneously on all bits that have to be changed at each address. The V_{pp} pin is connected to a +25 V supply (instead of the normal operating voltage of +5 V) and the output enable pin held at +5 V. After establishing the required address and data, the programming pin is held high for a period of 50 to 55 ms to record the data.

Although EPROMs are more expensive than mask programmed ROMs, they are extremely useful for prototypes or small volume applications.

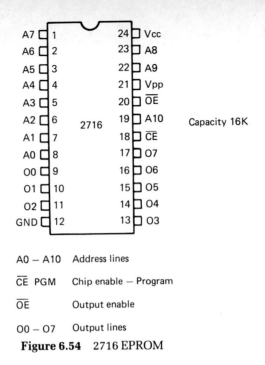

	2716		
A7 ☐ 1		24 ☐ Vcc	
A6 ☐ 2		23 ☐ A8	
A5 ☐ 3		22 ☐ A9	
A4 ☐ 4		21 ☐ Vpp	
A3 ☐ 5		20 ☐ OE	
A2 ☐ 6		19 ☐ A10	Capacity 16K
A1 ☐ 7		18 ☐ CE	
A0 ☐ 8		17 ☐ O7	
O0 ☐ 9		16 ☐ O6	
O1 ☐ 10		15 ☐ O5	
O2 ☐ 11		14 ☐ O4	
GND ☐ 12		13 ☐ O3	

A0 – A10   Address lines

$\overline{CE}$ PGM   Chip enable – Program

$\overline{OE}$ Output enable

O0 – O7   Output lines

Figure 6.54   2716 EPROM

4. *Electrically Alterable ROMs* or EAROMs have two main advantages over EPROMs: they can be both erased and programmed using electrical signals, while still within a circuit. However, at present they remain expensive.

Read/write memories
Read/write memory, commonly known as RAM, forms the main working store for programs and data in almost all microcomputers. There are two common forms of RAM currently available: static and dynamic.

Static RAM   Each cell in a static RAM is a basic circuit element called a 'flip-flop' made up of two or more transistors. Each flip-flop can exist in one of two states: the set state represents logic 1 and the reset state corresponds to logic 0.
    The memory is termed static since each flip-flop or cell will remain in its programmed state indefinitely, unless the power is removed or new data is recorded.
    Figure 6.55 illustrates a 6116, 2 K × 8-bit static RAM, one of a new breed of devices offered in a 24 pin package, pin compatible with standard 16 K EPROMs and ROMs. Using CMOS chip fabrication technology, the 6116 uses considerably less power than earlier NMOS static RAMs, making it an ideal candidate for appications requiring battery back-up.

Dynamic RAM   Dynamic memory, unlike static memory, cannot hold its recorded data indefinitely without the help of external support circuitry.

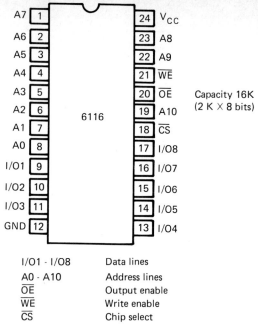

A7	1	24	V_{CC}

Capacity 16K
(2 K × 8 bits)

Figure 6.55   6116 static RAM

I/O1 - I/O8	Data lines
A0 - A10	Address lines
$\overline{OE}$	Output enable
$\overline{WE}$	Write enable
$\overline{CS}$	Chip select

The problem arises from data being stored as electrical charge in tiny capacitors (in reality each capacitor is formed by the gate input on a transistor). No charge represents the logic 0 state and a fully charged capacitor represents logic 1. Unfortunately over a period of a few milliseconds the capacitors will discharge, with a resulting loss of data. To overcome this problem, external refresh circuitry performs a periodic read operation (typically every 2 ms), replacing any charge lost by leakage.

In addition to increased storage capacity (64 K × 1-bit devices are now commonplace), dynamic RAMs have a relatively low cost and power consumption. However, on the debit side, they require the extra complexity and expense of additional refresh circuitry.

The 4816 is an example of a recent 16 K × 1-bit dynamic RAM, Figure 6.56. Unlike earlier devices which required a dual +5 V, +12 V supply, the 4816 operates from a single +5 V supply. Internally the 16 384 storage cells are arranged in the form of a lattice with 128 rows and 128 columns.

To reduce the overall package size, the 4816, in common with other dynamic RAMs, makes use of multiplexed addressing. As a result, only seven address lines are needed, along with two control signals: Row Address Select (RAS) and Column Address Select (CAS), to address the chip's 16 K locations.

Figure 6.57 illustrates one method of interfacing the 4816 to a microprocessor's address bus. Memory access begins with the processor, along with some additional circuitry, supplying a valid row address (the least significant seven address lines in the Figure) and activating the RAS

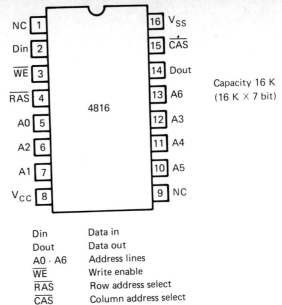

NC	1	16	V_{SS}
Din	2	15	$\overline{CAS}$
$\overline{WE}$	3	14	Dout
$\overline{RAS}$	4	13	A6
A0	5	12	A3
A2	6	11	A4
A1	7	10	A5
V_{CC}	8	9	NC

4816

Capacity 16 K
(16 K × 7 bit)

Din	Data in
Dout	Data out
A0 - A6	Address lines
$\overline{WE}$	Write enable
$\overline{RAS}$	Row address select
$\overline{CAS}$	Column address select

Figure 6.56   4816 dynamic RAM

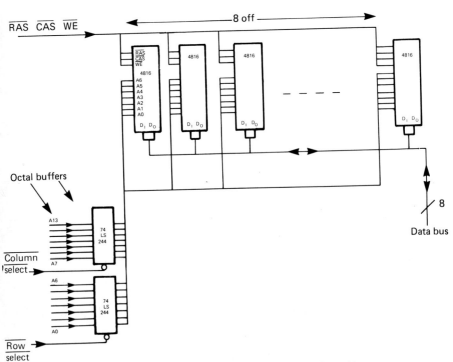

Figure 6.57   Interfacing the 4816's multiplexed address lines to a
microprocessor's address bus

control line. A valid column address is then supplied (from address bus lines A7 to A13) and the column address select line, CAS, activated. The chip now has the full 14-bit address required to locate the desired cell and the interchange of data can take place.

The extra circuitry required to perform memory refresh is shown in Figure 6.58. If each cell had to be refreshed independently, the whole process would take an unacceptably long time. In common with other dynamic memories, the 4816 can refresh a complete row of cells in one operation. As a result, only 128 refresh cycles are required every 2 ms.

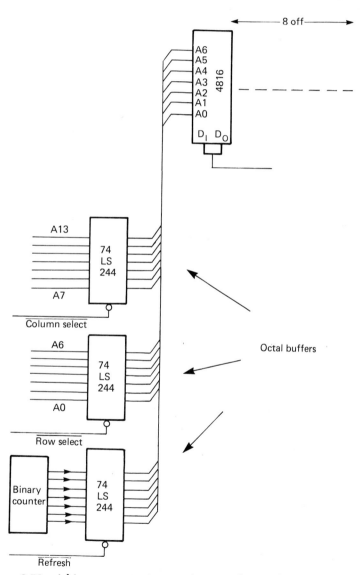

Figure 6.58 A binary counter is sometimes used to perform dynamic memory refresh

To ensure that each row obtains the necessary refresh activity, many systems make use of a binary counter to supply a refresh address at some convenient time in the system cycle, e.g. when the microprocessor is not making use of the memory.

Some microprocessors (e.g. the Zilog Z80) come complete with a built-in counter or *refresh register*. During periods when the processor is decoding operation codes, the current contents of the counter are placed on the lower half of the address bus performing a 'transparent' refresh of a number of dynamic memory cells.

Selecting RAM When selecting RAM for either a new system or to provide a memory expansion to an existing system, a number of factors have to be taken into account. Manufacturer's literature will provide details of the memory's speed, capacity and power consumption. However, prior to any detailed investigation, a decision has to be made on the memory type: static or dynamic.

Static memories are much easier to interface and are usually the best choice for small systems (up to about 8 Kbytes). In larger systems, the cost and power savings associated with dynamic memory will override the expense of the extra control circuitry.

It is worth drawing attention to one application area where dynamic memory has proved to be the ideal choice. Many general purpose microcomputers utilise a memory mapped screen, making use of a CRT controller chip, or discrete logic, to periodically read the display memory and update the screen (e.g. the BBC micro, Apple II). With careful circuit design, this periodic access can also act as the memory refresh, cancelling the need for special refresh circuitry.

6.6 FLOPPY AND HARD DISK SYSTEMS

Although magnetic tape provides a low cost method of storing information, it suffers from a major disadvantage in that all data must be accessed sequentially. Some tape devices utilise fast forward and reverse techniques to reduce the time needed to reach a desired data item, but compared with other media, it remains slow. As a result, tape in the form of cassettes or cartridges is employed mainly for archiving or backing up important programs and files.

Most microcomputer systems today make use of magnetic disks for 'on-line' storage applications where information has to be located, read and then modified in real time. Disks are available in a number of different forms ranging from miniature removable floppies to fixed high storage capacity Winchesters. Unlike tape systems, disk drives are designed to allow random/sequential access to data and as a result are much faster. However, on the debit side, they also require more sophisticated control electronics at a correspondingly higher cost.

Floppy disks
The recording medium on a floppy disk is a coating of magnetic material on both sides of a thin plastic disk. To provide protection and help maintain its shape while spinning within the drive, the disk is enclosed

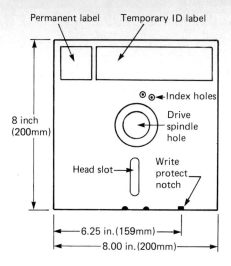

SA 104/105/124

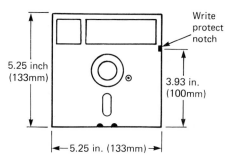

Figure 6.59 Floppy disk

within a protective jacket, Figure 6.59. In most drives the disk rotates at a fixed speed of approximately 360 rpm.

Until recently only two disk sizes were in common use: The 8 inch and the 5¼ inch or mini-floppy. However, rapid market changes have seen the appearance of sub-5¼ inch drives, from America and Japan, in a range of sizes: 3 inch, 3¼ inch and 3½ inch, Figure 6.60.

Tracks All formats give the read/write head access to the magnetic coating through a radial slot. Similar to a domestic tape recorder, the head contains tiny coils that enable it to write or read magnetic pulses on the disk surface. The drive mechanism only allows the head to move in radial increments or steps to one of a number of fixed positions where data is written or read in circular paths called tracks. The beginning of each track is located optically by means of a small index hole punched through the disk.

The standard 8 inch IBM 3740 disk format has 77 concentric tracks numbered 0 to 76, with track 0 lying around the outside edge of the disk.

Figure 6.60   Sub-5 ¼ inch disks

No real standard exists for miniature floppies. However, the latest advances have led to 5¼ inch drives with 80 tracks at track densities of 96 tracks/inch being commonplace.

Double sided drives employ two read/write heads to effectively double the number of tracks and hence the storage capacity. With double sided disks, two track numbering or access schemes are commonly in use: *wrap access* and *incremental access*. With the former, track 0 starts at the outside edge of one side (side 0) and continues on the outside edge of the other side (side 1). Track 1 is then made up of the next pair of top and bottom tracks, etc. Therefore a double sided disk with 80 tracks on each side, configured for wrap access, would contain tracks numbered from 0 to 79.

Incremental access again labels the outside track on side 0 as track zero, but then continues the numbering down the same side towards the centre of the disk. On reaching the innermost track on side 0, the numbering then continues on the innermost track on side 1, and increments as the head moves back towards the outside edge. Taking a double sided 80 track drive as an example would give track 0 at the outside edge of side 0, track 79 at the inside edge of side 0, track 80 on the inside edge of side 1, and finally track 159 on the outside edge of side 1.

Sectors   Each track is divided into a number of sectors, splitting the disk into regions shaped like slices of cake, Figure 6.61. Two techniques are used to define the sector boundaries: *hard sectoring* and *soft sectoring*.

With hard sectoring, holes similar to the index hole divide the disk into a number of sectors (32 with an 8 inch disk, 10 with a 5¼ inch disk).

In the soft sectoring technique the number of sectors is defined by the user. Each sector is identified by a marker or code written to the disk by the disk controller. (The 8 inch IBM format mentioned earlier uses soft sectoring to divide each track into 26 sectors.)

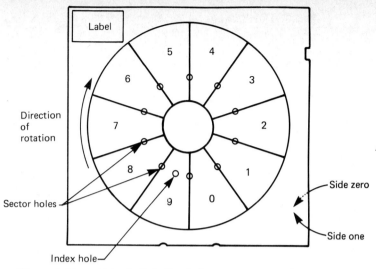

Figure 6.61   5 ¼ inch disk divided into 10 sectors (hard sectoring)

Both techniques are widely adopted with both 5¼ inch and 8 inch disks, with no significant advantage of one over the other. However, by eliminating the need for sector markers, hard sectoring will allow slightly more information to be stored on the disk. On the other hand, soft sectoring provides a unique identifier for each sector resulting in higher reliability.

Data recording   Data is recorded along tracks in a bit serial, byte serial format. Two standard recording techniques are used to combine data together with a clock signal onto a floppy. The single density technique is known as Frequency Modulation (FM) or double frequency recording. FM is the simplest to implement with each data bit written to the disk framed between two clocking bits. Therefore when reading the disk, each data bit is self-clocked into the controller by the clock bits already on the disk, Figure 6.62. Using this technique, 256 bytes of data can be stored in each sector, leading to a total storage capacity of $256 \times 10 \times 80 \times 2$ or 400 Kbytes on a single density, 80 track, double sided disk 5¼ inch floppy.

The encoding technique used for double density recording is known as Modified Frequency Modulation (MFM). Unlike FM encoding, MFM is not self clocking, with clock bits only written to the disk if both the previous and the present data bit is a zero, Figure 6.63. As a result, MFM encoded disks need improved decoding techniques to recover the data,

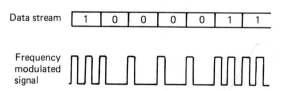

Figure 6.62   Frequency modulation or double frequency recording

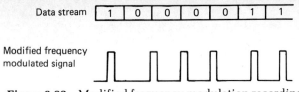

Figure 6.63 Modified frequency modulation recording

requiring the generation of a clock signal locked in time and phase to the incoming data stream.

With a double density technique, 512 bytes can be stored in each sector, with the result that the total capacity of a double sided 80 track disk increases to 800 Kbytes.

Disk controller The disk controller provides the interface between the micro and the disk drive, converting software commands issued by the Disk Operating System (DOS) into the electrical signals needed to control the drive. A number of different designs are available ranging from boards containing discrete logic to special purpose LSI single chip controllers such as Intel's 8272. Some controller boards contain their own microprocessor (e.g. Comart's C-IFDC employs a Z80) to form an 'intelligent floppy disk interface' which performs a number of high level functions, including:

- track buffering
- on-board diagnostics available through its own RS-232 serial interface
- error detection and reporting with automatic retry
- software configuration for different types of drive.

However, the following list represents the basic functions required of any controller:

Select drive typically one controller is capable of managing four separate drives. Each drive is given a unique identity, usually by configuring small jumpers. Issuing a drive select command to the controller allows it to enable the selected drive.

Seek track a sequence of step pulses together with a direction input are used to move the head to a given track. A special track 0 signal informs the controller that the head has reached the outermost track and can move no further even if extra step commands are given.

Read/write sector the controller is responsible for choosing when the head has to be brought in contact with the disk and also when the head has settled sufficiently to allow data transfer. In a similar manner to RAM, a write gate signal is used to define the direction of data transfer.

Data separation the information read from the disk is a serial stream made up of data and clock pulses. Before transfer to the micro system the two signals have to be separated and the data converted to parallel format.

Error detection   errors can occur while transferring data to or from a disk. Write operations are usually checked by performing a read during the next revolution of the disk. Normally the software will simply retry up to a maximum of about 10 times. If the sector still cannot be written to, it is then classed as unusable.

There are two classifications of errors. Soft errors are those that result from temporary conditions, such as electrical noise. Normally repeating the operation will eventually give a correct result. Hard errors, on the other hand, are the result of some more permanent defect, such as dirt or stray magnetic fields on the disk, and will never recover no matter how many retries are made.

Error checking is based on forming a cyclic redundancy check (a sensitive form of checksum, see Chapter 8), which is stored on the disk with the data. When the data is read the same algorithm is used to form a CRC which is then compared with the one on the disk.

Figure 6.64 illustrates a typical controller, disk drive interface.

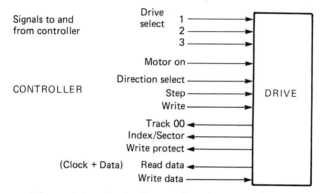

Figure 6.64   Typical controller/drive interface

There are two techniques used to interface the controller to the host microprocessor. In the simplest the controller occupies several port addresses in the processor's input/output map. Normally an interrupt strategy is then employed with the controller performing an interrupt whenever it is ready to perform some activity. The processor then has to intervene to carry out the required task. In the second technique the disk controller is not interfaced directly onto the system buses, but instead gains access to the bus through a Direct Memory Access (DMA) controller. This device is capable of taking over control of the system buses and communicating directly with memory. Hence whenever the disk controller requires to read or write data it uses the DMA controller to perform the transfer to or from memory. Although the latter obviously requires additional hardware, its increased efficiency has proved attractive to many system manufacturers (e.g. IBM with their Personal Computer).

Hard disks
Current 5¼ inch floppy disk systems are limited to a maximum disk capacity of approximately 1 Mbyte. A similar sized Winchester hard disk

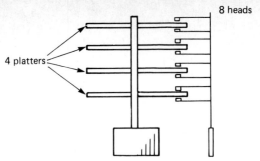

8 heads

4 platters

Figure 6.65 Platter/head assembly for typical 22 Mbyte Winchester

can store up to 40 Mbytes and provide data a factor of ten faster than a floppy. However, on the debit side costs, although falling, still remain high. Further, the fixed disk or platter prevents normal file back-up, where a copy of important files is kept on a separate disk in case of possible disaster. However, to a limited extent this can be overcome by copying files onto a series of floppies or to a cartridge tape unit.

In many ways Winchester drives (which incidentally obtained their

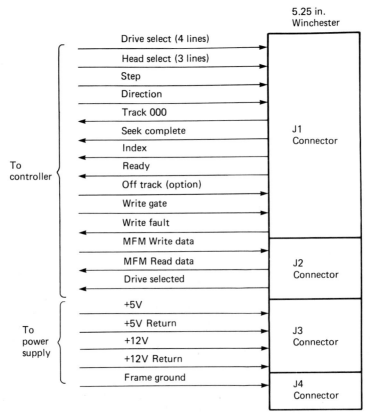

Figure 6.66 Standard 5 ¼ inch Winchester interface

name from an IBM project code name rather than from the inventor) are organised and operate in a similar manner to floppy drives. However, the main difference lies in the head/disk assembly, which is manufactured under extremely clean conditions and then sealed from outside air and dust. As a result the read/write head can operate much closer than normal to the disk surface (typically 20 micro-inches), giving rise to higher magnetic flux densities and correspondingly higher recording densities on the disk.

Figure 6.65 shows the four platters and eight heads found on a typical 22 Mbyte drive. The platters rotate at 3600 rpm, with the drive providing a data transfer rate of 5 Megabits/second. Each platter contains 640 tracks (320 each side), divided into 17 sectors each containing 512 bytes.

The standard 5¼ inch Winchester interface shown in Figure 6.66 contains many of the signals found on the floppy interface given earlier. Signals on the Winchester interface can be divided into three groups. The first group contains the power signals of +5 volts and +12 volts DC. In the second group are the data transfer signals conveying data serially in a MFM format. Finally, the third group contains a number of drive control signals selecting the drive and the head as well as the individual track.

Problems

6.1 Draw a voltage vs. time diagram of the signals found on an RS232 link when transmitting the ASCII codes for the following characters:

'*', 'U', <c-return>, <line-feed>

Assume the link is operating at 9600 baud with 1 start bit, 2 stop bits, 8 data bits and an even parity scheme.

6.2 Distinguish between the following terms used with the general purpose interface bus (GPIB):

a) device address
b) listen address
c) talk address

If a voltmeter has a device address of 21, find its talk and listen addresses. Why are they different?

6.3 Evaluate the storage capacity of a single-sided 5¼ inch floppy disk containing 40 tracks, divided into 10 sectors, each containing 256 bytes (single density).

6.4 Draw a circuit diagram for a 1K × 8 memory that uses 1K × 4 static RAM chips.

6.5 Outline the factors that would determine whether you would use static or dynamic RAM for a particular application.

FURTHER READING

Three excellent books dealing with microcomputer interfacing in general are:

Stone, H.S., 1982. *Microcomputer Interfacing.* Reading, MA: Addison-Wesley.

Zaks and Lesea, 1979. *Microprocessor Interfacing Techniques*. Sybex.

Artwick, B.A., 1980. *Microcomputer Interfacing*. Englewood Cliffs, NJ: Prentice-Hall.

A full treatment of RS-232C and other standards is given in:

Nichols, E.A., Nichols, J.C. and Musson, K.R., 1982. *Data Communications for Microcomputers*. New York, NY: McGraw-Hill.

Information on the IEEE 488 can be obtained from a number of equipment manufacturers, usually free of charge. Hewlett Packard's *Tutorial Description of the HP Interface Bus* provides an ideal introduction to all aspects of the bus.

Chapter 7

Local area networks

The objectives of this chapter are:

- to examine a number of local area network topologies;
- to describe the channel control and access techniques adopted by a number of commercial systems;
- to describe a typical Ethernet controller;
- to give an example of low level driver software and its use in a simple 'mail-box' application.

Local area networks (LANs) are a relatively recent innovation in micro-computer development. In the 1970s the use of versatile and inexpensive microcomputers became firmly established as people moved away from the constraints imposed by large mainframe installations. However, within an organisation this independence did not always work to advantage, resulting in duplication of programs, data files and expensive peripheral devices.

The advent of the local area network offered a solution, providing a data transmission system linking computers and associated peripheral devices within a restricted geographical area. However, real life installations have highlighted many problem areas. The diversity of systems: transmission media, topologies, access techniques and signal levels has emphasised the need for standardisation. The American Institute of Electrical and Electronic Engineers is at present tackling this problem and preparing a family of standards related to local area networks (IEEE project 802 standards 802.1 to 802.6).

This chapter examines the basic principles behind most of the systems currently available and looks at one contender, Ethernet, which is arguably the market leader.

7.1 NETWORK TOPOLOGY

The topology of a network is the arrangement of the stations and their interconnections. A number of simple patterns are currently employed e.g. star, bus, ring, tree.

Traditionally topology forms the basis of classification of network types, however, care must be taken as the same network topology can operate in many different ways. Some of the basic characteristics of the more common structures are outlined below.

Star

In the star configuration a number of stations are connected to a central node, Figure 7.1a. The centre of the star can function in several ways. In some systems it acts like the PABX (Private Automatic Branch Exchange) in a telephone network, forming connections between pairs of stations (e.g. the CASE Grapevine system uses a Data Concentrating Exchange (DCX) to perform this task). In other installations the hub of the star is a micro or mini-computer with large disk storage capacity and printer that acts as a file and print server to the outlying stations. Often with this arrangement the file server 'polls' the stations, interrogating each in turn to determine if any service is required, Figure 7.1b. An alternative and more efficient strategy uses interrupt techniques, with a station demanding attention from the file server when required (e.g. the Comart Multi-

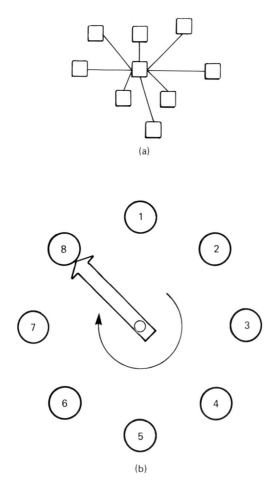

(a)

(b)

Figure 7.1　(a) Star topology; (b) file server polling stations

processor system, Corvus Constellation and Compustar networks).

Although relatively simple to design and implement, all star networks have a common weakness, namely the central node. If it goes down so does the network. As a result, some systems have built-in standby redundancy to protect against potential disaster. An example of this is the Tandem file server developed by GB Techniques for use with their newspaper word processing network *Speednet*.

Ring

Stations in a ring topology are connected by point-to-point links to form an unbroken circular configuration. Most rings are unidirectional and operate by passing packets of data from one node to the next, Figure 7.2. All stations on the ring will receive the information packet and examine its destination address before re-transmitting it on to the next station. If it is intended for them, the packet is first marked as having been received before it is re-transmitted. When the packet returns to the original transmitter the 'marker' indicates safe reception and the transmitter removes the packet from the ring.

Since every member of the network can receive each packet, it is simple to implement a broadcast feature. However, the need for each node to re-transmit every packet can lead to reliability problems requiring careful station interface design to cope with station or power failures.

Many techniques have been employed to distribute control and ensure that only one station is allowed to transmit at any time. The two most popular methods are token passing and empty slot (Cambridge Ring). Both work by giving permission to talk to a station which is then allowed to transmit a limited amount of information on the network before passing control to another station.

A monitor station is usually found in most ring configurations. Its main function is to monitor the data traffic and remove corrupted or unwanted packets which would otherwise continue to circulate round the ring.

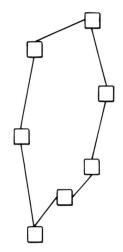

Figure 7.2 Ring topology

Bus

A bus network is an extension of the system that connects components inside the computer, i.e. the processor, memory and I/O devices. The concept uses a common data highway to connect nodes together, with each station having a unique identity or address, Figure 7.3. Unlike nodes in a ring configuration, stations do not have to repeat messages intended for other nodes. The passive nature of each node in transmission improves efficiency and reliability, resulting in a network inherently resistant to node failures.

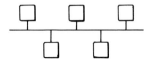

Figure 7.3 Bus topology

Sharing a single transmission path between several systems requires some scheme for dividing its use equally between the stations. A number of strategies are currently available, ranging from systems using control and status lines similar to those found inside the microcomputer (e.g. the IEEE 488 General Purpose Interface Bus) to systems employing a completely random method where a station can send information at any time but has sufficient intelligence to avoid talking when the bus is already in use and to detect a collision should it occur. (This is the basis of Ethernet which is described later.)

7.2 CHANNEL CONTROL AND ACCESS

The mechanism by which a network operates forms a much better criterion than topology on which to base a classification. Many different strategies exist based on mechanisms for controlling and gaining access to the channel connecting the stations or nodes. The control of a channel can be either centralised in a single node, as in star configurations, or distributed to all the nodes. Access techniques are the methods by which a station gains the use of the common channel to transmit information.

In this section three of the most popular schemes used today are examined.

Token passing

Token passing systems use a special packet or token to pass control from one node to another. In a ring configuration the token is passed around the ring from one station to its neighbour. Any station wanting to transmit information waits until it is in possession of the token. On completion, the token is passed on to the next station, Figure 7.4a.

Token passing schemes are also found in bus networks, Figure 7.4b. Again with this topology each station has a unique identity or address. On establishing the network, one station (usually that with the highest address) has the token. If it has nothing to say, a packet containing the token is sent to the station with the nearest ID number. Whenever a station

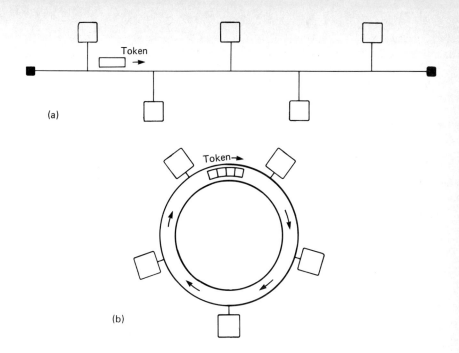

Figure 7.4 (a) Token bus network; (b) token ring network

with information to transmit receives the token, it transmits its data and passes the token on to the next station.

Example – Arcnet   Standard Microsystems Corporation of New York, together with the Datapoint Corporation, have recently launched a chip set that uses this technique in a network called Arcnet. Arcnet employs a 'modified token passing protocol' where all token passes are acknowledged by the node accepting the token by transmitting a short acknowledge packet containing an ACK character – ASCII code 06. Up to 255 stations can be connected to the network, which operates using data packets containing up to 512 bytes transmitted over either twisted pair or coaxial media at a data rate of 2.5 megabits/second.

An interesting feature of Arcnet is its ability to configure itself at power-up or to reconfigure if extra stations are added. Each station on the network expects to receive an invitation to transmit within a given time period (approximately 840 msec). If it does not, it emits a reconfigure burst to all stations, forcing them to enter network reconfiguration. During this phase each station, starting with the node with the highest ID number finds and stores the address of the station with the nearest ID. This ensures that control of the network is passed directly from one node to the next with no time wasted giving invitations to transmit to ID numbers not present.

Several manufacturers have adopted this scheme, including Zynar who are producing add-on interface boards for the IBM and Apple personal computers and Tandy for their range of microcomputers.

Contention techniques – CSMA/CD

The scheme described above in Arcnet was designed to avoid conflict between nodes wishing to transmit. In such a system collisions should never occur, the token ensuring that only one node is talking at any instant. Contention techniques, however, do not regulate when a station can talk. All stations are free to contend for the use of the medium at any time. The most popular scheme using this philosophy is that used by Ethernet, namely Carrier Sense Multiple Access with Collision Detection (CSMA/CD).

The *carrier sense* feature means that before talking a station listens to the transmission medium to see if there is a carrier signal present, indicating that some other station is already using the network. A station will then defer transmission whenever traffic is sensed on the channel, Figure 7.5a.

Multiple access allows any station to transmit immediately it senses the channel is free. This ensures a more efficient use of the transmission medium, reducing the waiting time characteristic of token and empty slot techniques.

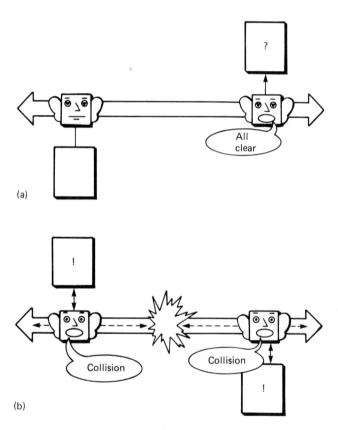

Figure 7.5 (a) Carrier sense: listening before talking to avoid collision; (b) collision detection: listen while talking to detect collisions

The 'listen before talking' strategy reduces but does not eliminate the possibility of two or more nodes colliding.

Collision detection is the ability of a station to listen to the network as it transmits – 'listen while talking' – and to sense any increase in the energy level of the channel and interpret it as a collision. The transmission is then abandoned and the station 'backs off' delaying its attempt for a short interval before trying to transmit again. The back-off time is random, thus reducing the chance of further collisions. If further collisions do occur, the back-off time is increased. Adopting this procedure, stations using the network adapt to the traffic: during quiet spells the time between collisions is relatively short but as the load increases so does the waiting time, thus reducing the chance of multiple collisions, Figure 7.5b.

To ensure that all nodes in the system are aware of a collision, any node involved emits a short burst of noise called a jam, reinforcing the collision state on the transmission medium.

Empty slot

A technique often employed with ring topologies uses one or more circulating data packets or slots. If a station has information to transmit it waits until it receives an empty slot upon which it loads it with data, the address of the destination node, its own address and a flag to say the slot is currently in use, Figure 7.6. The packet is then passed from node to node until it reaches its destination where it is read and a flag set to signify that it has been received satisfactorily. The packet then passes off round the ring to the original source station, which on sensing that it has been received, declares the slot empty and passes it on to the next node. Most slot rings need a monitor station to detect and remove defective packets, along with circuitry that ensures safe relay of packets whenever intermediate stations are powered down.

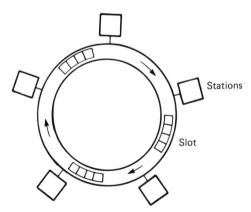

Stations

Slot

A number of SLOTS or FRAMES of fixed size circulate around the ring

Figure 7.6 Empty slot technique

227

One popular system using this technique is the Cambridge Ring in which two twisted pair cables are used to transmit data and provide power for the station repeaters. Among others, Acorn Computers, manufacturers of the BBC micro, Seel Transring and Racal Planet are all supporting this format.

7.3   ETHERNET

Ethernet has grown from collaboration between the three American corporations – Digital Equipment, Intel and Xerox (DIX). In 1980 the consortium published a booklet outlining the specification for a bus topology network employing the CSMA/CD technique outlined earlier. The document was based on a successful experimental system developed by Xerox at their Palo Alto Research Centre. The DIX specification was designed to encourage a standardised approach for different manufactur-

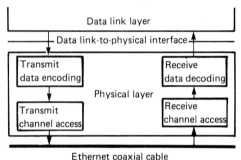

Data encoding/decoding

- Generation and removal of 64 preamble bits before each packet is transmitted for synchronisation and timing of messages.
- Bit encoding and decoding – between the binary encoded form of the Data Link level and the *phase encoded* form required for transmission on the coaxial cable. *Manchester phase encoding* is specified, for all data transmitted on the Ethernet, at a data transmission rate of ten million bits per second.

Channel access

- Transmission and reception of encoded data.
- Carrier sense – monitoring the channel for traffic and signalling the Data Link layer if traffic is detected.
- Collision detect – signalling the Data Link layer, *during* transmission, when a collision is detected.

Physical interface

- Transceiver cable interface
- Coaxial cable interface

Figure 7.7   Ethernet: physical layer (Courtesy of Digital Equipment Corporation)

228

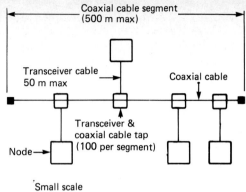

Small scale

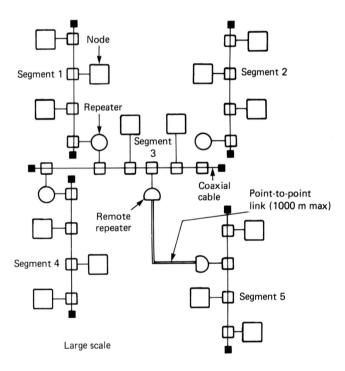

Large scale

Figure 7.8 Typical Ethernet installations: small and large scale (Courtesy of Digital Equipment Corporation)

ers wishing to design equipment capable of utilising Ethernet, detailing the lowest two levels of an overall network architecture, namely the physical layer and the data link layer.

The *physical layer* specification gives details of the most primitive level in the Ethernet architecture, Figure 7.7. Coaxial cable segments up to 500 m long with a maximum of 100 stations are used to transmit data at 10 megabits/second. Repeater stations can link segments together to form a network of maximum length 2.8 km with up to 1024 stations, Figure 7.8.

At each station the Ethernet interface is made up of two parts:

1. A transceiver unit containing a limited amount of electronics, together with a 'vampire' tap that uses a gold plated pin to penetrate through the coaxial cable insulation to make contact with the inner conductor. The transceiver electronics is responsible for the transmission and reception of encoded data together with the detection of collisions due to multiple transmission attempts on the Ether.

2. The controller performs a number of functions including encapsulating the data into packets, appending or checking cyclic redundancy checks as well as initiating or deferring transmission onto the bus, Figure 7.9.

The *data link layer* details both the link management, i.e. the CSMA/CD technique, and the packet format, defining packet addressing, framing and error detection, Figure 7.10.

Ethernet packets can contain between 46 and 1500 bytes of data along with a system overhead of 18 bytes giving packet lengths of 64 to 1518

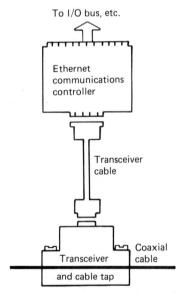

Figure 7.9 An Ethernet interface is made up of two parts: the transceiver and the controller (Courtesy of Digital Equipment Corporation)

230

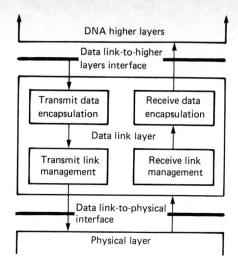

DNA higher layers

Data link-to-higher layers interface

Transmit data encapsulation

Receive data encapsulation

Data link layer

Transmit link management

Receive link management

Data link-to-physical interface

Physical layer

Data encapsulation/decapsulation

- Defining the format of message packets – the different fields of information within packets.
- Constructing packets from data supplied by the nodes through the higher levels ; disassembling network messages and supplying data to the higher level protocols of the node.
- Addressing – handling of source and destination addresses.
- Error detection – physical channel transmission errors.

Link management

- Channel allocation – amount of channel use is determined by the definition of packet size.
- Channel access – access to the channel is controlled by a contention-avoidance-and-resolution technique, called CSMA/CD, part of which is carried out in each of the two layers. The Data Link level responds to the channel or carrier sensing of the Physical layer. This means it defers sending in the case of traffic, sends in the absence of traffic, and backs off and resends in the case of a collision.

Figure 7.10   Ethernet: data link layer (Courtesy of Digital Equipment Corporation)

bytes. In addition to the packet itself all transmissions are accompanied by an 8-byte preamble made up of the sequence 10101010 . . . and ending . . . 10101011 to ensure that the receiver electronics in each transceiver is locked onto the transmitting station before the packet proper is released.

The minimum packet size of 64 bytes ensures that two stations transmitting simultaneously from opposite ends of a maximum length 2.8 km network will still register a collision (i.e. the minimum packet size

231

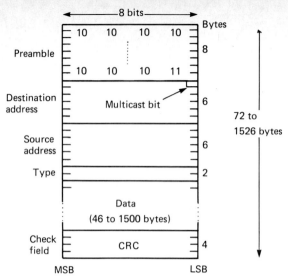

Figure 7.11 Ethernet frame format showing preamble, destination and source addresses (Courtesy of Digital Equipment Corporation)

must be greater than the 'round trip' propagation time of a packet on the network). If smaller packets were allowed it would become possible for a station to think it had successfully transmitted a packet, which had in fact taken part in a collision somewhere in the network.

The Ethernet frame format is shown in Figure 7.11. After the preamble the packet contains a 6-byte destination and a 6-byte source address. At first glance a 48-bit address might seem excessive since any network can only support 1024 stations. However, Xerox view the address as being global, with each piece of Ethernet equipment having a unique identity. This philosophy is supported by Xerox issuing manufacturers of Ethernet products with a block of addresses with their licensing agreement.

Finally, the least significant bit in the destination address is known as a Multicast bit. If set, all devices within the block will receive the transmission. The corresponding bit in the source address is always zero.

Ethernet interfaces – the LRT filtabyte
At present the cost of an Ethernet interface remains relatively high with the market eagerly awaiting low cost VLSI components, notably the Intel 82586 LAN controller and the 82501 Ethernet serial interface. Other manufacturers, for example Advanced Micro Devices with its AM7990 Ethernet family and Fujitsu with its MB8795 controller and MB502 interface have already entered the market place. (The latter is being employed in the 3COMS Ethernet interface board for the Altos 586 and the IBM PC.)

Several relatively high cost discrete component controllers are currently in use providing interfaces between Ethernet industry standard buses such as Intel's Multibus and Digital Equipment's Q-bus. A British company, based in Reading, Logic Replacement Technology, are at

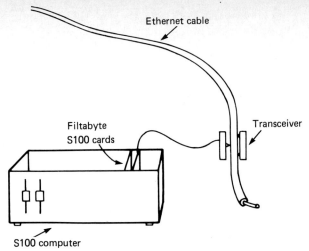

Ethernet cable

Filtabyte
S100 cards

Transceiver

S100 computer

Figure 7.12   LRT's Ethernet interface installed in an S100 system

present producing a low cost S100 interface together with network software that runs under CP/M and provides basic file exchange over Ethernet ('Pipe Package' – Program Interchange Package over Ethernet).

The interface itself is in two parts: a transceiver unit that forms the vampire tap onto the cable and two S100 cards that slot into the S100 motherboard, Figure 7.12. Along with the controller circuitry the cards contain 16 Kbytes of random access memory organised as eight 2 Kbyte buffers. (The memory on the card can be expanded to 64 Kbytes providing 32 buffers.) Each buffer is large enough to hold a maximum size Ethernet packet.

From a programmer's viewpoint the interface appears as four registers that are port mapped and a 2 Kbyte block of RAM. On-board links allow the customer to position the cards at a suitable port and memory range within his system. Figure 7.13 shows a possible arrangement for both the Comart Communicator CP200 and the North Star Horizon, namely ports located at F0H to F3H and RAM at F800H through to FFFFH.

Only one of the eight buffers is visible in the host microcomputer memory map at any instant, and the programmer uses the Window View Register (WVR) to select the required buffer. Before operation buffers are assigned to act as either transmit buffers, holding packets that are to be sent over the Ether, or receive buffers accepting packets received from the Ether with the correct destination address. Figure 7.14 shows a typical configuration with one transmit buffer (number 0) and seven receive buffers (numbers 1 to 7).

Packet transmission   The first step in preparing a packet for transmission is to move the selected transmit buffer into the host micro's memory map. The programmer then begins constructing the packet for transmission, inserting the destination address together with the data into the buffer RAM, Figure 7.15. The controller hardware automatically adds the following before the packet is transmitted:

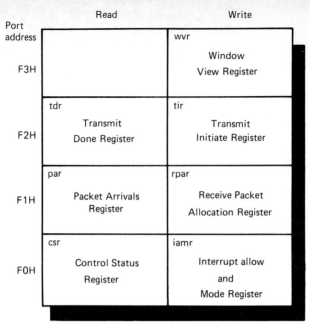

	Read	Write
Port address		
F3H		wvr Window View Register
F2H	tdr Transmit Done Register	tir Transmit Initiate Register
F1H	par Packet Arrivals Register	rpar Receive Packet Allocation Register
F0H	csr Control Status Register	iamr Interrupt allow and Mode Register

Filtabyte's 7 registers occupy 4 port addresses

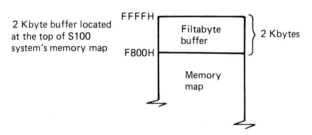

2 Kbyte buffer located at the top of S100 system's memory map

FFFFH — Filtabyte buffer — 2 Kbytes

F800H — Memory map

Figure 7.13 Filtabyte port and memory addresses in the Comart Communicator and the North Star Horizon

1. the 8-byte preamble on the front of the packet
2. the 6-byte source address of the transmitting station
3. a cyclic redundancy check (CRC) of the enclosed data

Once complete the programmer then places the packet's buffer number in the Transmit Initiate Register (TIR) and the controller hardware then takes on the task of transmitting the packet, deferring to other users and retransmitting should a collision occur. If 15 attempts at retransmission fail the controller sets a transmit error flag warning the station that the Ethernet probably has some problem, e.g. a missing terminator or a short circuit on the coaxial cable.

Packet reception After configuration the controller will work in the background automatically receiving packets whose address matches the

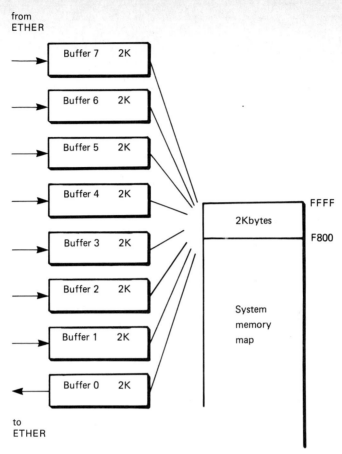

Figure 7.14 Filtabyte has eight 2 Kbyte buffers. The Window View
Register selects the buffer that appears in the memory map

station's identity. (Unless it has been configured in the promiscuous
mode when it will eavesdrop on all transmissions.)

When a packet is received it is automatically loaded onto the first
available receive buffer and a flag set (Packet Available bit in the
Controller Status Register). The programmer can either poll this register or
use an interrupt strategy to detect an incoming packet. Once detected the
buffer number of the received packet is obtained by reading the Packets
Arrival Register (PAR). To inspect the packet the buffer number just
extracted from the PAR is entered into the window view register transferring the newly arrived packet into the host micro's memory map.

Figure 7.15 outlines the format of the receive buffer showing the
position of the source address together with status bits added by the
controller. The I or 'integral number of bytes' flag is set if the frame
contains a whole number of bytes and the C flag is set if the receiver
evaluates the same cyclic redundancy check as that received at the end of
the packet. It is then up to the programmer to accept or reject a packet if
either of these flags reports a problem.

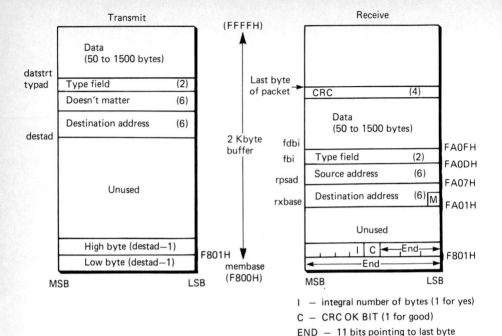

Figure 7.15 Filtabyte transmit/receive buffer formats

After the source and integrity of a packet have been tested its data can then be copied down into the system RAM and the buffer re-allocated for reception of future packets.

Filtabyte driver routines – a simple 'mail-box' program The file transfer utilities accompanying the Filtabyte Controller have been written in the 'C' programming language and then compiled to Z80 code using the BDS 'C' compiler. Although 'C' is probably one of the better languages for writing this type of package it is arguably terse and difficult to follow, especially by those meeting it for the first time. With this in mind the following driver routines have been written in BBC BASIC. Programs written in BASIC would of course be relatively inefficient and slow, but the intention here is to present an easily understood set of building blocks that illustrate the procedures involved in driving a typical Ethernet controller.

The LRT interface can be used to transmit packets containing between 46 and 1500 bytes of data. In the following routines the interface is configured to handle packets containing 256 bytes of data in the form of short text messages. Programs 7.1 to 7.14 give listings of the low level driver routines together with some useful procedures for generating and viewing short text messages. The routines include:

1. `PROCdefinitions` – contains definitions of all the filtabyte registers and buffer RAM locations. This procedure should be called at the start of any application, Program 7.1.

```
9020 DEF PROCdefinitions
9030
9040 REM *********** HARDWARE ADDRESSES ***************
9050
9060 REM i/o registers.......port addresses
9070 csr=&F0   :REM controller status register
9080 iamr=csr :REM interrupt allow and mode register
9090 par=csr+1:REM packet arrivals register
9100 rpar=par :REM receive packet allocation register
9110 tdr=par+1:REM transmit done register
9120 tir=tdr  :REM transmit initiate register
9130 wvr=tdr+1:REM window view register
9140
9150 REM buffer RAM - transmission format (256 bytes data)
9160 membase=&F800      :REM start of buffer memory
9170 destad=membase+&6F2 :REM destination address
9180 typad=destad+12     :REM ethernet type field
9190 datstrt=typad+2     :REM data start address
9200
9210 REM buffer RAM - receive format
9220 rxbase=membase+&201 :REM receive packet base address
9230 rpsad=rxbase+6      :REM receive packet source address
9240 fbi=rpsad+6         :REM type field address
9250 fdbi=fbi+2          :REM address of first data byte
9260 REM define some working space
9270 DIM A(6),text 256
9280 ENDPROC
```

Program 7.1 Procedure: definitions

2. `PROCbinit` – this is the initialisation routine for filtabyte and should be called after `PROCdefinitions` at the start of the main program, Program 7.2.

```
9300 DEF PROCfbinit
9310
9320 REM ******* INITIALISE FILTABYTE **********
9330
9340 PUT csr,&20          :REM initialise the controller
9350 PUT csr,0            :REM release initialisation
9360 REM allocate receive buffers
9370 FOR buffer=1 TO 7
9380   PUT rpar,buffer
9390 NEXT buffer
9400 REM allocate 1 buffer for transmission (number 0)
9410 REM (involves transmitting a dummy packet)
9420 PUT wvr,0           :REM select buffer 0
9430 REM set up dummy packet to ether address 00 00 00 00 00 00
9440 PROCdest_addr(00,00,00,00,00,00)
9450 PUT tir,0           :REM transmit packet
9460 ENDPROC
```

Program 7.2 Procedure to initialise the Filtabyte interface

237

3. `PROCdest_addr (A(0), A(1), A(2), A(3), A(4), A(5))` – this routine places the 6-byte destination address into the transmit buffer, Program 7.3.

PROCdest_addr(A(6))

```
9500 DEF PROCdest_addr(A(0),A(1),A(2),A(3),A(4),A(5))
9510 REM slot destination address into transmit buffer
9520 FOR S=0 TO 5
9530    ?(destad+S)=A(S)
9540 NEXT S
9550 REM also slot in address of first data byte in buffer (lowbyte
                                                          /highbyte)
9560 ?membase=(destad-1) MOD 256 :membase?1=(destad-1) DIV 256
9570 ENDPROC
```

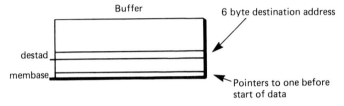

Program 7.3   Procedure to place destination address in buffer

4. `PROCload_buf_from (start)` – loads the buffer in the window view register, with the 256 bytes starting at `start`, Program 7.4.

PROCload_buf_from(start)

```
9590 DEF PROCload_buf_from(start)
9600 REM loads 256 bytes from location 'start' upwards into buffer
9610 FOR N=0 TO 252 STEP 4
9620    !(datstrt+N)=!(start+N)
9630 NEXT N
9640 ENDPROC
```

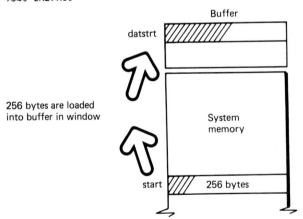

Program 7.4   Procedure to load a transmit buffer with data

5. `PROCempty_buf_to(start)` — empties buffer in window view register into memory starting at `start`, Program 7.5.

```
9660 DEF PROCempty_buf_to(start)
9670 REM loads 256 bytes from buffer into memory beginning at 'start'
9680 FOR N=0 TO 252 STEP 4
9690    !(start+N)=!(fdbi+N)
9700 NEXT N
9710 ENDPROC
```

Program 7.5   Procedure to empty a receive buffer into system memory

6. `PROCpacin` — this routine sets the variable `return` to FALSE if no packets have been received. If a packet has been received `return` is set to TRUE and its buffer number is placed in the window view register, Program 7.6.

PROCpacin

```
9730 DEF PROCpacin
9740 REM sets return=TRUE, rxbufno and wvr to buffer number
9750 REM if packet has arrived, otherwise return=FALSE
9760 IF (&01 AND GET(csr))=0 THEN return=FALSE:ENDPROC
9770 REM packet must have arrived, place its number in rxbufno and wvr
9780 rxbufno=GET(par):PUT wvr,rxbufno:return=TRUE
9790 ENDPROC
```

Wait for packet (poll bit 0 in csr)

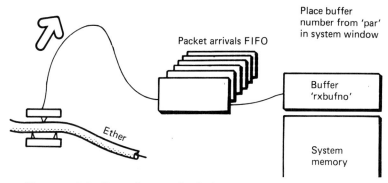

Place buffer number from 'par' in system window

Packet arrivals FIFO

Buffer 'rxbufno'

Ether

System memory

Program 7.6   Procedure to check if a packet has been received from the Ether

7. `PROCcheck_crc` — routine sets `return` TRUE if the received packet's cyclic redundancy check is good. Otherwise `return` is set FALSE, Program 7.7.

PROCcheck_crc

```
9810 DEF PROCcheck_crc
9820 REM routine sets return=TRUE if crc ok else return=FALSE
9830 IF (&08 AND GET(membase+1))=0 THEN return=FALSE : ENDPROC
9840 return=TRUE
9850 ENDPROC
```

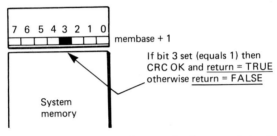

Program 7.7 Procedure to check CRC 'ok' bit for received packet

8. **PROCrelbuf** – after a packet has been received and placed in the window view register for examination this routine re-allocates the buffer for future packet reception, Program 7.8.

PROCrelbuf

```
9870 DEF PROCrelbuf
9880 REM routine to release buffer for receive allocation
9890 PUT rpar,rxbufno
9900 ENDPROC
```

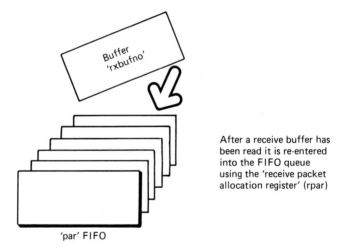

After a receive buffer has been read it is re-entered into the FIFO queue using the 'receive packet allocation register' (rpar)

'par' FIFO

Program 7.8 Procedure to re-allocate a receive buffer for future packet reception

9. **PROCselect (buffer)** — brings selected buffer into window view register, Program 7.9.

PROCselect (buffer)

```
9920 DEF PROCselect(buffer)
9930 REM brings selected buffer into window
9940 PUT wvr,buffer
9950 ENDPROC
```

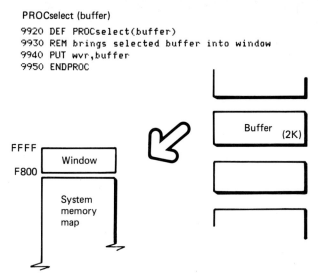

Program 7.9 Procedure to move the selected buffer into host micro's memory map

10. **PROCtxpac (buffer)** — routine transmits packet pointed to by buffer, Program 7.10.

PROCtxpac (buffer)

```
9970 DEF PROCtxpac(buffer)
9980 REM routine to transmit packet pointed to by 'buffer'
9985 REM assumes transmit buffer is free!
9990 PUT tir,buffer
10000 ENDPROC
```

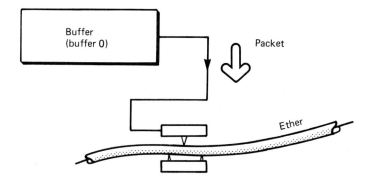

Program 7.10 Procedure to transmit a packet

11. **PROCvu(S)** – allows you to examine 256 bytes of memory, starting at S, in hex and ASCII, Program 7.11.

```
10020 DEF PROCvu(S)
10030 REM procedure to display memory contents
10040 FOR N=S TO S+239 STEP 16
10050   PRINT';~N;" ";
10060   FOR R=0 TO 15
10070     T=?(N+R):IF T<16 PRINT;0;
10080     PRINT;~T;" ";
10090   NEXT R
10100   FOR R=0 TO 15
10110     T=?(N+R)
10120     IF T>&1F AND T<&7F THEN PRINT CHR$(T); ELSE PRINT CHR$(&2E);
10130   NEXT R:NEXT N:PRINT
10140 ENDPROC
```

Program 7.11   Procedure to view 256 bytes of memory in ASCII and hex

12. **PROCwrite_text_to(S)** – simple editor routine that allows you to write up to 255 bytes of text to an area of memory starting at S. Control Z is used to exit the routine, Program 7.12.

```
10160 DEF PROCwrite_text_to(S)
10170 REM routine to write text...ctl Z finishes
10180 N=0
10190 REPEAT
10200   X=GET:?(S+N)=X
10210   IF X=&0D THEN PRINT CHR$(&0A);
10220   PRINT CHR$(X);:N=N+1
10230 UNTIL X=&1A OR N=255:PRINT
10240 ENDPROC
```

Program 7.12   Simple editor routine to store text in a buffer

13. **PROCvu_text_at(S)** – displays text starting at S up to control Z, Program 7.13.

```
10260 DEF PROCvu_text_at(S)
10270 REM routine to view text up to ctl Z
10280 N=1:X=?S
10290 REPEAT
10300   IF X=&0D THEN PRINT CHR$(&0A);
10310   PRINT CHR$(X);
10320   X=?(S+N):N=N+1
10330 UNTIL X=&1A OR N=255
10340 ENDPROC
```

Program 7.13   Routine to view text in the buffer

14. **PROCsource_addr** – obtains the 6-byte source address from received packet and places in vector A, Program 7.14.

```
10350 DEF PROCsource_addr
10360 REM get source address from packet
10370 FOR S=0 TO 5
10380   A(S)=?(rpsad+S)
10390 NEXT S
10400 ENDPROC
```

Program 7.14   Procedure to obtain the source address from a packet received from the Ether

```
10 CLS
20 PRINT"ETHERNET TRANSMITTER/RECEIVER ROUTINE ":PRINT:PRINT
30 PROCdefinitions·
40 PROCfbinit
60 REPEAT
65    PRINT
70    PRINT" Command?....(W,T,D,Q,H-HELP) "
80    A$=GET$
90    IF A$="W" THEN PRINT"Enter message....CTL Z to finish":PROCwrite_text_to
      (text)
100   IF A$="T" THEN PROCtransmit
110   IF A$="D" THEN PROCdisplay
120   IF A$="H" THEN PROChelp
130 UNTIL A$="Q"
150 END
400 DEFPROCdisplay
410 PROCpacin                        :REM has a  packet arrived?
420 IF return=FALSE THEN PRINT"No messages..":ENDPROC
430 PROCempty_buf_to(text)           :REM empty packet for display
440 PROCrelbuf                       :REM release receive buffer for use
450 PROCvu_text_at(text)             :REM display text received
460 ENDPROC
500 DEFPROCtransmit
510 PROCselect(0)
520 PROCload_buf_from(text)
530 PROCdest_addr(02,&60,&86,00,00,&91)
540 PROCtxpac(0)
544 PRINT
545 PRINT"TRANSMISSION COMPLETE"
550 ENDPROC
600 DEFPROChelp
610 PRINT:PRINT"W....TO WRITE TEXT...CTL Z TO FINISH "
620 PRINT"T....TO TRANSMIT TEXT "
630 PRINT"D....TO DISPLAY TEXT "
640 PRINT"Q....TO QUIT"
650 ENDPROC
```

Program 7.15   Mail-box program written in BBC BASIC. The program
makes use of the driver routines given in Programs 7.1 to 7.14

Program 7.15 makes use of some of these procedures to implement a
simple 'mail-box' program that allows several stations to pass short text
messages between each other. When running, the program presents the
operator with a menu offering the following options:

```
W ..... to Write text  ..... CTLZ to finish
T ..... to Transmit message
D ..... to Display any messages received
Q ..... to Quit program.
```

The routine shown has been left relatively simple. There are several
modifications that would increase its versatility and make it more robust.
For example:

- a procedure that would allow the operator to select the address of a
  destination station by name rather than by its 6-byte Ethernet
  address
- all messages contain a source address that could be used to display
  the name of the transmitting station

- a simple broadcast facility could be implemented by setting the Multicast bit in the destination address of a transmitted packet
- on reception the CRC flag should be monitored to ensure that the packet has not been involved in a collision

How would you implement these improvements? Are there any others you would make?

Problems

7.1 Give a brief account of the functions associated with the physical layer and the data link layer of an Ethernet network.

7.2 Write a routine that implements the modifications suggested in the text to the 'mail-box' program (Program 7.15).

7.3 Ethernet uses a self-clocking encoding technique (Manchester encoding) where the first half of each bit cell is the complement of the binary digit being transmitted. Sketch the signal found on an Ethernet cable during the first two octets that form the start of the preamble in an Ethernet frame.

FURTHER READING

Several books provide a good introduction to local area networks, describing topologies and access techniques.

Hirschheim, R. and Cheong, V., 1983. *Local Area Networks: Issues, Products and Developments*. Chichester: Wiley.

Gee, K. 1982. *Local Area Networks*. Manchester: NCC Publications.

For a more in-depth treatment of network architectures and protocols:

Meijer, A. and Peeters, P., 1982. *Computer Network Architectures*. London: Pitman.

Tanenbaum, A. 1981. *Computer Networks*. Englewood Cliffs, NJ: Prentice-Hall.

The Digital, Intel, Xerox publication *The Ethernet* is available from any Intel distributor (e.g. Rapid Recall, High Street, Nantwich).

Further details of the Filtabyte Ethernet controller can be obtained from Logic Replacement Technology Ltd., 9 Arkwright Road, Reading.

Chapter 8

System servicing

The objectives of this chapter are:

- to highlight the problems associated with fault-finding a micro-processor system;
- to examine simple self-diagnostic routines;
- to introduce the concept of stimulus testing;
- to examine the role of in-circuit emulation as a servicing tool;
- to describe the operation of the signature analyser;
- to outline the application of signature analysis to a microprocessor based product.

Servicing a microprocessor based system employs fundamentally the same strategy as that used with any electronic circuit. A good knowledge of the circuit and a basic understanding of how it works are essential. Circuit diagrams along with additional documentation in the form of a memory map and even program listings can all help.

Many of the problems found in microcomputers are common to those found in any electronic circuit: bad connections, faulty power supplies, leaky capacitors etc. However, along with these the microprocessor system brings a whole range of new problems:

- Buses do not always carry meaningful information. At times they may be undergoing switching transients or be inactive, if driven by tri-state outputs.
- Processors are programmable devices with the result that two identical pieces of hardware can display completely different electrical signals.
- Many components are connected in parallel on the system buses. Even when a fault is discovered on a bus line (node) there still remains the problem of identifying the component generating the fault.

The problems look formidable and finding a solution with conventional test equipment can be difficult if not impossible. Fortunately, a range of new techniques has been developed to ease the task. This chapter examines some of these techniques.

Good design at the development stage of a product will certainly minimise the probability of future failure. However, faults will still occur and it is unfortunate that, due to financial considerations or just neglect, most microprocessor based products are not designed to be easily serviced. Clearly the time to make provision for servicing is in the early stages of development so that any additional components (e.g. test-points, jumpers, ROMs containing test-routines) can be included before the final design is reached.

8.1 SELF DIAGNOSTICS

Some systems make use of test programs either already present in firmware, or loaded from tape or disk, to perform system verification, checking the ROM, RAM and to some extent any input/output devices. The results of these tests are usually communicated to the operator using the computer's display or through an indicator (e.g. a light emitting diode) that confirms satisfactory completion, or otherwise, of the tests. Test routines resident in ROM obviously make fewer assumptions on the system's performance than those loaded from disk or tape where the majority of the computer has to be operational in order to load the test software. However, diagnostic disks do have a part to play, exercising the 'edges' of the system, e.g. serial and printer ports, video displays and RAM not used by the operating system etc.

RAM testing

The usual technique for testing RAM involves writing a pattern into a memory location, reading it back and then checking that both operations were successful. A number of strategies can be employed to detect the different types of RAM failure. Some test programs, although thorough, can take several hours to complete and would only be used if a complex fault was suspected. One of the simplest algorithms uses a checkerboard pattern of 1s and 0s to test each memory location. The test begins by filling the RAM under test with 0AAH, i.e. 10101010 in binary. Each location is then read and checked. The memory block is then filled with 55H, i.e. 01010101 in binary and again checked. If a fault is discovered the test reports the address of the faulty location.

Program 8.1 lists a checkerboard test routine issued by Comart of Cambridge as a quick test for their memory boards. Note how the routine expects at least 10 bytes of RAM are operative to act as a system stack. Making this assumption simplifies the test routine which can then make use of subroutine calls.

ROM testing

The normal method of testing ROM involves forming a checksum. The contents of each memory location within the ROM are added together and then truncated to form a checksum byte or word. A simple program initiated during the self-check sequence computes the checksum and compares it with a stored value. If they don't match a ROM failure has been detected. If they do match the ROM is probably functional but there

```
0001          COMART LTD.
0002          8 LITTLE END ROAD
0003          EATON SOCON
0004          ST. NEOTS
0005          CAMBRIDGESHIRE
0006
0007          SEPTEMBER 1980
0008
0009   THIS IS A QUICK TEST FOR COMART MEMORY BOARDS. IT IS DESIGNED
0010   FOR THE OPERATOR TO TYPE IN THE OBJECT CODE, SET UP THE START
0011   AND END ADDRESS, AND RUN UNDER CONTROL OF A MONITOR, SUCH AS
0012   THE NORTH STAR MONITOR OR THE CROMEMCO DEBUGGER.
0013
0014   THE PROGRAM IS ORIGINED AT 100HEX BUT OTHER ORIGINS MAY BE
0015   USED EITHER BY RELOCATION BY THE OPERATOR OR BY REQUESTING A
0016   LISTING FROM COMART AT THE SPECIFIED ORIGIN
0017   THE PROGRAM EXPECTS TO FIND THE START AND END ADDRESS AT LOCATIONS
0018   ORIGIN AND ORIGIN+2 RESPECTIVELY.(THESE ADDRESSES MUST BE STORED
0019   IN THE INTEL REVERSE FORMAT). NO CHECK IS MADE ON THE VALIDITY OF
0020   THESE ADDRESSES.   THE REQUIRED CONDITIONS ARE :-
0021          START+1<END
0022
0023   ENSURE THAT THE PROGRAM AREA IS NOT INSIDE THE TEST AREA!!!
0024
0025   A SUCCESSFUL TEST WILL TERMINATE AT TESTEND AND A JUMP MAY BE PUT
0026   HERE TO YOUR MONITOR (OR A BREAKPOINT IF YOU HAVE THIS FACILITY)
0027
0028   AN ERROR CONDITION WILL TRANSFER CONTROL TO ERROR AND ONCE AGAIN
0029   A JUMP TO YOUR MONITOR OR A BREAKPOINT MAY BE PLACED HERE. AT THE
0030   ERROR ADDRESS THE REGISTERS MAY BE INTERPRETED AS FOLLOWS:-
0031          A=ACTUAL DATA
0032          B=EXPECTED DATA
0033          HL=ERROR ADDRESS
0034
0035   IF A JUMP TO YOUR MONITOR IS USED AT THE ERROR LOCATION IT IS RECOMMENDED
0036   THAT THE REGISTERS ARE SAVED FIRST TO AVOID CORRUPTION BY THE MONITOR
0037   TO FACILITATE THIS THE ERROR ADDRESS IS THE LAST LOCATION IN THE PROGRAM
0038
```

Program 8.1   Checkerboard test program for RAM (Courtesy of Comart Limited)

```
0039  ;     ALLOWING FOR EXPANSION
0040  ;
0041  ;     THE PROGRAM REQUIRES AT LEAST 10 BYTES OF STACK. THE STACK POINTER
0042  ;     MUST BE SET UP PRIOR TO PROGRAM EXECUTION.NOTE THAT THE ERROR EXIT DOES
0043  ;     NOT RECOVER THE STACK
0044  ;
0045  ;     THE TEST WILL FIND ANY STUCK BITS AND SOME ADDRESSING FAULTS
0046  ;
0047  ;
0000' (0002)   0048  START    DS    2            ;START ADDRESS
0002' (0002)   0049  END      DS    2            ;END ADDRESS
0004' 06AA     0050  QUIKTST  LD    B,0AAH       ;FIRST WRITE AA TO EVERY MEMORY LOCATION
0006' CD1100'  0051           CALL  TEST         ;THEN READ IT BACK AND VERIFY
0009' 0655     0052           LD    B,055H       ;THEN WRITE AND VERIFY 55'S
000B' CD1100'  0053           CALL  TEST         ;NOTE THAT THIS TESTS EVERY BIT AT 1 AND 0
000E' C30E00'R 0054  TESTEND  JP    $            ;END OF TEST
               0055  ;
               0056  ;   TEST FILL MEMORY AND READ BACK FROM B
               0057  ;
0011' CD2500'  0058  TEST     CALL  GETEND       ;GET END ADDRESS IN DE
0014' CD2B00'  0059           CALL  FILL         ;FILL MEMORY FROM B
0017' 2A0000'  0060           LD    HL,(START)   ;GET START ADDRESS FROM LOC 100
001A' 7E       0061  TEST100  LD    A,(HL)       ;GET BACK NEXT BYTE
001B' B8       0062           CP    A,B          ;SAME AS WRITTEN?
001C' 2048     0063           JR    NZ,ERROR     ;NO SO FAIL!
001E' CD3600'  0064           CALL  CHLDE        ;SEE IF WEVE REACHED THE END YET
0021' C8       0065           RET   Z            ;YEP SO GO HOME
0022' 23       0066           INC   HL           ;INC POINTER FOR NEXT BYTE
0023' 18F5     0067           JR    TEST100      ;LOOP FOR ALL MEMORY UNDER TEST
0025' 2A0200'  0068  GETEND   LD    HL,(END)     ;GET END ADDRESS FROM LOC 102
0028' E5       0069           PUSH  HL
0029' D1       0070           POP   DE           ;TRANSFER TO DE AND RETURN
002A' C9       0071           RET
002B' 2A0000'  0072  FILL     LD    HL,(START)   ;GET START ADDRESS IN HL
002E' 70       0073  FILL100  LD    (HL),B       ;WRITE B INTO MEMORY UNDER TEST
002F' CD3600'  0074           CALL  CHLDE        ;FINISHED YET?
0032' C8       0075           RET   Z
0033' 23       0076           INC   HL           ;INC POINTER AND LOOP FOR ALL MEMORY
```

Program 8.1 Continued

248

```
0034'  18F8              JR FILL100
                 0077  ;
                 0078  ;
                 0079  ; CHLDE COMPARE HL AND DE FOR EQUALITY
                 0080  ;
0036'  7C        0081  CHLDE   LD A,H           ;GET H
0037'  BA        0082          CP A,D           ;COMPARE WITH D
0038'  C0        0083          RET NZ           ;NOT EQUAL
0039'  7D        0084          LD A,L
003A'  BB        0085          CP A,E           ;COMPARE AN L.S.BYTE
003B'  C9        0086          RET
                 0087  ;
                 0088  ;ADTEST ADDRESS TEST WRITE AND VERIFY ADDRESS TO EACH LOC
                 0089  ;
003C'  CD2500'   0090  ADTEST  CALL GETEND      ;GET END ADDRESS TO DE
003F'  2A0000'   0091          LD HL,(START)    ;START ADDRESS TO HL
0042'  74        0092  ADT100  LD (HL),H        ;WRITE MSB OF ADDRESS
0043'  CD3600'   0093          CALL CHLDE       ;CHECK FOR END
0046'  2808      0094          JR Z,ADT200      ;END FOUND
0048'  23        0095          INC HL           ;INC POINTER
0049'  75        0096          LD (HL),L        ;AND WRITE LSB OF ADDRESS
004A'  CD3600'   0097          CALL CHLDE       ;CHECK FOR END
004D'  23        0098          INC HL
004E'  20F2      0099          JR NZ,ADT100     ;NOT END SO LOOP
0050'  2A0000'   0100  ADT200  LD HL,(START)    ;GET START ADDRESS BACK AGAIN
0053'  7E        0101  ADT300  LD A,(HL)        ;GET NEXT BYTE
0054'  BC        0102          CP A,H           ;VERIFY HIGH ADDRESS BYTE
0055'  200F      0103          JR NZ,ERROR      ;WRONG!!!!
0057'  CD3600'   0104          CALL CHLDE       ;CHECK FOR END
005A'  C8        0105          RET Z
005B'  23        0106          INC HL           ;INC POINTER
005C'  7E        0107          LD A,(HL)        ;GET NEXT BYTE
005D'  BD        0108          CP A,L           ;VERIFY LOW ADDRESS BYTE
005E'  2006      0109          JR NZ,ERROR
0060'  CD3600'   0110          CALL CHLDE       ;CHECK FOR END
0063'  C8        0111          RET Z
0064'  18ED      0112          JR ADT300        ;LOOP FOR ALL MEMORY
0066'  C36600' R 0113  ERROR   JP $
0069'  (0000)    0114          END
```

Program 8.1 Continued

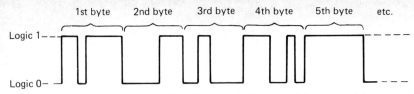

Figure 8.1 Contents of a ROM laid out in bit serial, byte serial format

still remains a possibility that several errors have cancelled each other out resulting in a falacious 'correct' checksum.

A more sensitive technique, less likely to mask errors, involves forming a Cyclic Redundancy Check (CRC). The method finds its origin as a means of error checking data transfers between computers and their peripherals e.g. disks or tapes. To understand how the technique is applied to ROM testing imagine the entire contents of a ROM chip are laid out end to end forming one large linear bit stream, Figure 8.1. The bit stream is then fed into a shift register with feedback paths that effectively perform an addition to the modulo–2 between the feedback data and the new data from the bit stream. The remainder left in the register after all the data bits within the ROM have been entered is the cyclic redundancy check. (The technique forms the basis of signature analysis which is described later in this chapter, see Figure 8.11.) As with most tasks in computing the procedure can also be implemented in software. Program 8.2 shows a routine, written in 6502 assembly language, to evaluate a cyclic redundancy check of a 2 Kbyte block of data. The sensitivity of the technique follows from the feedback paths that ensure that every single bit fed into the register contributes towards the final signature. If even one bit is missing the probability is high that the final CRC will differ greatly from the original.

Input/output devices
The complexity of I/O devices poses problems for effective self-testing. Many modern devices encompass several functions: e.g. the 6522 VIA contains 2 parallel ports with 4 handshake lines, 2 counter/timers and a serial to parallel shift register. One limited test strategy that can be easily implemented is to perform a read/write test on those registers that are known to have this capability. A second strategy, often employed with parallel port chips or UARTs involves installing a special port fixture that links neighbouring ports together, Figure 8.2. One port is configured as an input and the other as an output. A test pattern is then fed to the output port and checked at the input port. Their roles are then reversed and the test repeated.

8.2 EMULATION IN SERVICING

To the service engineer in-circuit emulation provides a method of gaining control of the Unit Under Test (UUT), and injecting test or stimulus programs onto its buses. This can prove an essential facility if the UUT does not respond to normal keyboard operation or perhaps, as in the case of come controllers, does not contain a keyboard. Once in control the

```
 1  ;••••••••••••••••••••••••••••••••••••••••••••••••••••••••••••••••
 2  ; PROGRAM TO EVALUATE SIGNATURE
 3  ;OF 2KBYTE BLOCK (C800-CFFF)
 4  ;EACH BYTE IS SERIALIZED BIT0-BIT7
 5  ;••••••••••••••••••••••••••••••••••••••••••••••••••••••••••••••••
```

NEXT OBJECT FILE NAME IS APPSIG.OBJ0

```
 9                       ORG         $2000
10  COUNT                EQU         $1900       ;STORE FOR SUM
11  SIGL                 EQU         $1901       ;CURRENT SIGNATURE LOW BYTE
12  SIGH                 EQU         $1902       ;CURRENT SIGNATURE HIGH BYTE
13  POINT                EQU         $0008       ;BYTE COUNTER
14  TEMP                 EQU         SIGH + 1    ;TEMPORARY STORE
15  PRBYTE               EQU         $FDDA       ;PRINT A HEX BYTE
16  CROUT                EQU         $FD8E       ;GENERATE C-RETURN
17  ;
18  START                LDA         #00         ;ZERO SHIFT REGISTER
19                       STA         SIGL
20                       STA         SIGH
21  WSTART               LDA         #00         ;WARM START
22                       STA         POINT
23                       TAY
24                       LDA         #$C8        ;START OF BLOCK C800
25                       STA         POINT + 1
26  NBYTE                LDA         (POINT),Y   ;GET BYTE
27                       STA         TEMP
28                       LDX         #08         ;FOR 8 BITS
29  NBIT                 LDA         TEMP
30                       AND         #01         ;BIT0 INTO COUNT
31                       STA         COUNT
32                       JSR         FEEDBACK    ;APPLY FEEDBACK
33                       ROR         TEMP        ;READY FOR NEXT BIT
34                       DEX
35                       BNE         NBIT        ;BACK FOR NEXT BIT
36                       INC         POINT       ;NEXT BYTE
37                       BNE         NBYTE
38                       INC         POINT + 1
39                       LDA         POINT + 1
40                       CMP         #$D0
41                       BNE         NBYTE       ;END OF BLOCK? CFFF
42                       RTS
45  ;FEEDBACK ALGORITHM—SUMS BITS
46  ;15,11,8 AND 6 WITH INCOMING BIT
47  ;ON ENTRY 'COUNT' CONTAINS INPUT BIT
48  ;
49  FEEDBACK             LDA         SIGH        ;TOP HALF OF SIG
50                       BPL         NEX1        ;TEST BIT15
51                       INC         COUNT
52  NEX1                 ROR         A
53                       BCC         NEX2        ;TEST BIT 8
54                       INC         COUNT
55  NEX2                 ROR         A
56                       ROR         A
57                       ROR         A
58                       BCC         NEX3        ;TEST BIT 11
59                       INC         COUNT
60  NEX3                 LDA         SIGL        ;BOTTOM HALF OF SIG
61                       ROL         A
62                       ROL         A
63                       BCC         NEX4        ;TEST BIT 6
64                       INC         COUNT
65  NEX4                 ROR         COUNT       ;SUM INTO CARRY
66                       ROL         SIGL        ;CARRY INTO BIT0 LBYTE
67                       ROL         SIGH        ;CARRY INTO BIT0 HBYTE
68                       RTS
69  DISPLAY              LDA         SIGH        ;MSB TO DISPLAY
70                       JSR         PRBYTE      ;ONTO APPLE DISPLAY
71                       LDA         SIGL        ;LSB TO DISPLAY
72                       JSR         PRBYTE      ;ONTO APPLE DISPLAY
73                       JSR         CROUT       ;C-RETURN
74                       RTS
```

Program 8.2   Routine to evaluate a signature or CRC of a 2 Kbyte
ROM

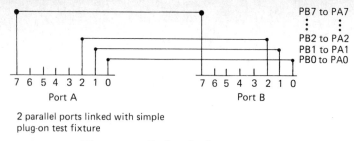

PB7 to PA7
⋮ ⋮
PB2 to PA2
PB1 to PA1
PB0 to PA0

7 6 5 4 3 2 1 0   7 6 5 4 3 2 1 0
Port A   Port B

2 parallel ports linked with simple
plug-on test fixture

Figure 8.2   Back to back testing ports

emulator can run routines to check the operation of the target system's functional components using routines similar to those employed in self-testing. If a fault is discovered the emulator's display reports its location giving the serviceman clues to the possible source of trouble. The Fluke 9010A troubleshooter, outlined below, is an example of this type of instrument. However, not all emulators contain a keyboard and display. For example, the Solartron Micropod is designed to be used with test software developed on another machine and loaded into the emulator in EPROM. The test routines exercise the target system generating data streams that are monitored using a signature analyser (described later).

Fluke troubleshooter

The 9010A troubleshooter, manufactured by the John Fluke company, is representative of a new breed of servicing tools in which in-circuit emulation is an essential ingredient, Figure 8.3. Connection to the unit under test is made through an interface pod that plugs into the target system's processor socket. Each pod employs a microprocessor of the

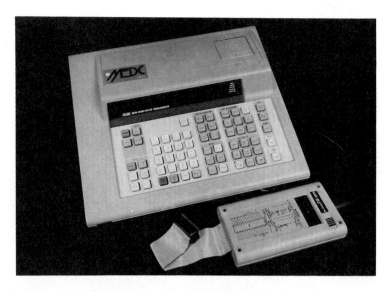

Figure 8.3   Fluke 9010A troubleshooter

252

same type it is replacing, and forms the basis of the 9010A's emulation capability. The *mainframe* (host) contains a miniature tape cassette system on which programs and UUT details can be stored and retrieved, together with a keyboard and 32 character wide LED display.

In operation the 9010A acts as an in-circuit emulator gaining control of the UUT's address, data and control buses through the processor socket. Its advantage over other emulators stems from the range of special functions that simplify and speed up the generation of a test program. These functions range from a LEARN mode where the memory map of the UUT is logged (i.e. the address range of ROM, RAM and I/O) to a TEST mode that uses 'canned' test routines in firmware or 'tailor-made' test programs downloaded from the cassette tape.

Example – a test routine for a single board computer

The AIM 65, described in Chapter 5, contains the major components found in most popular microcomputers and serves as a good example to illustrate the implementation of a test program with the 9010A. The first step involves some investigations on a known working system. This procedure begins by removing the microprocessor from the board and inserting the interface pod in its place. Power is then applied to the board and the operator commences investigation of the system memory map using the Fluke's LEARN mode. In this mode an algorithm explores the UUT's address space, writing and reading data to and from each location. Depending on the data read-back, the algorithm dimensions and classifies the regions of the map occupied by ROM, RAM and I/O devices. For each block of ROM detected a signature is generated based on a cyclic redundancy check of its contents. If desired, the LEARN phase can be edited or bypassed by entering address information directly at the keyboard. Figure 8.4 shows the map produced for the AIM 65.

After the memory map of a good working system has been defined, the Fluke can then undertake testing of identical boards immediately, using its built-in test programs. Routines are provided in the mainframe's firmware to exercise and test the system's buses, ROM, RAM, and to a limited extent, I/O devices.

```
ADDRESS SPACE INFORMATION

RAM @ 0000-0FFF
RAM @ A400-A47F

ROM @ B000-BFFF SIG EA7C
ROM @ C000-CFFF SIG E7E4
ROM @ D000-DFFF SIG 7915
ROM @ E000-EFFF SIG 6E7E
ROM @ F000-FFFF SIG BD87

I/O @ A002-A003 BITS FF
I/O @ A00A-A00C BITS FF
I/O @ A481 BITS FF
I/O @ A483 BITS FF
I/O @ A802-A805 BITS 86
I/O @ A80A BITS FF
I/O @ AC00-AC03 BITS 3F
```

Figure 8.4   9010A's LEARN mode produces a memory map and ROM
signatures for the AIM 65

- The BUS test checks the electrical integrity of the address, data and control buses by trying to establish test patterns and then reporting on its success. Typically a bus test might report that a particular node (e.g. A13 or D0) is stuck either high or low. However, the test is not capable of reporting the source of the fault, which may be due to a number of factors, including a faulty chip or a solder bridge on the printed circuit board. Finding the source of the problem often requires a separate instrument such as a *current probe*. This device makes use of the magnetic field generated by a current to provide a non-intrusive (the probe is held over the conductor and does not become part of the circuit) method of monitoring current flow and hence detecting any sources or sinks along a selected node.
- The ROM test performs the same CRC carried out during the LEARN mode. Any departures from the original signature are reported on the display.
- Two tests are provided for RAM: RAM SHORT and RAM LONG. The former tests the read/write capability of each data bit and proper functioning of the RAM's address decoder. RAM long goes a stage further, including a pattern sensitivity test.
- INPUT/OUTPUT testing is similar to the RAM short test with a check on the bits declared capable of read/write activity in the learn mode.

All of the built-in tests described can be initiated directly from the keyboard or called from within a program. The 9010A uses a programming language, in many respects similar to BASIC, that allows the programmer to combine tests to form a complete test sequence involving messages that guide the operator, specifying what action he has to perform. This programming facility is not restricted to sequencing on-board tests. It also provides a simple method of implementing 'tailor-made' routines to perform more efficient testing of I/O devices. The following examples illustrate possible routines for three of the interface chips found on the AIM 65, namely the VIA, PIA and RIOT.

1. *Testing the 6522 VIA* The VIA dedicated to user applications provides two input/output ports on the J1 application connector at the rear of the machine. During testing a special plug is attached, shorting port A to port B (PA0 to PB0, PA1 to PB1 ... etc.). The test program begins by configuring port A as an input and port B as an output. A test pattern is written to port B and then read at port A and checked. The procedure continues using a 'ramping test pattern', transmitting data between 00H and FFH. On completion, the role of each port is reversed and the procedure repeated. Any failures are reported to the operator, with the message "VIA ERROR", together with an audible bleep, and the test stops, Program 8.3.

The 9010A contains sixteen 32-bit registers, REG0 to REGF, that can be used as variables along with arithmetic and logical operations. Some registers are given dedicated tasks. For example, register E stores the last piece of data used by the operator or generated by the 9010A.

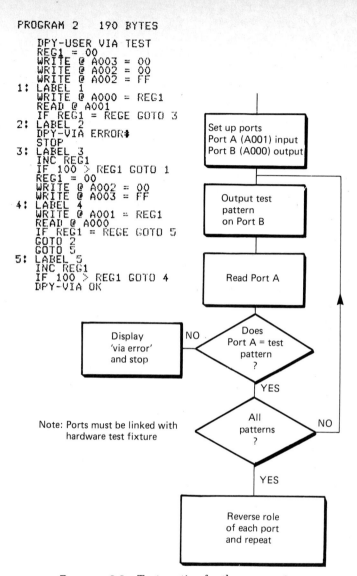

```
PROGRAM 2    190 BYTES
     DPY-USER VIA TEST
     REG1 = 00
     WRITE @ A003 = 00
     WRITE @ A002 = 00
     WRITE @ A002 = FF
1:   LABEL 1
     WRITE @ A000 = REG1
     READ @ A001
     IF REG1 = REGE GOTO 3
2:   LABEL 2
     DPY-VIA ERROR$
     STOP
3:   LABEL 3
     INC REG1
     IF 100 > REG1 GOTO 1
     REG1 = 00
     WRITE @ A002 = 00
     WRITE @ A003 = FF
4:   LABEL 4
     WRITE @ A001 = REG1
     READ @ A000
     IF REG1 = REGE GOTO 5
     GOTO 2
     GOTO 5
5:   LABEL 5
     INC REG1
     IF 100 > REG1 GOTO 4
     DPY-VIA OK
```

Set up ports
Port A (A001) input
Port B (A000) output

Output test
pattern
on Port B

Read Port A

Display
'via error'
and stop

NO

Does
Port A = test
pattern
?

YES

Note: Ports must be linked with
hardware test fixture

All
patterns
?

NO

YES

Reverse role
of each port
and repeat

Program 8.3   Test routine for the user ports

In this example REG1 is used to store the current value of the test pattern written to the output and register E yields the data received at the input port after the read operation.

   2.   *Display test – 6520 PIA*   The 20 character LED display is made up of five, four-digit display modules, each with its own internal memory and driver circuitry, Figure 8.5. A 6520 PIA parallel port chip interfaces the complete array to AIM 65's address, data and control bus. To display a character on the screen, port A of the PIA is used to select the display module and the individual character position within the module. The

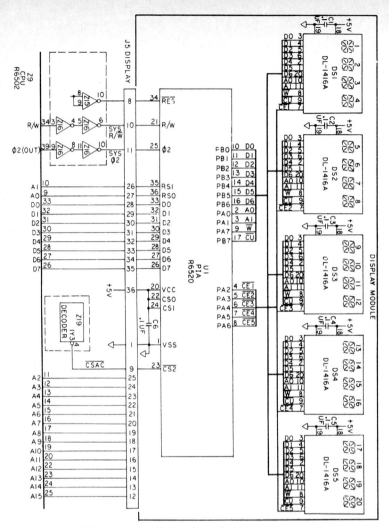

Figure 8.5 AIM 65 LED display interface

ASCII code for the character is then transmitted to the selected position through port B.

The test program begins by initialising both ports as outputs, Program 8.4. The character position is then selected using port A and the character code latched out through port B. The program emables all five modules together and uses a software loop to write the character onto each character position on each element. The next character code is then adopted and the process repeats itself until the entire character set has been written into every position on the screen. The speed of the test procedure is slow enough for an observer to check visually that all character codes appear at every position.

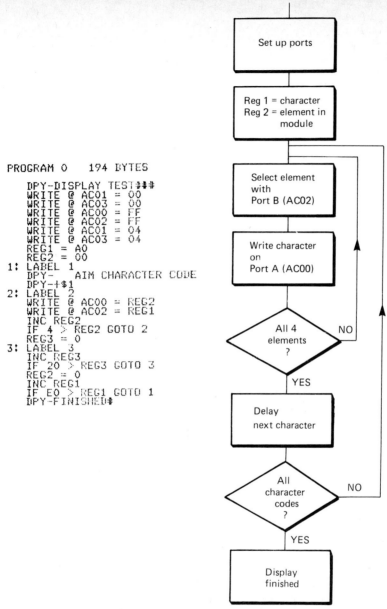

```
PROGRAM 0    194 BYTES

    DPY-DISPLAY TEST***
    WRITE @ AC01 = 00
    WRITE @ AC03 = 00
    WRITE @ AC00 = FF
    WRITE @ AC02 = FF
    WRITE @ AC01 = 04
    WRITE @ AC03 = 04
    REG1 = A0
    REG2 = 00
1:  LABEL 1
    DPY-    AIM CHARACTER CODE
    DPY-+$1
2:  LABEL 2
    WRITE @ AC00 = REG2
    WRITE @ AC02 = REG1
    INC REG2
    IF 4 > REG2 GOTO 2
    REG3 = 0
3:  LABEL 3
    INC REG3
    IF 20 > REG3 GOTO 3
    REG2 = 0
    INC REG1
    IF E0 > REG1 GOTO 1
    DPY-FINISHED*
```

Flowchart:

- Set up ports
- Reg 1 = character / Reg 2 = element in module
- Select element with Port B (AC02)
- Write character on Port A (AC00)
- All 4 elements ? — NO (loop back)
- YES
- Delay next character
- All character codes ? — NO (loop back)
- YES
- Display finished

Program 8.4   Test routine for the AIM 65 LED display

3. *Keyboard test – 6532 RIOT*   The matrix keyboard is interfaced to the processor through a 6532 RIOT, Figure 8.6. Port A is used as an output and strobes the matrix columns. Port B is configured as an input and monitors the matrix rows looking for a depressed key. The keyboard test program shown in Program 8.5 begins by configuring the ports on the RIOT. It then continues by latching out the binary patterns shown below on port A and prompting the operator to press the relevant key.

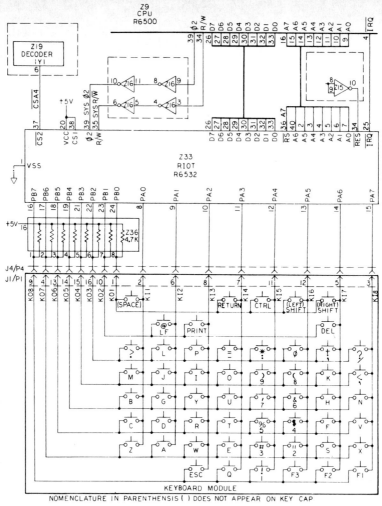

Figure 8.6 Keyboard interface on the AIM 65

Pattern on Port A	Key Requested
01111111	Space
10111111	LF
11011111	P
11101111	0
11110111	7
11111011	4
11111101	5
11111110	F1

By following this pattern, the program performs a short test of every row and every column on the keyboard (obviously a more exhaustive test could be designed to monitor correct operation of every key and to detect

258

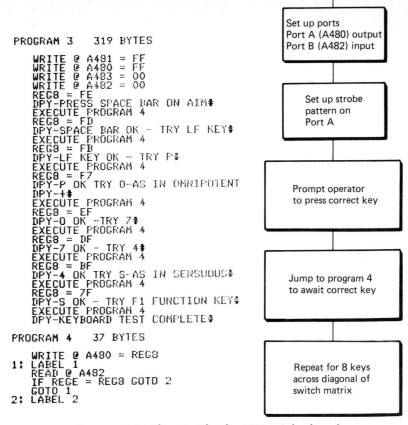

```
PROGRAM 3    319 BYTES

     WRITE @ A481 = FF
     WRITE @ A480 = FF
     WRITE @ A483 = 00
     WRITE @ A482 = 00
     REG8 = FE
     DPY-PRESS SPACE BAR ON AIM↓
     EXECUTE PROGRAM 4
     REG8 = FD
     DPY-SPACE BAR OK -- TRY LF KEY↓
     EXECUTE PROGRAM 4
     REG8 = FB
     DPY-LF KEY OK -- TRY P↓
     EXECUTE PROGRAM 4
     REG8 = F7
     DPY-P OK TRY O--AS IN OMNIPOTENT
     DPY-↓
     EXECUTE PROGRAM 4
     REG8 = EF
     DPY-O OK --TRY 7↓
     EXECUTE PROGRAM 4
     REG8 = DF
     DPY-7 OK - TRY 4↓
     EXECUTE PROGRAM 4
     REG8 = BF
     DPY-4 OK TRY S-AS IN SENSUOUS↓
     EXECUTE PROGRAM 4
     REG8 = 7F
     DPY-S OK -- TRY F1 FUNCTION KEY↓
     EXECUTE PROGRAM 4
     DPY-KEYBOARD TEST COMPLETE↓

PROGRAM 4    37 BYTES

     WRITE @ A480 = REG8
1:   LABEL 1
     READ @ A482
     IF REGE = REG8 GOTO 2
     GOTO 1
2:   LABEL 2
```

Set up ports
Port A (A480) output
Port B (A482) input

Set up strobe
pattern on
Port A

Prompt operator
to press correct key

Jump to program 4
to await correct key

Repeat for 8 keys
across diagonal of
switch matrix

Program 8.5   Short test for the AIM 65's keyboard

possible shorts between rows or columns). When the correct key is pressed the program moves on to prompt the operator to press the next key in the sequence.

Finally Program 8.6 shows the final test program for the AIM 65. The routine links together the built-in tests for the system buses, RAM and ROM along with the special I/O routines described above. In this example the program is a straightforward linear sequence of tests. However, it is relatively simple to create a test program that is sophisticated enough to call up more detailed tests if a failure is detected. The operator can then be guided to the root of a problem, where a message is displayed specifying what action has to be performed, e.g. replace IC number, etc.

8.3 SIGNATURE ANALYSIS

The traditional approach to fault finding in an analogue system is to produce an *annotated schematic* that clearly shows the voltage levels and waveforms expected at different points within the circuit, Figure 8.7. Voltmeter readings and oscilloscope traces are compared with those given

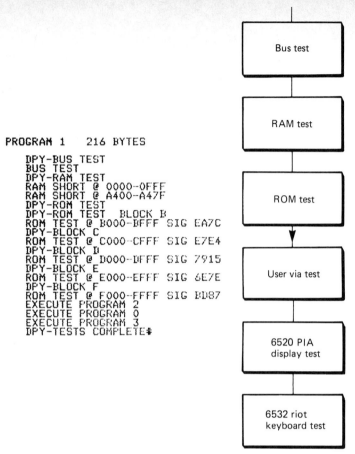

```
PROGRAM 1     216 BYTES
    DPY-BUS TEST
    BUS TEST
    DPY-RAM TEST
    RAM SHORT @ 0000-0FFF
    RAM SHORT @ A400-A47F
    DPY-ROM TEST
    DPY-ROM TEST    BLOCK B
    ROM TEST @ B000-BFFF  SIG EA7C
    DPY-BLOCK C
    ROM TEST @ C000-CFFF  SIG E7E4
    DPY-BLOCK D
    ROM TEST @ D000-DFFF  SIG 7915
    DPY-BLOCK E
    ROM TEST @ E000-EFFF  SIG 6E7E
    DPY-BLOCK F
    ROM TEST @ F000-FFFF  SIG BD87
    EXECUTE PROGRAM 2
    EXECUTE PROGRAM 0
    EXECUTE PROGRAM 3
    DPY-TESTS COMPLETE*
```

Bus test

RAM test

ROM test

User via test

6520 PIA display test

6532 riot keyboard test

Program 8.6 Main program controlling the test sequence for the
AIM 65

on the diagram allowing a serviceman to detect faults and make repairs
without necessarily having a detailed knowledge of the system. Adopting
the same approach with digital circuits meets with several problems.
Neither voltmeters nor oscilloscopes yield meaningful information:
voltage levels lie at either 0 V or +5 V, waveforms are long, complex and
have a random appearance that makes all data streams look much alike.
Clearly what is required is an instrument capable of recording these
complex data streams and yet able to present them to the serviceman in a
compact form. The signature analyser fills this role ideally. Like the
oscilloscope it monitors the logic activity at a circuit node, but instead of
replaying a picture of this activity it produces a four-digit code or
signature to represent the data stream, Figure 8.8. The signature itself has
no meaning and serves only as a token representing the pattern of logic
ones and zeros forming the data stream. If the pattern changes, by even
one bit, there is a high probability that the signature will also change.

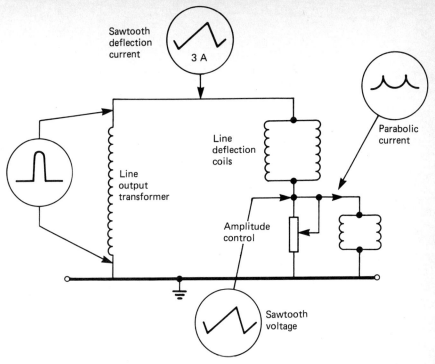

Figure 8.7 Conventional annotated schematic showing voltage levels and expected waveforms at different circuit nodes

Using signature analysis an annotated schematic for a digital circuit might look like Figure 8.9. Instead of voltages and sample waveforms each circuit node is labelled with a signature that characterises the data stream at that point.

In microprocessor based systems the activity at a circuit node, and hence the signature, will depend on the program being executed. An integral part of signature analysis is the *stimulus* or test program that exercises circuit components generating data streams. Only limited information can be obtained from a circuit node that remains in one state. The stimulus program should ensure that circuit nodes are 'wiggled' between logic 0 and logic 1 creating meaningful data streams that reflect the system's performance.

The signature analyser
The function of the signature analyser is to monitor the logic levels at some point in a circuit and produce a code or signature that characterises the activity at that point. Figure 8.10 shows the layout of a typical instrument. In operation five connections are made to the circuit under test. Data from the selected node enters the analyser directly through the data probe; the other connections, namely START, STOP, CLOCK and EARTH are made via an external POD. Similarly to the logic analyser a CLOCK signal is used to strobe data into the signature analyser. Typically

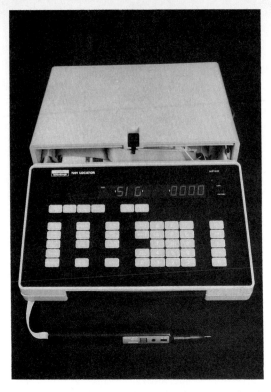

Figure 8.8 The signature analyser produces a 4-digit code to represent a data stream

clock frequencies between DC and 10 MHz are acceptable and switches on the front panel allow the operator to choose either a rising or a falling edge as the active transition. The START and STOP signals define the length of the data stream or the *signature window*.

At the heart of the instrument lies a 16-bit shift register with feedback. On receipt of a valid START signal the register is reset to zero and data is shifted in using the selected clock edge. The feedback paths 'scramble' the data entering the register and ensure that all the bits forming the data stream, not just the last 16, contribute to the final signature. On receipt of a STOP signal the 16 bits remaining in the register are displayed, in a hexadecimal format, to give the signature of the data stream, Figure 8.11.

Some time spent examining how the analyser deals with two simple data streams should help illustrate the function of the feedback shift register. Consider first a data stream constantly at ground potential. At each CLOCK edge a logic zero enters the analyser. As the feedback mechanism is also delivering logic zeros to the exclusive OR gate at the input of the shift register the register remains filled with zeros. Therefore, the signature of a node at ground potential is always 0000. If, however, the probe monitors a point constantly at logic one (e.g. the V_{cc} line) the contents of the register will change as the feedback algorithm alters the bit

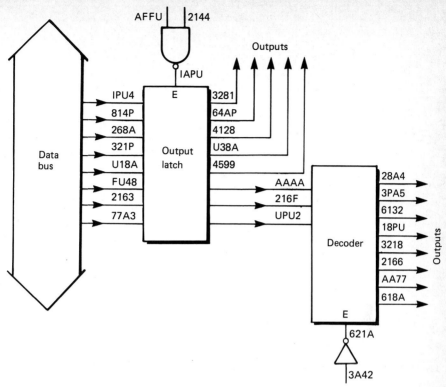

Figure 8.9 Signatures displayed on a digital annotated schematic

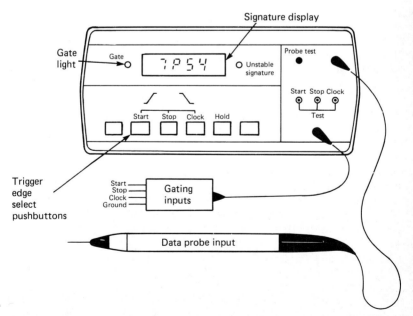

Figure 8.10 Layout and connections required by signature analyser

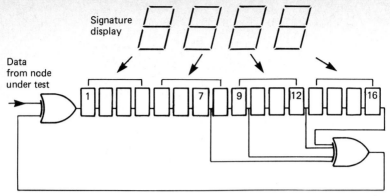

Figure 8.11   A 16-bit shift register with feedback lies at the heart of the signature analyser

stream entering the register. The final signature obviously depends only on the number of clock pulses within the signature window. For this reason the V_{cc} (+5 V) signature is often used as a preliminary check on the gate, to ensure the correct number of clock edges are occurring between the START and STOP signals, before proceeding to measurements that use the same gate with more complicated data streams.

The signature analyser's display uses a non-standard hexadecimal character set: 01234...9ACFHPU. Two LED indicators labelled GATE and UNSTABLE SIGNATURE give information on the signals used by the analyser. The GATE light turns on when the window opens and off when it closes. If the window is continuously opening and closing the GATE light flashes at about 10 Hz. The UNSTABLE SIGNATURE indicator flashes if the signatures obtained in successive windows differ.

Implementing signature analysis
The ideal time to implement signature analysis is at the product design stage. At this point thought can be given by the engineer to the design of stimulus software and to the inclusion of any extra hardware that may be required, e.g. an extra ROM socket, latches to provide START and STOP signals, switches or jumpers to enable ROMs or break feedback paths. Some systems, notably those from manufacturers of signature analysers, do come with signature analysis built-in. Unfortunately the majority do not. Whatever the reasons, failure to include the necessary hardware and software does not close the door. Existing products can be 'retrofitted' with the technique. To help with this task, several manufacturers, notably Hewlett Packard and Solartron, have developed exercisers or emulators that 'inject' stimulus signals into the system under test, Figure 8.12.

With the Solartron Micropod the microprocessor is removed from the unit under test and connection made through the processor socket. The processor is then inserted into the Micropod where it can be tested before being used as part of the emulator.

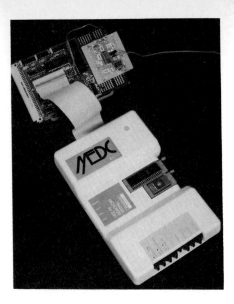

Figure 8.12 The Solartron Micropod: an exerciser or emulator to 'inject' stimulus software into a target system

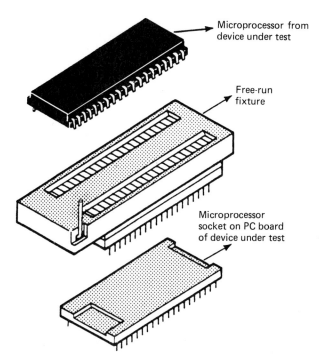

Figure 8.13a Free-run fixture: hardwiring a NOP instruction onto the processor's data bus

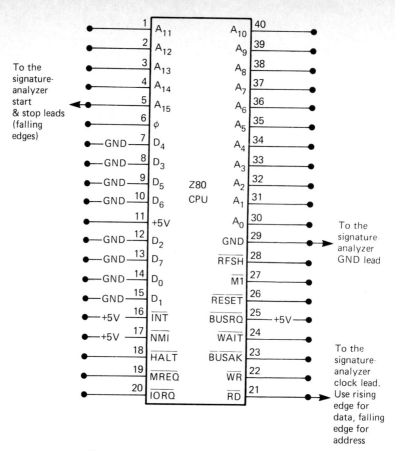

Figure 8.13b Example of a Z80 fixture

Along with its emulation capability the Micropod provides other useful test functions:

1. **Free-run** Free-running the microprocessor provides a relatively simple method of stimulating a large part of a microcomputer system to allow testing by signature analysis. The technique makes use of a simple piece of circuitry to hardwire the code for NOP (no-operation) onto the processor's data bus pins. Figure 8.13 shows how this is achieved.

    After reset the microprocessor reads the NOP code and then increments the program counter and the contents of the address bus to read the next location. As NOP appears at every location the processor is forced to cycle through its entire address range, exercising any address decode circuitry on the board and drawing data from the ROM and RAM chips onto the system data bus, generating data streams suitable for testing with signature analysis.

2. *Normal*   Selecting this function forms normal connections between the microprocessor pins and the buses on the board allowing the unit under test to run its own system program.

3. *Microprocessor test*   A stimulus program supplied in ROM, inside the Micropod, exercises the microprocessor itself. The routine uses most of the instruction set and generates characteristic signatures on the processor's pins.

4. *Stimulus*   Alongside the microprocessor socket the Micropod contains another zero force insertion socket to hold a 4 Kbyte EPROM with test or stimulus routines. (Micropod does not offer any programming facilities and test programs have to be prepared on another system and transferred in EPROM.)

   When stimulus is selected, the Micropod overwrites a 4 Kbyte block of memory on the target system with its on-board EPROM. The block overwritten depends on the version of the Micropod and is chosen to include either the reset address or the reset vectors of the microprocessor. For example with the Z80 Micropod, memory addresses between 0000H and 0FFFH are overwritten by the test EPROM; in the 6502 pod the stimulus EPROM sits in the top 4 Kbytes, i.e. F000H to FFFFH.

   To ease the problem of finding suitable control signals to define the signature window, Micropod provides a START/STOP output that can be driven under software control. To toggle the START/STOP output HIGH or LOW the stimulus program merely has to write to a control address in the Micropod (F000H in the 6502 and 0000H in the Z80). The least significant bit written to the control address is latched out at the STOP/START pin.

   Hence

```
LDA    XXXX XXX0B
STA F000H
```

   would toggle the output low, and

```
LDA    XXXX XXX1B
STA F000H
```

   would set it high.

An example   To be of any use to a service engineer a signature analyser must be accompanied by documentation from a known working system. The following example details how this documentation can be obtained for a relatively simple single board microcomputer, the AIM 65.

   Tests on the system are divided into two groups:

1. Tests on the address bus, decode logic circuitry and ROM using the hardware free-run fixture to generate *free-run signatures*.

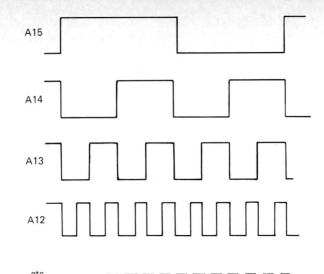

Figure 8.14 When free-running the microprocessor's address bus behaves like a binary counter

2. Tests on the system RAM and I/O devices using a software stimulus program to create *software stimulus signatures*.

Free-run signatures When free-running the address bus is cycling through the processor's entire address range with each address line producing a characteristic repeatable voltage pattern, Figure 8.14.

To obtain signatures on each, address line A15 provides the START/ STOP signals for the signature window. Figure 8.15 shows its behaviour as the processor increments through its address range. On reaching address 8000H, A15 toggles high and remains high up to address FFFFH after which it falls low at the start of a new scan. Choosing falling edges for the START and STOP signals defines a signature window in which the processor places all possible addresses on the bus. With the 6502 the falling edge of the phase 1 clock defines a time at which an address is

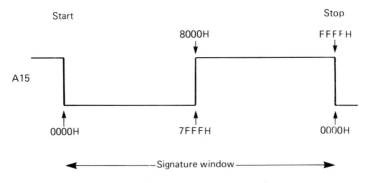

Figure 8.15 Address line A15 provides a signature window that encompasses all the addresses generated by the processor in 'free-run'

FUNCTION	START	STOP	CLOCK	MODE	VCC SIGN	START ID	STOP ID	CLOCK ID
	_/	_/	_	1	0003	A15	A15	P1

CLOCK QUALIFIER	N/A	N/A	N/A	N/A	N/A	N/A

NODE	CIRCUIT ID	CIRCUIT ID	CIRCUIT ID	CIRCUIT ID	CIRCUIT ID	SIGNATURE
A0	Z1-38	Z2-5	Z3-5	Z6-5	Z7-5	UUUU
	Z9-9	Z11-5	Z12-5	Z17-5	Z18-5	
	Z22-8	Z23-8	Z24-8	Z25-8	Z26-8	
	Z32-38	Z33-7	U1-36			
A1	Z1-37	Z2-6	Z3-6	Z6-6	Z7-6	FFFF
	Z9-10	Z11-6	Z12-6	Z17-6	Z8-6	
	Z22-7	Z23-7	Z24-7	Z25-7	Z26-7	
	Z32-37	Z33-6	U1-35			
A2	Z1-36					

Figure 8.16 Free-run address bus and decode circuitry signatures for the AIM 65

established and stable. Using it as a CLOCK signal for the analyser ensures that only valid address information is used to form a signature.

Figure 8.16 shows the signatures obtained from the address bus and the address decode circuitry. Beside each circuit node and its signature the table lists all the components and pin numbers that are attached to that node, a useful list for the service engineer allowing him to check the continuity and integrity of nodes from their source at the processor to various circuit components.

While free-running, the microprocessor attempts to read every possible address drawing information from memory onto the data bus and generating data streams that characterise its contents. The break in the data bus formed by the free-run fixture prevents any of this information reaching the processor and also separates the NOP code at the processor from the system bus. However, before taking signatures on the data bus two changes are required. Firstly, to observe data as opposed to address the CLOCK used by the analyser has to be moved to a point later in the timing cycle, namely to the falling edge of the processor's phase 2 clock. Secondly, leaving the signature window to encompass the processor reading the entire 64 K would yield signatures formed by ROM and RAM. As there is no simple method of ensuring the system is always powered

FUNCTION	START	STOP	CLOCK	MODE	VCC SIGN	START ID	STOP ID	CLOCK ID
	_/	_/	_	1	P254	CSF	CSF	P2

CLOCK QUALIFIER	N/A	N/A	N/A	N/A	N/A	N/A

NODE	CIRCUIT ID	CIRCUIT ID	CIRCUIT ID	CIRCUIT ID	CIRCUIT ID	SIGNATURE
D0	Z1-33	Z2-14	Z6-14	Z9-33	Z11-14	524P
	Z17-14	Z22-9	Z23-9	Z24-9	Z25-9	
	Z26-9	Z32-33	Z33-33	U1-33		
D1	Z1-32	Z2-13	Z6-13	Z9-32	Z11-13	AFUU
	Z17-13	Z22-10	Z23-10	Z24-10	Z25-10	
	Z26-10	Z32-32	Z33-32	U1-32		
D2	Z1-31	Z2-12	Z6-12	Z9-31	Z11-12	6076
	Z17-12	Z22-11	Z23-11	Z24-11	Z25-11	
	Z26-11	Z32-31	Z33-31	U1-31		

Figure 8.17 Free-run ROM signatures for the AIM 65 monitor ROM (F000H to FFFFH)

up with the same RAM contents these signatures would be unrepeatable and therefore useless. However, meaningful signatures can be obtained if the signature window is redefined to enclose only data streams from ROM. Normally this is achieved by connecting the START/STOP inputs to the ROM chip select signal which becomes active when the first location is selected and stays true until the last.

The eight data bus signatures obtained from one of the AIM 65's monitor ROM chips (F000H–FFFFH) are shown in Figure 8.17. Similar tables can be obtained for the other ROMs (e.g. the Assembler, Basic, etc). Also it is possible to use a signature window that encompasses all the ROM devices in the AIM (i.e. from B000H to FFFFH) and obtain a set of signatures that form a check on the five system ROMs.

Software stimulus signatures   Random access memory and input/output devices can only be effectively tested when driven by a stimulus program. Figure 8.18 gives a flowchart of a routine to exercise the RAM and the user ports on the AIM 65. The program is designed to operate from the 6502 Micropod and makes use of the pod's single pin output to generate START and STOP signals.

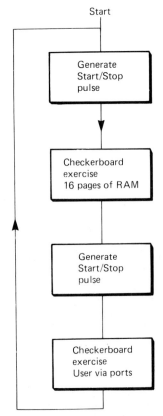

Figure 8.18   Flowchart of software stimulus program for RAM and user ports on the AIM 65

Program 8.7 lists the stimulus program. After ensuring the reset vectors FFFCH and FFFDH are set up to point to the start address of the routine, namely F800H, the program begins by driving the START/STOP pin low with a dummy write to the control address F000H. Each of the AIM 65's RAM locations is then exercised using a checkerboard pattern, writing and reading 55H and AAH. At first glance the routine may appear clumsy since it does not utilise subroutine calls or indirect addressing. However, this is intentional as both operations rely on satisfactory operation of two pages of RAM, namely page 0 and page 1.

On completing RAM stimulus the program toggles the START/STOP pin high and then performs a similar checkerboard test of the two user ports before returning to the start to repeat the whole procedure.

```
LOCATION OBJECT CODE LINE      SOURCE LINE

                     1  "650X"
                     2  ****************************************************
                     3  *AIM65 STIMULUS PROGRAM FOR SIGNATURE ANALYSIS.
                     4  *THIS PROGRAM IS DESIGNED TO TEST THE 4K RAM IN
                     5  *THE AIM IN REPETITIVE 255 BYTE BLOCKS.
                     6  *THE VIA I/O PORTS ARE ALSO TESTED.
                     7  *BY M. BROWN
                     8  ****************************************************
                     9  *
                    10  *FOR COMMENCEMENT OF PROGRAM RESET VECTOR MUST
                    11  *CONTAIN START ADDRESS.
                    12
                    13          ORG      0FFFCH
   FFFC 00F8        14          HEX      00,F8      ;START ADDRESS LOADED
                    15
                    16  ;TEST PATTERN IS 55H THEN AAH WRITTEN TO AND READ
                    17  ;FROM RAM THIS IS CALLED A CHECKERBOARD PATTERN.
                    18
                    19  ;EQUATE ALL RAM BLOCKS
        <0000>      20  RAMST0   EQU      00000H
        <0100>      21  RAMST1   EQU      00100H
        <0200>      22  RAMST2   EQU      00200H
        <0300>      23  RAMST3   EQU      00300H
        <0400>      24  RAMST4   EQU      00400H
        <0500>      25  RAMST5   EQU      00500H
        <0600>      26  RAMST6   EQU      00600H
        <0700>      27  RAMST7   EQU      00700H
        <0800>      28  RAMST8   EQU      00800H
        <0900>      29  RAMST9   EQU      00900H
        <0A00>      30  RAMSTA   EQU      00A00H
        <0B00>      31  RAMSTB   EQU      00B00H
        <0C00>      32  RAMSTC   EQU      00C00H
        <0D00>      33  RAMSTD   EQU      00D00H
        <0E00>      34  RAMSTE   EQU      00E00H
        <0F00>      35  RAMSTF   EQU      00F00H
                    36          ORG      0F800H
                    37          EXTEND
                    38  ;LOAD ACCUMULATOR WITH 55 TEST DATA
   F800 A955        39          LDA      #055H
                    40  ;CLEAR X REGISTER
   F802 A200        41          LDX      #000H
                    42
                    43  ;START PULSE FOR RAM,STOP FOR VIA
   F804 8DF000      44  START   STA      0F000H
                    45
                    46  ;NOW TO TEST RAM 256 BYTES AT A TIME
                    47  ; COMMENCING ON PAGE 0
                    48
   F807 9D0000      49  LOOP0   STA      >RAMST0,X ;STORE 01010101B
   F80A DD0000      50          CMP      >RAMST0,X ;READ LOCATION
   F80D 0A          51          ASL      A         ;SHIFT LEFT ALL BITS
   F80E 9D0000      52          STA      >RAMST0,X ;STORE 10101010B
   F811 DD0000      53          CMP      >RAMST0,X ;READ LOCATION
   F814 4A          54          LSR      A         ;SHIFT RIGHT ALL BITS
   F815 E8          55          INX                ;NEXT LOCATION
   F816 D0EF        56          BNE      LOOP0     ;DO FOR 256 BYTES
                    57
```

Program 8.7 Stimulus program for testing RAM and user ports on the AIM 65

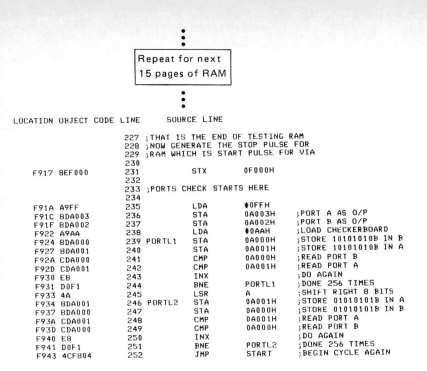

```
                    •
                    •
                    •
              ┌─────────────────────┐
              │ Repeat for next     │
              │ 15 pages of RAM     │
              └─────────────────────┘
                    •
                    •
                    •

  LOCATION OBJECT CODE LINE       SOURCE LINE

                          227  ;THAT IS THE END OF TESTING RAM
                          228  ;NOW GENERATE THE STOP PULSE FOR
                          229  ;RAM WHICH IS START PULSE FOR VIA
                          230
  F917 8EF000             231          STX     0F000H
                          232
                          233  ;PORTS CHECK STARTS HERE
                          234
  F91A A9FF               235          LDA     #0FFH
  F91C 8DA003             236          STA     0A003H    ;PORT A AS O/P
  F91F 8DA002             237          STA     0A002H    ;PORT B AS O/P
  F922 A9AA               238          LDA     #0AAH     ;LOAD CHECKERBOARD
  F924 8DA000             239 PORTL1   STA     0A000H    ;STORE 10101010B IN B
  F927 8DA001             240          STA     0A001H    ;STORE 10101010B IN A
  F92A CDA000             241          CMP     0A000H    ;READ PORT B
  F92D CDA001             242          CMP     0A001H    ;READ PORT A
  F930 E8                 243          INX               ;DO AGAIN
  F931 D0F1               244          BNE     PORTL1    ;DONE 256 TIMES
  F933 4A                 245          LSR     A         ;SHIFT RIGHT 8 BITS
  F934 8DA001             246 PORTL2   STA     0A001H    ;STORE 01010101B IN A
  F937 8DA000             247          STA     0A000H    ;STORE 01010101B IN B
  F93A CDA001             248          CMP     0A001H    ;READ PORT A
  F93D CDA000             249          CMP     0A000H    ;READ PORT B
  F940 E8                 250          INX               ;DO AGAIN
  F941 D0F1               251          BNE     PORTL2    ;DONE 256 TIMES
  F943 4CF804             252          JMP     START     ;BEGIN CYCLE AGAIN
```

Program 8.7 Continued

The START/STOP signal effectively defines two signature windows; the first encompassing the RAM test and the second the port test. Figure 8.19 shows the eight data bus signatures obtained from the RAM test. To capture data the clock input to the analyser was connected to the processor's phase 2 clock. A clock qualifier attached to the RAM $\overline{CS}$ signal ensured that only data in transit to or from the RAM contributed to the final signatures, i.e. the data that appeared on the bus due to the program itself is not clocked into the analyser. Hence alternate data lines have identical signatures.

```
MEDC SIGNATURE REPORT FORM          TITLE:AIM SIG 9:    STIMULUS: RAM
-----------------------------------------------------------------------------
FUNCTION  : START : STOP  : CLOCK : MODE : VCC   : START : STOP  :CLOCK
          :       :       :       :      : SIGN  : ID    : ID    : ID
          : _/    : \_    : \_    :  2   : P254  : M/P   : M/P   : M/P

CLOCK QUALIFIER :\_ ON CS : ON RAM :SELECTED :  N/A   :  N/A   :  N/A

NODE :CIRCUIT ID :CIRCUIT ID :CIRCUIT ID :CIRCUIT ID :CIRCUIT ID :SIGNATURE
D0   :   Z2-14   :   Z6-14   :  Z11-14   :  Z17-14   :           : 958F
D1   :   Z2-13   :   Z6-13   :  Z11-13   :  Z17-13   :           : 9CU7
D2   :   Z2-12   :   Z6-12   :  Z11-12   :  Z17-12   :           : 958F
D3   :   Z2-11   :   Z6-11   :  Z11-11   :  Z17-11   :
D4   :   Z3-14   :   Z7-14   :
```

Figure 8.19 Signatures from RAM test

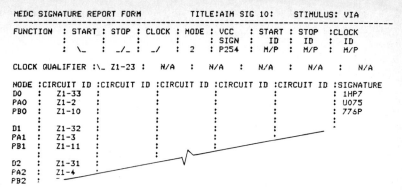

```
MEDC SIGNATURE REPORT FORM          TITLE:AIM SIG 10:    STIMULUS: VIA
------------------------------------------------------------------------
FUNCTION  : START : STOP  : CLOCK : MODE : VCC   : START : STOP  :CLOCK
          :       :       :       :      : SIGN  :  ID   :  ID   :  ID
          :  \_   :  _/_  :  _/   :  2   : P254  :  M/P  :  M/P  :  M/P

CLOCK QUALIFIER :\_ Z1-23 :   N/A    :   N/A   :   N/A   :   N/A   :   N/A

NODE :CIRCUIT ID :CIRCUIT ID :CIRCUIT ID :CIRCUIT ID :CIRCUIT ID :SIGNATURE
D0   :   Z1-33   :           :           :           :           : 1HP7
PA0  :   Z1-2    :           :           :           :           : U075
PB0  :   Z1-10   :           :           :           :           : 776P

D1   :   Z1-32   :           :           :           :           :
PA1  :   Z1-3    :           :           :           :           :
PB1  :   Z1-11   :           :           :           :

D2   :   Z1-31   :           :           :
PA2  :   Z1-4    :
PB2  :    -
```

Figure 8.20   Signatures from user port test

Finally, Figure 8.20 lists the signatures obtained from the port test. Again a $\overline{\text{CS}}$ signal (this time to the user port chip) was used as a clock qualifier, restricting the data bus activity clocked by the analyser to those read or write operations directed at the user ports.

Problems

8.1 Discuss the role of the in-circuit emulator as a servicing tool.

8.2 Decribe how you would induce a microprocessor to 'free-run'. What functional areas of a microcomputer can be tested by 'free-running' the microprocessor.

8.3 Why is it sensible to check the V_{cc} signature before commencing signature testing on other circuit nodes?

8.4 What approach would you take when fault-finding a 'dead' micro-computer for which no service documentation was available?

FURTHER READING

There is a definite lack of textbooks covering many of the new techniques used in microprocessor system servicing. The following list includes two books (Goodman and Leuk) covering general aspects of troubleshooting. Slater and Bronson's text is really a handbook for Hewlett Packard's HP5036A Microprocessor Lab course, but also provides a good introduction to signature analysis.

Slater, H. and Bronson, B., 1979. *Practical Microprocessors – Hardware, Software and Troubleshooting.* Hewlett Packard.

Goodman, 1981. *Troubleshooting Microprocessors and Digital Logic.* Tab.

Leuk, 1979. *Handbook of Practical Microcomputer Troubleshooting.* Englewood Cliffs, NJ: Prentice-Hall.

Rhodes-Burke, February 1981. 'Applying Signature Analysis to Existing Processor-based Products' *Electronics.*

Hewlett Packard Application Notes:

A Designer's Guide to Signature Analysis (No. 222)

Guidelines for Signature Analysis (No. 222-4)

A Signature Analysis Case Study of a Z80 based Personal Computer (No. 222-10)

Appendix A

Glossary

A

Absolute Addressing   An addressing mode in which the instruction is accompanied by an address required for its execution.

Absolute Indexed Addressing   Indexed addressing in which the instruction combines a 16-bit base address with the contents of another register, e.g. the X or Y index register on the 6502.

Accumulator   The principal working register that is normally the destination of the result for most arithmetic and logic operations.

ACIA   Asynchronous Communications Interface Adapter chip. A serial interface device. See UART.

Alphanumeric   The character set A–Z, a–z and 0–9.

Analogue to Digital Converter (A to D)   A device that converts an analogue signal (e.g. voltage level) to a digital value.

AND   A logical operation which for two inputs generates a true (1) result only if both inputs are also true.

Array   A collection of related data items, usually stored in consecutive memory addresses.

ASCII (American Standard Code for Information Interchange)   A 7-bit character code widely used in computers and communications.

Assembler   A program that converts assembly language statements into a form (machine code) that the computer can execute directly. The assembler translates mnemonic operation codes and labels into their numeric equivalents and assigns locations in memory to data and instructions.

Assembly Language   A computer language in which the programmer can use mnemonic operation codes, labels, and names to refer to their numerical equivalents.

Assignment Statement   A statement that assigns the value of an expression on the right hand side of an equals sign to the variable on the left hand side.

Asynchronous   Operating without reference to any timing source, i.e. at irregular intervals.

B

Back-Up   A copy of a file or disk made for safe keeping.

Bank Switching   A technique used to increase the memory available to a microprocessor by using a number of overlapping banks of memory. The processor uses control circuitry to select which bank is currenty in use.

Base Address   The address in memory at which an array or table starts as used in indexed addressing.

BASIC (Beginners All-purpose Instruction Code)   The most commonly used programming language for microcomputers.

Baud   A measure of the rate at which serial data is transmitted in bits per second. Common baud rates are 110, 300, 1200, 2400, 4800, and 9600.

BCD (Binary-Coded Decimal)   A representation of decimal numbers in which each decimal digit 0–9 is coded separately into four bits.

Bit-Slice   A processing system made up of a number of identical parallel components, each performing operations on a part of the total processed word.

Bit Test   An operation that determines whether a bit is 0 or 1. Usually refers to a logical AND operation with an appropriate mask.

Block Move   Moving an entire set of data from one area of memory to another.

Boolean Operators   The logical operators AND, OR, XOR and NOT.

Bootstrap   An initialisation program used to load a larger operating system program into a computer's memory.

Branch Instructions   A group of instructions that enable conditional jumps to be performed. Each instructions action is determined by one of the flags of the processor status register.

Break Flag   A flag of the processor status register that is set to 1 if the microprocessor encounters a break instruction.

Break Instruction   An instruction that forces a jump to a specific address (a software interrupt) often used to produce breakpoints or to indicate hardware or software errors. e.g. BRK on the 6502.

Breakpoint   A condition specified by the user under which program execution is to end temporarily. Breakpoints are used as an aid in debugging.

Buffer   Temporary storage area generally used to hold data before it is transferred to its final destination.

Bug   An error.

Byte   A unit of eight bits.

C

C A highly portable programming language developed by Bell Laboratories.

CAD Computer Aided Design.

CAE Computer Aided Engineering.

Call (a subroutine) Transfers control to the subroutine while retaining the information required to resume the current program. A call differs from a jump or branch in that a call retains information concerning its origin, whereas a jump or branch does not.

CAM Computer Aided Manufacture.

Carry A bit that is 1 if an addition overflows into the succeeding digit position.

Carry Flag A flag that is 1 if the last operation generated a carry from the most significant bit and 0 if it did not.

CCITT Consultative Committee on International Telephony and Telegraphy.

Central Processing Unit (CPU) The microprocessor is the CPU of a microcomputer. When dealing with microcomputers the terms CPU and microprocessor are synonomous. Larger computers have other components that form the CPU and perform the corresponding function of the microcomputer's microprocessor.

Clear Set to zero.

COBOL A high level language used primarily in business applications.

Complement Invert – 0 becomes 1 and 1 becomes 0.

Concatenation Uniting in a continuous series. In string operations, placing of one string after another.

Conditional Jump A programmed jump that takes place only if some specific condition is true.

CP/M Control Program for Microcomputers – an operating system developed by Digital Research.

CPU See Central Processing Unit.

CSMA/CD Carrier sense multiple access with collision detection – a technique used with some computer networks to share a common data highway, while avoiding collisions.

D

Data Direction Register A register that determines whether bidirectional I/O lines are being used as inputs or outputs. Often abbreviated to DDR.

Data Register In a PIA or VIA, the actual input/output port. Also called an output register or a peripheral register.

Debugger   A program intended as an aid to locating and correcting errors in a program.

Device Address   The address of a port associated with an input or output device.

Digital to Analogue Converter (D to A)   A device that forms an analogue output given a digital input.

Direct Addressing   An addressing mode in which the instruction is accompanied by an address required for its execution. The 6502 microprocessor has two types of direct addressing: zero page addressing (requiring only an 8-bit address on page 0) and absolute addressing (requiring a full 16-bit address in two bytes of memory).

DMA   Direct Memory Access – a method of carrying out fast data transfer between a peripheral device and a computer's memory. The transfer does not involve the microprocessor.

Duplex   Bidirectional data communication capability.

E

Editor   A utility program used to create and modify text files.

Effective Address   The actual address used by an instruction to fetch or store data.

Emulate   The process of simulating the action of a device or system in real time.

Endless Loop   An instruction that transfers control to itself, thus executing indefinitely (or until interrupted).

Even Parity   A 1-bit error detecting code that makes the total number of 1 bits in a unit of data (including the parity bit) even.

Exclusive OR   A logical function that is true if either of its inputs is true but not both.

F

File   A collection of related information that is treated as a unit for purposes of storage or retrieval.

Firmware   Programs stored in ROM.

Flag (or status bit)   A single bit that indicates a condition within the computer.

Flag Register   See Processor Status Register.

Free-Running the Microprocessor   A technique used in fault-finding where the code for NOP is 'hardwired' onto the processor's data pins and the microprocessor induced to cycle through its entire address range.

Free-Running Mode   An operating mode for a timer in which it indicates the end of a time interval and then starts another of the same length. Also referred to as a continuous mode.

G

Gateway   An exchange in one network that allows access to and from another network.

Glitch   A transient noise pulse, usually of very short duration.

Global   Relevant throughout an entire program.

H

Handshake   An asynchronous transfer in which sender and receiver exchange predetermined signals to establish synchronisation and to indicate the status of the data transfer. Typically, the sender indicates that new data is available and the receiver reads the data and indicates that it is ready for more.

Hexadecimal (or hex)   Number system with base 16. The digits are the decimal numbers 0 through 9, followed by the letters A through F.

Hex Code   See Object Code.

I

IEEE   Abbreviation for Institute of Electrical and Electronic Engineers, an American body of professional engineers.

Immediate Addressing   An addressing mode in which the data required by an instruction is part of the instruction. The data immediately follows the operation code in memory.

Index   A data item used to identify a particular element of an array or table.

Indexed Addressing   An addressing mode in which the address is modified by combining the contents of an index register to a base address to determine the effective address (the actual address used).

Indexed Indirect Addressing   An addressing mode in which the effective address is determined by indexing from the base address and then using the indexed address indirectly.

Index Register   A general purpose register that can be used as a counter or pointer, e.g. the X or Y register of the 6502.

Indirect Addressing   An addressing mode in which the effective address is the contents of the address included in the instruction, rather than the address itself.

Indirect Indexed Addressing   An addressing mode in which the effective address is determined by first obtaining the base address indirectly and then indexing from that base address.

Indirect Jump   A jump instruction that transfers control to the address stored in the memory location accompanying the instruction.

Instruction   A group of bits that defines a microprocessor operation and is part of the instruction set.

Instruction Cycle The process of fetching, decoding, and executing an instruction.

Instruction Execution Time The time required to fetch, decode, and execute an instruction.

Instruction Fetch The process of addressing memory and reading an instruction into the microprocessor for decoding and execution.

Instruction Set The set of general purpose instructions available on a given computer; the set of inputs to which the microprocessor will produce a known response when they are fetched, decoded, and executed.

Interrupt A signal that temporarily suspends the microprocessor's normal sequence of operations and transfers control to a special routine.

Interrupt-Driven Dependent on interrupts for its operation, may wait indefinitely until it receives an interrupt.

Interrupt Flag A flag that is set automatically when the processor is interrupted or encounters an interrupt disable instruction. (Only on some microprocessors.)

Interrupt Request A signal that is active when a peripheral is requesting service, often used to cause a microprocessor interrupt.

Interrupt Service Routine A program that performs the actions required when responding to an interrupt.

ISO Abbreviation for International Organisation for Standardisation.

J

Jump Instruction An instruction that places a new value in the program counter, thus departing from the normal sequential flow. Jump instructions may be conditional, i.e. a new value is placed in the program counter only if a certain condition is true.

Jump Table A table consisting of the starting addresses of executable routines, used to transfer control to one of them.

L

Label A name attached to an instruction or statement in a program that identifies the address or assignment produced from that instruction or statement.

Latch A device that retains its contents until new data is specifically entered into it.

Leading Edge The edge that marks the beginning of a pulse.

Least Significant Bit The right-most bit in a group of bits.

Lookup Table An array of data items where the required element can be accessed using indexed addressing if the position of that element in the table is known.

M

Machine Language   The language of the microprocessor executed directly with no translation.

Macro   A set of program instructions defined by a single name.

Mask   A bit pattern that isolates one or more bits from a group of bits.

Maskable Interrupt   An interrupt that the system can disable.

Microcomputer   A computer that has a microprocessor as its central processing unit.

Microcontroller   A microprocessor system designed for control applications.

Microprocessor   A complete central processing unit for a computer constructed from one or a few integrated circuits.

Mnemonic   A name that suggests the meaning or purpose of the instruction e.g. LDA for LoaD the Accumulator.

Modem (Modulator/Demodulator)   A device that adds or removes a carrier frequency, thereby allowing data to be transmitted on a high-frequency channel or received from such a channel.

Modular Programming   A programming method whereby the overall program is divided into logically separate sections or modules.

Module   A part or section of a program.

Monitor   A program that allows the computer user to enter programs and data, run programs, examine the contents of the computer's memory and registers.

Most Significant Bit   The left-most bit in a group of bits.

MP/M   A multi-tasking operating system developed by Digital Research.

Multiplexer   A logic circuit that selects one of its several inputs to become its output.

Multi-Tasking   The ability of a computer system to run more than one application program at one time.

Multi-User   The ability of a computer system to support a number of users, each with their own keyboard and display.

N

Negate   Form the Two's Complement (negative) of a number.

Negative Flag   A flag of the processor status register used as the sign flag of Two's Complement arithmetic. The negative flag of the 6502 represents the current status of bit 7 of the accumulator.

Negative Logic   Circuitry in which a logic zero is the active or 'on' state.

Nesting   Programs constructed with one level contained within another and so on.

Nibble (or nybble) A unit of four bits. A byte may be described as consisting of a high nibble (four most significant bits) and a low nibble (four least significant bits).

Non-maskable Interrupt An interrupt that cannot be disabled or ignored.

Non-volatile Memory Memory that retains its contents when power is removed.

No-op (or no operation) An instruction that does nothing other than increment the program counter.

O

Object Code (or object program) The program that is the output of an assembler. Usually a machine language program ready for execution.

Odd Parity A 1-bit error detecting code that makes the total number of 1 bits in a unit of data (including the parity bit) odd.

Offset Distance from a starting point or base address.

Operating System (OS) A computer program that controls the overall operations of a computer and performs such functions as assigning places in memory to programs and data, handling input/output of keyboard, display, disks etc.

Operation Code (op-code) The part of an instruction that specifies the operation to be performed.

Output Register In a PIA or VIA, the input/output port. Also called a data register or a peripheral register.

Overflow Flag A flag of the processor status register is set when the result of Two's Complement arithmetic overflows in either the positive or negative sense.

P

PABX Private Automatic Branch Exchange.

Page A subdivision of the memory area. A 256-byte section of memory in which all addresses have the same eight most significant bits (or page number). For example, page 6 consists of memory addresses 0600 through 06FF.

Page 0 The lowest 256 addresses in memory (addresses 0000 through 00FF).

Parallel Interface An interface between two devices that handles data in parallel (more than one bit at a time).

Parity A 1-bit error detecting code that makes the total number of 1 bits in a unit of data, including the parity bit, odd (odd parity) or even (even parity).

Pascal   A general purpose high level language named after the French mathematician Blaise Pascal.

Peripheral Register   In a PIA or VIA, the input or output port. Also called a data register or an output register.

PIA (Peripheral Interface Adapter)   The common name for the 6522 or 6821 device which consists of two bidirectional 8-bit I/O ports, two status lines, and two bidirectional status or control lines.

Pointer   A register or memory location that contains the address of a data item rather than the item itself.

Polling   Determining which I/O devices are ready by examining the status of each device in turn.

Polling Interrupt System   An interrupt system in which a program determines the source of a particular interrupt by examining the status of potential sources one at a time.

Port   The basic addressable unit of the computer's input/output section.

Priority Interrupt System   An interrupt system in which some interrupts have precedence over others, that is, they will be serviced first or can interrupt the others' service routines.

Processor Status Register   The register of a processor containing the flags which are set (1) or cleared (0) as the microprocessor executes the instructions of a program. Also known as the Flag register or Status register.

Program Counter   A register that contains the address of the next instruction to be fetched from memory and executed by the microprocessor.

Programmable Timer   A device that can handle a variety of timing tasks, including the generation of delays, under program control.

Programmed Input/Output   Input or output performed under program control without using interrupts or other special hardware techniques.

Pull   Removes data from a stack.

Push   Stores data on a stack.

R

Random Access Memory (RAM)   Memory that can be both read and altered (written) in normal operation.

Read Only Memory (ROM)   Memory that can be read but not altered in normal operation.

Re-entrant   A program or routine that can be executed concurrently while the same routine is being interrupted or otherwise held in abeyance.

Register   A storage location inside the microprocessor.

Relational Operator   A relational operator states a relationship between two expressions, e.g. GT, LT, EQ, NE etc.

Relative Addressing   An addressing mode in which the address specified in the instruction is the offset from a base address.

Relocatable   A program that will execute identically when placed anywhere in memory without changes.

Return (from a subroutine)   Transfers control back to the program that originally called the subroutine.

Rotate   A shift operation that treats the data as if it were arranged in a circle, that is, as if the most significant and least significant bits were connected either directly or through a carry bit.

RS-232 (or EIA RS-232)   A standard interface for the transmission of serial digital data.

RS-423   A similar standard to RS-232 but with different signal level definitions.

S

Scratchpad   An area of memory that is especially easy and quick to use for storing variable data or intermediate results.

Sequential Access   A type of file structure where data can only be accessed serially, one record at a time.

Serial   One bit at a time.

Serial Interface   An interface between two devices that handle data serially, i.e. one bit at a time.

Shift Instruction   An instruction that moves all the bits of the data left or right a bit at a time.

Signed Number   A number in which one bit (left-most) represents whether the number is positive or negative. Usually 0 represents positive and 1 represents negative as in Two's Complement.

Sign Flag   See Negative Flag.

Simplex   Unidirectional data transfer scheme.

Software Delay   A program that has no function other than to waste time.

Software Interrupt   See Break Instruction.

Source Code (or source program)   A computer program written in assembly language or in a high level language.

Stack   A section of memory that can be accessed only in a last-in / first-out manner. That is, data can be added to or removed from the stack only through its top; new data is placed above the old data and the removal of a data item makes the item below it the new top. The stack grows downwards through memory.

Stack Pointer   Register that contains the address on page 1 of the next available (empty) stack location or in some cases the last item on the stack.

Status Register   See Processor Status Register.

Subroutine   A subprogram that can be executed (called) from more than one place in a main program.

Synchronous   Operating according to an overall timing source or clock, that is, at regular intervals.

T

Terminator   A data item that has no function other than to signify the end of an array or list of items.

Tri-state Logic   TTL circuits that behave as normal when enabled but exhibit a high impedence when disabled.

TTL   Abbreviation for Transistor Transistor Logic.

Two's Complement   A binary number system that includes the representation of negative numbers. The Two's Complement of a number may be obtained by subtracting the number from zero or by adding 1 to the one's complement.

Two's Complement Overflow   A situation in which a signed arithmetic operation produces a result that cannot be represented correctly, that is, the magnitude overflows into the sign bit.

U

UART (Universal Asynchronous Receiver/Transmitter)   A device that acts as an interface between systems that handle data in parallel and devices that handle data in asynchronous serial form.

UNIX   Operating system developed by Bell Laboratories.

Unsigned Number   A number in which all the bits are used to represent magnitude.

V

VDU   Visual Display Unit.

Versatile Interface Adapter (VIA)   The name commonly given to the 6522 parallel interface device; it consists of two 8-bit bidirectional I/O ports, four status and control lines, two 16-bit timers, and a shift register.

VIA   See Versatile Interface Adapter.

VLSI   Very large scale integration components have in excess of 10000 transistors on a single chip.

Volatile Memory   A memory that loses its contents when power is removed.

W

Wraparound   Organisation in a circular manner as if the ends were connected.

X

XOR   See Exclusive OR function.

Z

Zero Flag   A flag of the processor status register set to 1 if an operation produces a result of zero and 0 otherwise.

Zero Page   The lowest 256 memory addresses (addresses 0000 through 00FF).

Zero Page Addressing   A form of absolute addressing in which the instruction contains only an 8-bit address on page 0. That is, zero is implied as the more significant byte of the absolute address.

Zero Page Indexed Address   A form of indexed addressing in which the instruction contains a base address and need not be included explicitly in the instruction.

Appendix B

MEDC Z80
single board controller

The MEDC single board controller was designed as a minimum Z80 system that could be used in a range of development projects. The on-board circuitry contains all the components required to form a stand alone microcomputer with a limited amount of I/O capability. To cope with possible future expansion, the board contains an expansion connector that carries a buffered address bus along with other processor signals.

In the following description the circuit, Figure B.1, is divided into three sections:

1. the Z80 processor, memory and associated control circuitry
2. on-board input/output circuitry
3. expansion bus

1. The Z80 processor, memory and associated control circuitry
The Z80 processor and other major components obtain their timing from a clock generator circuit consisting of two inverters and a crystal oscillator. The output of the clock generator is buffered using an additional inverter before it is distributed to the various devices on the board.

A reset switch is provided on board which in addition to resetting the Z80 will also reset the I/O devices by activating their $\overline{M1}$ inputs.

The read/write memory consists of two 2114 static RAM chips arranged to form 1 K × 8 bits of R/W memory. The read only memory socket can support either a 2716, 2 K × 8 bit, or a 2532, 4 K × 8 bit EPROM. Address decode circuitry places the R/O memory at the bottom end of the address space while the R/W memory is placed at the top, Figure B.2.

Any memory read or write activity enables the processor's $\overline{\text{MREQ}}$ signal and provides one of the input signals required to enable the two NAND gates controlling the address decode circuitry. If the processor performs a READ operation to any address where A15 is low (ie. addresses 0000H to 7FFFH) the system ROM is enabled. This crude memory decoding results in a 4 Kbyte ROM appearing repeatedly within the bottom 32 Kbytes of the system memory map.

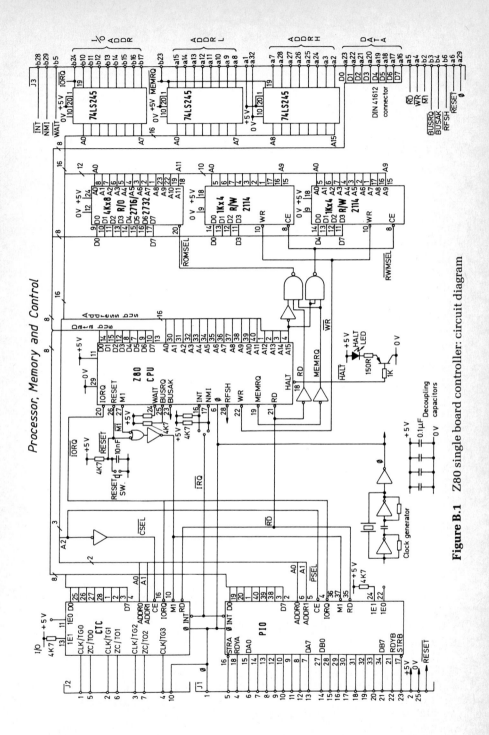

Figure B.1 Z80 single board controller: circuit diagram

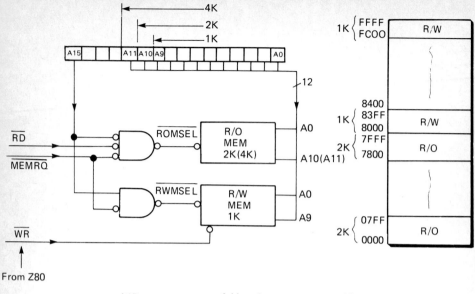

A15	Address bus		A0		
0 0 0 0	0 0 0 0	0 0 0 0	0 0 0 0	–0000 } 2K	
0 0 0 0	0 1 1 1	1 1 1 1	1 1 1 1	–07FF	} 4K
0 0 0 0	1 0 0 0	0 0 0 0	0 0 0 0	–0000 } 2K	
0 0 0 0	1 1 1 1	1 1 1 1	1 1 1 1	–0FFF	
0 1 1 1	1 0 0 0	0 0 0 0	0 0 0 0	–7800 } 2K	
0 1 1 1	1 1 1 1	1 1 1 1	1 1 1 1	–7FFF	
1 0 0 0	0 0 0 0	0 0 0 0	0 0 0 0	–8000 } 1K	
1 0 0 0	0 0 1 1	1 1 1 1	1 1 1 1	–83FF	
1 0 0 0	0 1 0 0	0 0 0 0	0 0 0 0	–8400 } 1K	
1 0 0 0	0 1 1 1	1 1 1 1	1 1 1 1	–87FF	
1 1 0 1	0 1 0 0	0 0 0 0	0 0 0 0	–D400 } 1K	
1 1 0 1	0 1 1 1	1 1 1 1	1 1 1 1	–D7FF	
1 1 1 1	1 1 0 0	0 0 0 0	0 0 0 0	–FC00 } 1K	
1 1 1 1	1 1 1 1	1 1 1 1	1 1 1 1	–FFFF	

$\overline{ROMSEL}$ = '0' applies to the first block; $\overline{RWMSEL}$ = '0' applies to the lower block.

Figure B.2 Memory select circuitry and memory map

When the processor performs READ or WRITE activity with memory in the top 32 Kbytes of the memory map (i.e. 8000H to FFFFH) the second NAND gate enables the 1 Kbyte of static RAM. Again, like the ROM, the system RAM appears repeatedly within the memory map.

This appearance of the same memory at different addresses (degeneracy) is a feature of systems where the address decoding is simple and the select line for a particular memory device is active for a processor address range greater than the number of locations in the device.

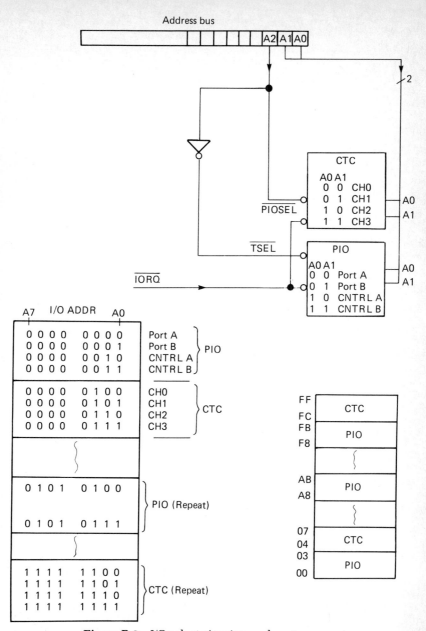

Figure B.3   I/O select circuitry and port map

2.   On-board input/output circuitry

The I/O facilities provided on the board consist of a PIO – Parallel Input/Output chip, and a CTC – Counter/Timer Circuit. Both of these devices are designed to be used with the port addressing mode of the Z80 which transfers data to and from the processor on the execution of IN and OUT instructions. The 8-bit address of the port appears on the lower half of the address bus. Both the PIO and CTC have four addressable registers and require two address lines. These lines are connected to A0 and A1 on the processor. Read and write operations are controlled by the single line RD from the processor.

Address line A2 is used in the I/O select circuitry to ensure that the PIO is selected when A2='0' and the CTC when A2='1'. I/O addresses 00, 01, 02, 03 and 08, 09, 0A, 0B . . . F8, F9, FA, FB will select the PIO registers for port A, port B, control A and control B, i.e. the same registers appear repeatedly in the I/O map. Similarly the CTC channels CH0, CH1, CH2 and CH3 will appear first at 04, 05, 06, 07 and then 0C, 0D, 0E, 0F and so on up to FC, FD, FE and FF, Figure B.3.

3. Expansion bus

The expansion bus is intended to match as closely as possible the Acorn bus. All the address lines are buffered using 74LS245 chips and the I/O address is obtained by gating the bottom nine address lines with the processor's $\overline{\text{IORQ}}$ signal.

Care is required when extending the system using this bus connector in order to avoid conflict with the on-board memory, e.g. to extend the R/W memory the on-board memory would have to be removed.

FURTHER INFORMATION

For further details of the MEDC single board computer, contact:

> The Information Officer
> MEDC
> Paisley College
> High Street
> Paisley, PA1 2BE

Appendix C

S100 interface

Pin number	Signal	Active level		Description
1	+8 VOLTS (B)			
2	+16 VOLTS (B)			
3	XRDY (S)	H		One of two ready inputs to the current bus master. The bus is ready when both these ready inputs are true. See pin 72
4	VI0*(S)	L	O.C.	Vectored interrupt line 0
5	VI1*(S)	L	O.C.	Vectored interrupt line 1
6	VI2*(S)	L	O.C.	Vectored interrupt line 2
7	VI3*(S)	L	O.C.	Vectored interrupt line 3
8	VI4*(S)	L	O.C.	Vectored interrupt line 4
9	VI5*(S)	L	O.C.	Vectored interrupt line 5
10	VI6*(S)	L	O.C.	Vectored interrupt line 6
11	VI7*(S)	L	O.C.	Vectored interrupt line 7
12	NMI*(S)	L	O.C.	Non-maskable interrupt
13	PWRFAIL*(B)	L		Power fail bus signal
14	DMA3*(M)	L	O.C.	Temporary master priority bit 3
15	A18 (M)	H		Extended address bit 18
16	A16 (M)	H		Extended address bit 16
17	A17 (M)	H		Extended address bit 17
18	SDSB* (M)	L	O.C.	The control signal to disable the 8 status signals
19	CDSB* (M)	L	O.C.	The control signal to disable the 5 control output signals
20	GND (B)			Common with pin 100
21	NDEF			Not to be defined. Manufacturer must specify any use in detail
22	ADSB* (M)	L	O.C.	The control signal to disable the 16 address signals
23	DODSB* (M)	L	O.C.	The control signal to disable the 8 data output signals
24	φ (B)	H		The master timing signal for the bus
25	pSTVAL* (M)	L		Status valid strobe
26	pHLDA (M)	H		A control signal used in conjunction with HOLD* to coordinate bus master transfer operations

Figure C.1 S100 interface

Pin number	Signal	Active level		Description
27	RFU			Reserved for future use
28	RFU			Reserved for future use
29	A5 (M)	H		Address bit 5
30	A4 (M)	H		Address bit 4
31	A3 (M)	H		Address bit 3
32	A15 (M)	H		Address bit 15
33	A12 (M)	H		Address bit 12
34	A9 (M)	H		Address bit 9
35	DO1 (M)/DATA1 (M/S)	H		Data out bit 1, bidirectional data bit 1
36	DO0 (M)/DATA0 (M/S)	H		Data out bit 0, bidirectional data bit 0
37	A10 (M)	H		Address bit 10
38	DO4 (M)/DATA4 (M/S)	H		Data out bit 4, bidirectional data bit 4
39	DO5 (M)/DATA5 (M/S)	H		Data out bit 5, bidirectional data bit 5
40	DO6 (M)/DATA6 (M/S)	H		Data out bit 6, bidirectional data bit 6
41	DI2 (S)/DATA10 (M/S)	H		Data in bit 2, bidirectional data bit 10
42	DI3 (S)/DATA11 (M/S)	H		Data in bit 3, bidirectional data bit 11
43	DI7 (S)/DATA15 (M/S)	H		Data in bit 7, bidirectional data bit 15
44	sM1 (M)	H		The status signal which indicates that the current cycle is an op-code fetch
45	sOUT (M)	H		The status signal identifying the data transfer bus cycle to an output device
46	sINP (M)	H		The status signal identifying the data transfer bus cycle from an input device
47	sMEMR (M)	H		The status signal identifying bus cycles which transfer data from memory to a bus master, which are not interrupt acknowledge instruction fetch cycle(s)
48	sHLTA (M)	H		The status signal which acknowledges that a HLT instruction has been executed
49	CLOCK (B)			2 MHz (0.5%) 40–60% duty cycle. Not required to be synchronous with any other bus signal
50	GND (B)			Common with pin 100
51	+8 VOLTS (B)			Common with pin 1
52	−16 VOLTS (B)			
53	GND (B)			Common with pin 100
54	SLAVE CLR* (B)	L	O.C.	A reset signal to reset bus slaves. Must be active with POC* and may also be generated by external means
55	DMA0* (M)	L	O.C.	Temporary master priority bit 0
56	DMA1* (M)	L	O.C.	Temporary master priority bit 1
57	DMA2* (M)	L	O.C.	Temporary master priority bit 2
58	sXTRQ* (M)	L		The status signal which requests 16-bit slaves to assert SIXTN*
59	A19 (M)	H		Extended address bit 19

Figure C.1 Continued

292

Pin number	Signal	Active level		Description
60	SIXTN* (S)	L	O.C.	The signal generated by 16-bit slaves in response to the 16-bit request signal sXTRQ*
61	A20 (M)	H		Extended address bit 20
62	A21 (M)	H		Extended address bit 21
63	A22 (M)	H		Extended address bit 22
64	A23 (M)	H		Extended address bit 23
65	NDEF			Not to be defined signal
66	NDEF			Not to be defined signal
67	PHANTOM* (M/S)	L	O.C.	A bus signal which disables normal slave devices and enables phantom slaves – primarily used for bootstrapping systems without hardware front panels
68	MWRT (B)	H		pWR·–sOUT (logical equation). This signal must follow pWR* by not more than 30 ms
69	RFU			Reserved for future use
70	GND (B)			Common with pin 100
71	RFU			Reserved for future use
72	RDY (S)	H	O.C.	See comments for pin 3
73	INT* (S)	L	O.C.	The primary interrupt request bus signal
74	HOLD* (M)	L	O.C.	The control signal used in conjunction with pHLDA to coordinate bus master transfer operations
75	RESET* (B)	L	O.C.	The reset signal to reset bus master devices. This signal must be active with POC* and may also be generated by external means
76	pSYNC (M)	H		The control signal identifying BS_1
77	pWR* (M)	L		The control signal signifying the presence of valid data on DO bus or data bus
78	pDBIN (M)	H		The control signal that requests data on the DI bus or data bus from the currently addressed slave
79	A0 (M)	H		Address bit 0 (least significant)
80	A1 (M)	H		Address bit 1
81	A2 (M)	H		Address bit 2
82	A6 (M)	H		Address bit 6
83	A7 (M)	H		Address bit 7
84	A8 (M)	H		Address bit 8
85	A13 (M)	H		Address bit 13
86	A14 (M)	H		Address bit 14
87	A11 (M)	H		Address bit 11
88	DO2 (M)/DATA2 (M/S)	H		Data out bit 2, bidirectional data bit 2
89	DO3 (M)/DATA3 (M/S)	H		Data out bit 3, bidirectional data bit 3
90	DO7 (M)/DATA7 (M/S)	H		Data out bit 7, bidirectional data bit 7
91	DI4 (S)/DATA12 (M/S)	H		Data in bit 4 and bidirectional data bit 12

Figure C.1 Continued

Pin number	Signal	Active level	Description
92	DI5 (S)/DATA13 (M/S)	H	Data in bit 5 and bidirectional data bit 13
93	DI6 (S)/DATA14 (M/S)	H	Data in bit 6 and bidirectional data bit 14
94	DI1 (S)/DATA9 (M/S)	H	Data in bit 1 and bidirectional data bit 9
95	DI0 (S)/DATA8 (M/S)	H	Data in bit 0 (least significant for 8-bit data) and bidirectional data bit 8
96	sINTA (M)	H	The status signal identifying the bus input cycle(s) that may follow an accepted interrupt request presented on INT*
97	sWO* (M)	L	The status signal identifying a bus cycle which transfers data from a bus master to a slave
98	ERROR* (S)	L O.C.	The bus status signal signifying an error condition during present bus cycle
99	POC* (B)	L	The power-on clear signal for all bus devices; when this signal goes low, it must stay low for at least 10 ms
100	GND (B)		System ground

Key: S   Slave generated signal
      M   Master generated signal
      M/S   Master or slave generated signal
      B   Bus signal from power supply or front panel
      *   Signal is true when line is low
      H   Active high
      L   Active low
      O.C.   Open Collector

Figure C.1   Continued

Appendix D

ASCII codes

Computers work with numeric information. To handle letters of the alphabet or characters like + / - ?, a coding system is used in which each character is given a numeric value. The most common system used is the American Standard Code for Information Interchange, or ASCII code, Figure D.1

					b7	0	0	0	0	1	1	1	1
					b6	0	0	1	1	0	0	1	1
					b5	0	1	0	1	0	1	0	1
b4	b3	b2	b1	ROW	COLUMN	0	1	2	3	4	5	6	7
0	0	0	0	0		NUL	DLE	SP	0	@	P	`	p
0	0	0	1	1		SOH	DC1	!	1	A	Q	a	q
0	0	1	0	2		STX	DC2	"	2	B	R	b	r
0	0	1	1	3		ETX	DC3	#	3	C	S	c	s
0	1	0	0	4		EOT	DC4	$	4	D	T	d	t
0	1	0	1	5		ENQ	NAK	%	5	E	U	e	u
0	1	1	0	6		ACK	SYN	&	6	F	V	f	v
0	1	1	1	7		BEL	ETB	'	7	G	W	g	w
1	0	0	0	8		BS	CAN	(	8	H	X	h	x
1	0	0	1	9		HT	EM	)	9	I	Y	i	y
1	0	1	0	A		LF	SUB	*	:	J	Z	j	z
1	0	1	1	B		VT	ESC	+	;	K	[	k	{
1	1	0	0	C		FF	FS	,	<	L	\	l	|
1	1	0	1	D		CR	GS	-	=	M	]	m	}
1	1	1	0	E		SO	RS	.	>	N	^	n	~
1	1	1	1	F		SI	US	/	?	O	_	o	DEL

NUL	Null	DC1	Device control 1
SOH	Start of heading	DC2	Device control 2
STX	Start of text	DC3	Device control 3
ETX	End of text	DC4	Device control 4
EOT	End of transmission	NAK	Negative acknowledge
ENQ	Enquiry	SYN	Sychronous idle
ACK	Acknowledge	ETB	End of transmission block
BEL	Bell, or alarm	CAN	Cancel
BS	Backspace	EM	End of medium
HT	Horizontal tabulation	SUB	Substitute

Figure D.1   ASCII codes

LF	Line feed	ESC	Escape
VT	Vertical tabulation	FS	File separator
FF	Form feed	GS	Group separator
CR	Carriage return	RS	Record separator
SO	Shift out	US	Unit separator
SI	Shift in	SP	Space
DLE	Data link escape	DEL	Delete

Figure D.1 Continued

Appendix E

IEEE 488 code chart

In the command mode the GPIB uses its data lines to transmit a number of control signals, including:

- talk and listen addresses to select the devices that will take part in the following transaction
- universal commands that apply to all devices on the bus capable of responding
- addressed commands directed only at specific devices

Figure E.1 presents these GPIB codes in tabular form.

b7		0		0		0		0		1		1	
	b6		0		0		1		1		0		0
		b5		0		1		0		1		0		1
				Commands				*Listen*			*Talk*		
				Addressed				*addresses*			*addresses*		
b4 b3 b2 b1					*Universal*								
0 0 0 0				0	10		20	30			40	50	
							0	16			0	16	
0 0 0 1				1	11		21	31			41	51	
				GTL	LLO		1	17			1	17	
0 0 1 0				2	12		22	32			42	52	
							2	18			2	18	
0 0 1 1				3	13		23	33			43	53	
							3	19			3	19	
0 1 0 0				4	14		24	34			44	54	
				SDC	DCL		4	20			4	20	
0 1 0 1				5	15		25	35			45	55	
				PPC	PPU		5	21			5	21	

Figure E.1 IEEE-488 code chart (*Note:* secondary addresses and commands not shown)

b7		0	0	0	0	1	1
b6		0	0	1	1	0	0
b5		0	1	0	1	0	1
		Commands		Listen		Talk	
		Addressed	Universal	addresses		addresses	
b4 b3 b2 b1							
0 1 1 0		6	16	26	36	46	56
		6		6	22	6	22
0 1 1 1		7	17	27	37	47	57
		7		7	23	7	23
1 0 0 0		8	18	28	38	48	58
		GET	SPE	8	24	8	24
1 0 0 1		9	19	29	39	49	59
		TCT	SPD	9	25	9	25
1 0 1 0		A	1A	2A	3A	4A	5A
				10	26	10	26
1 0 1 1		B	1B	2B	3B	4B	5B
				11	27	11	27
1 1 0 0		C	1C	2C	3C	4C	5C
				12	28	12	28
1 1 0 1		D	1D	2D	3D	4D	5D
				13	29	13	29
1 1 1 0		E	1E	2E	3E	4E	5E
				14	30	14	30
1 1 1 1		F	1F	2F	3F	4F	5F
				15	UNL	15	UNT

Key: 8   Hex value
          GET   Mnemonic/Device address

Figure E.1   Continued

Appendix F

Answers to selected problems

Chapter 1

1.1 a) 0001001000110100
   b) 1010010000101000
   c) 1111001010101100
   d) 111111111111111
   Address line A7 is at logic 1 in answers (c) and (d).

1.2 a) 011064
   b) 122050
   c) 171254
   d) 177777

1.3 a) Place an invertor before the NAND gate on address line A15.
   b) Requires invertors in address lines A14 and A12.

1.5 The simplest circuit uses address line A15 directly for the ROM device and with an invertor for the RAM device. Examine the circuit diagram for the Z80 controller board in Appendix B.

Chapter 2

2.1 Refer to section 2.1.

2.2 Refer to Figure 2.14.

2.3 When reading an op-code from memory the Z80 expects the data to be available within 2 T states, i.e. ≈300 nsec. To operate with an 800 nsec EPROM a wait state generator would be required introducing four additional T states into the microprocessor's read cycle.

2.4 Intel and Zilog have a separate port map for input/output devices. To support this additional map two extra control signals are used, e.g. MREQ and IORQ. The former must be used along with any address decode circuit enabling memory devices, and the latter with decode circuitry enabling I/O devices.

2.5 Refer to section 2.4 and the 8088/8086 processor description.

Chapter 3

3.1 Refer to Program 2.2.

3.3 Refer to section 3.3.

Chapter 4

4.3 See Figure 4.14.

Chapter 6

6.2 Talk address=55H; Listen address=35H

Separate talk and listen addresses allow the system controller to select either a talker or a listener with a single code.

Chapter 7

7.1 See Figures 7.7 and 7.10.

7.2 Make use of the procedures given in Programs 7.7 and 7.14.

Chapter 8

8.2 Refer to Figure 8.13 and associated text.

8.3 The V_{cc} signature depends only on the number of clock signals occurring within the signature window. Checking the V_{cc} signature first gives confidence that the analyser's CLOCK, START and STOP controls and probes have been set up according to the documentation.

8.4 If simple checks for power and system clock fail to reveal the problem, beg, borrow or steal a functional tester such as the Fluke Troubleshooter!

Index